DUBLIN STREET GUIDE

GW00602835

contents

Key to map symbols	3
Street maps	4-77
Enlarged scale street maps	78-81
Index to streets	82-111
Index to suburbs & districts	111
Index to landmarks - buildings	111-116
Index to parks - golf courses - sports stadia	116

Includes **MALAHIDE** **TALLAGHT** **LUCAN** **BRAY**

Gill & Macmillan Ltd
Hume Avenue, Park West, Dublin 12
with associated companies throughout the world
www.gillmacmillan.ie
© Gill & Macmillan 2005, 2007
978 07171 4174 6

Atlas designed and produced by Oxford Cartographers
Map data © Mapflow, Dublin

Printed in China by Hing Yip Printing Company Ltd.

A CIP catalogue record for this book is available from the British Library.

1 3 5 4 2

DUBLIN STREET GUIDE

key to map symbols

transportation

- Motorway
- Port Tunnel
- Primary Route
- Secondary Road
- Main Road
- Minor Road
- **22** Inner Orbital Route Junction
- Pedestrian Access
- Path
- Railway
- LUAS, Station
- LUAS - proposed line
- Ferry

building colours/symbols

- Hotel
- ⊠ Post Office
- School/College
- ✚ Church
- ✚ Hospital
- ✚ Convent
- Bank
- Other Building
- Government Building
- ☜ Theatre
- Train/Bus Station
- Shopping Centre
- ▣ Police Station
- ▣ Fire Station
- ⋒ Museum
- Garda HQ

symbols

- **P** Car Park
- ⋒ Museum/Art Gallery
- ▦ Train Station
- *i* Information
- ⚑ Golf Course
- ← One-way Street

land use

- Green Area
- Park
- Low Urban
- Medium Urban
- High Urban

Scale for pages 4 - 77, 1:15,225

6.56cm = 1km (1000m), 4.16 inches = 1mile (1760yds)

| 200 | 100 | 0 | 200 | 400 | 600 | 800 | 1000m |

| 200 | 100 | 0 | 200 | 400 | 600 | 800 | 1000yds |

Scale for pages 78 - 81, 1:11,000

9.09cm = 1km (1000m), 5.76 inches = 1mile (1760yds)

| 200 | 100 | 0 | 200 | 400 | 600m |

| 200 | 100 | 0 | 200 | 400 | 600yds |

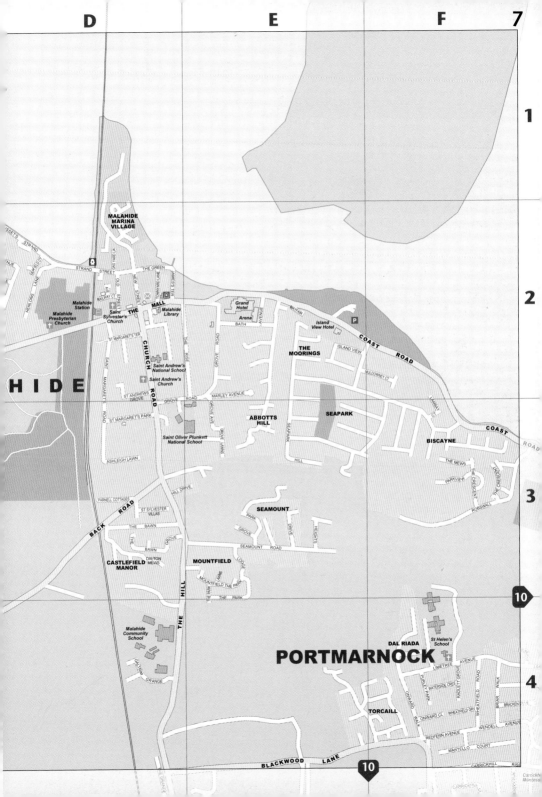

D
E
F
9

AIRSIDE RETAIL PARK

O'Scanaill Vet Hospital

Forte Travel Lodge

NEVINSTOWN

LANE

HOLYWELL

MELROSE PARK

DRYNAM ROAD

DRYNAM

Kingdom Hall of Jehovah's Witnesses

KETTLES LANE

KETTLES LANE

M1

STOCKLIDLE LANE

STOCKLIDLE LANE

M 1

TERM PARK

P

BASKIN LANE

5

6

1

2

3

4

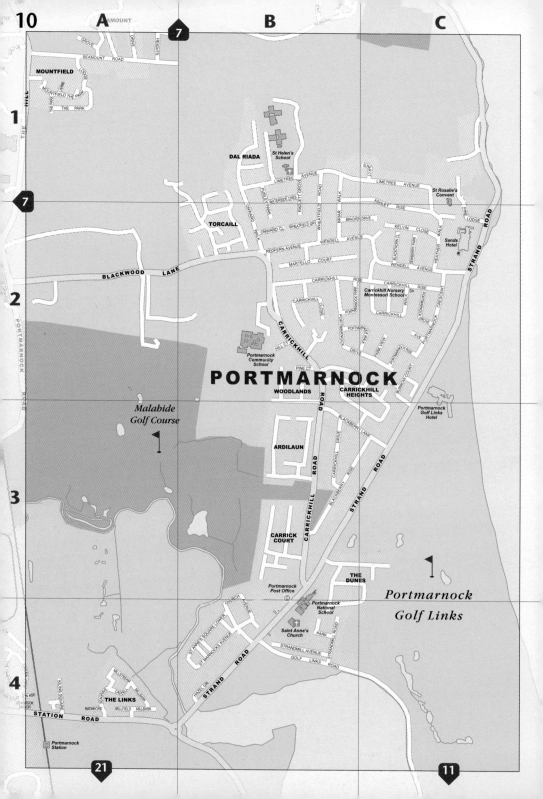

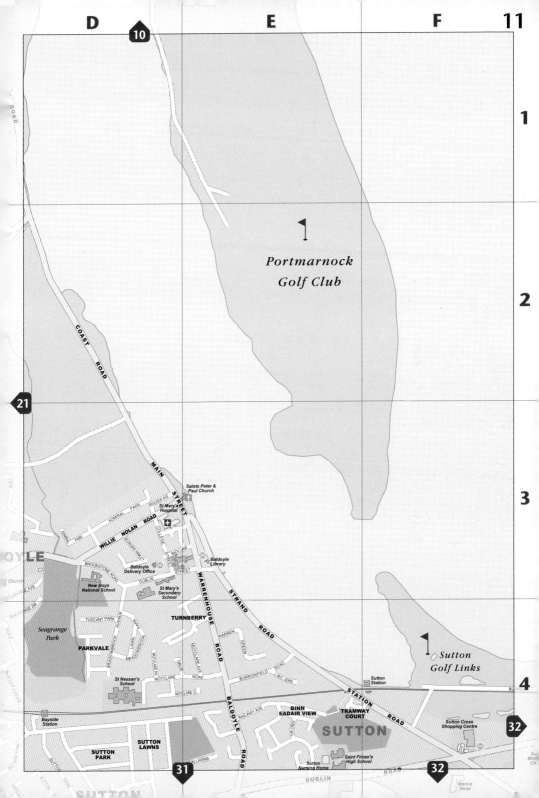

1

DAMASTOWN
INDUSTRIAL ESTATE

MACETOWN ROAD

TYRELLSTOWN

DAMASTOWN
INDUSTRIAL
ESTATE

DAMASTOWN   AVENUE

2

DAMASTOWN
INDUSTRIAL ESTATE

DAMASTOWN GREEN

DAMASTOWN   ROAD

DAMASTOWN CLOSE

DAMASTOWN CT.

WELLVIEW ROAD
WELLVIEW GREEN
WELLVIEW PARK
CRESCENT
WELLVIEW

PARSLICKSTOWN
GARDENS

COURT

LADY'S WELL

N 3

INDUSTRIAL
ESTATE

LADY'S   WELL   ROAD

FAS

PARSLICKSTOWN LANE

PARSLICKSTOWN
GREEN

LADY'S   WELL   ROAD

14

St Lu...
Chu...

THE GROVE

PHEASANT
RUN

SWALLOWBROOK

SWALLOWBROOK

HUNTERS RUN THE PARK

THE FERN

THE DRIVE

THE CLOSE

CRESCENT

BRAMBLEFIELD DRIVE

WALK

PARK

PARK

VIEW

SHACKLETON

BLANCHARDSTOWN

NAVAN   ROAD

BYPASS

MULHUDDART

CASTLECU
HEAT

NTSTOWN

THE GLADE

HUNTERS RUN THE PARK

THE CLOSE

THE DRIVE

DEEP HAVEN

AVENUE

ASHFIELD GROVE

ASHFIELD GREEN

HUNTSTOWN RISE

THE DRIVE

THE AVENUE

THE GREEN

RIVERPARK
VIEW

3

ttlepace
hopping
Centre

THE GROVE

THE CLOSE

THE DRIVE

HUNTERS RUN THE WAY

WEST HAVEN

DEEP HAVEN

School

HUNTSTOWN
WOOD

Sacred Heart
Church

LAWN

PINEROCK
COURT

ASHFIELD WAY

ASHFIELD GARDENS

HUNTSTOWN RISE

ASHFIELD PARK

SADDLERS

BLAKESTOWN   ROAD

Mulhuddart
National
School

SADDLERS

BLANCHARDSTOWN

NAVAN

HANSFIELD

HUNTERS
RUN

HUNTERS RUN

THE WAY

THE

WEST HAVEN

WALK

CARNE COURT

WAY

HUNTSTOWN   WAY

GREEN

HUNTSTOWN

HUNTSTOWN

DRIVE

PARK

GROVE

HUNTSTOWN   WAY

ASHFIELD

RISE

ASHFIELD CLOSE

HUNTSTOWN ROAD

CLOSE

SADDLERS

SADDLERS

CRESCENT

SADDLERS

BYPASS

CRESCENT

MANOR

RUSHEENEY

CLOSE

GREEN

AVENUE

GLENEAT DOWNS

HUNTSTOWN GLEN

HUNTSTOWN
COURT

HUNTSTOWN   AVENUE

FILMCOURT DRIVE

PARK

BROADWOOD LAWN

BROADWOOD

AVENUE

DRIVE

WHITESTOWN AVENUE

WHITESTOWN PARK

WHITESTOWN

BLAKESTOWN   WAY

GREEN

CRESCENT

AVENUE

RUSHEENEY

CASTLEWOOD

CASTLEWOOD
CLOSE

PINEBROOK

VALE

PINEBROOK PARK

WOODVALE

WOODLANDS

Scoil
Mhuire

House of
St Mary of
the Servants

DRIVE

4

MANORFIELDS DRIVE

GREEN

MANOR

CLOSE

MEADOW

WAY

RISE

BEECHWOOD DOWNS

CASTLEWOOD DOWNS

VIEW

GLEN

PINEBROOK DOWNS

PINEBROOK

WOODVALE

LAWN

Scoil
Chiarain

Hartstown
Park

GREEN

WOODVALE AVENUE

WOODVALE PARK

Blanchardstown
Community
School

LAWN

AVENUE

SHEEPMOOR GROVE

GARDENS

WHITESTOWN PARK

GARDENS

WALK

ROAD

Blancha
Shoppi

CHERRYFIELD

DRIVE

MEADOW

WAY

HAZELWOOD AVENUE

GREEN

COURT

PARK

BLAKESTOWN   ROAD

TSTOWN

Scoil Chiarain

Church of
t Ciaran

HARTS

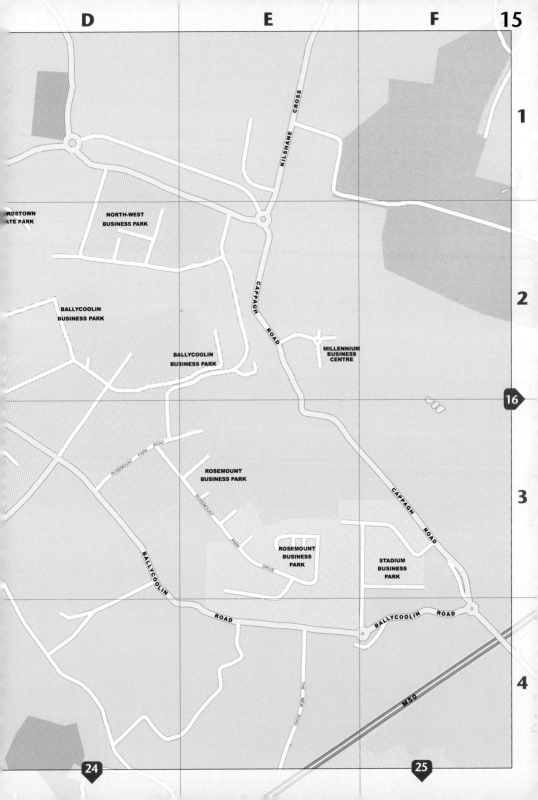

1

*Sillogue
Golf Course*

2

MEAKSTOWN COTTAGES

M50

*Sillogue
Park*

SAINT   MARGARET'S   ROAD

CASTLE
GARDENS

QUARE

HAMPTON
WOOD

POPPINTREE

18

LANESBOROUGH

LANES
DONOUGH ROAD
DRIVE
GROVE
GREEN
AVENUE

JAMESTOWN   ROAD

GROVE

POPPINTREE
INDUSTRIAL
ESTATE

BALBUTCHER   DRIVE

BALBUTCHER   WAY

GRAIGUE
COURT

CRANNOGE
CLOSE
CRANNOGE
ROAD

CRANNOGE
DONNET

GALLAUN ROAD

BALBUTCHER

LANE

TERMON
COURT

St Joseph's
Church

**BALLYMUN
INDUSTRIAL
ESTATE**

BALCURRIS

ROAD

MEWS

LANESBOROUGH ROAD

CRES

LANESBOROUGH
VIEW

MELVILLE PARK

CRESCENT

MELVILLE
DRIVE

Apple of
my Eye
Creche

O CT

GREEN

TER

CLOSE

WAY

WEST

LANE

POPPINTREE

PARK

LANE

BELCLARE
PARK

HOLYWELL

BELCLARE   GREEN

BELCLARE   GROVE

BELCLARE   AVENUE

BELCLARE   DRIVE

CAIRN ROAD

KNOWTH
CT

CARRIG ROAD

DRUID
COURT

DANE

ROAD

St Joseph's
School

CAIRN
COURT

DANE   ROAD

BALCURRIS ROAD

**BALCURRIS
GARDENS**

ARD NA MEALA

DOLMEN COURT

LANE

DANE CLOSE

COURT

BARNEWOOD DR

BELCLARE
PARK

CALE ENN

SANDYHILL AVE

**SANDYHILL
GARDENS**

SILLOGE

Holy Spirit School

SILLOGE
DRIVE

SILLOGE

BALCURRIS ROAD

GATEWAY

*Poppintree
Park*

**FINGLAS
BUSINESS
CENTRE**

JAMESTOWN   ROAD

SYCAMORE   ROAD

SYCAMORE PARK

OAKWOOD

CLOSE

OAKWOOD
ROAD

OAKWOOD
AVENUE

OAKWOOD
GROVE

CEDARWOOD   ROAD

CEDARWOOD GREEN

CEDARWOOD PARK

CEDARWOOD RISE

CEDARWOOD AVENUE

CEDARWOOD

WILLOW

WILLOW
PARK CLOSE

MOTTE

WILLOW PARK
LAWN

PINEWOOD

PINEWOOD   CRESCENT

PINEWOOD   AVENUE

SILLOGE

GROVE

AVENUE

CLANCY   ROAD

MCKEE ROAD

FINGLAS ROAD

CLANCY   AVENUE

GROVE WOOD

GROVE AVE

PARK   ROAD

WILLOW   PARK   CRESCENT

GROVE   PARK   DRIVE

WILLOW PARK DRES

WILLOW   PARK   AVENUE

3

4

26   27

1

M-1

CLONSHAUGH ROAD

2

N32

FAS
Workshop

TURVEY COTTAGES
SCORE ROAD
LANE
KING ROAD

CLONSHAUGH
INDUSTRIAL ESTATE

CLONSHAUGH ROAD

C'S GROVE
SWIFT'S GROVE
MOORFIELD DRIVE
CLONSHAUGH HEIGHTS
CLONSHAUGH CRESCENT
CLONSHAUGH CLOSE
CLONSHAUGH PARK
CLONSHAUGH DRIVE
MOATVIEW COURT
MOATVIEW AVENUE

St Francis
School

Priorswood
Post Office

St Francis
Church

CLONSHAUGH AVENUE

20

CLONSHAUGH
INDUSTRIAL ESTATE

WOODLAWN GREEN
WOODLAWN DRIVE
WOODLAWN AVENUE
WOODLAWN PARK
WOODLAWN CT.
WOODLAWN RISE
WOODLAWN INN
CRESCENT
THE PARK
THE GREEN
THE VILLA
WOODLAWN WAY
CLOSE
VIEW

NEWBURY TERRACE

NEWBURY AVENUE

NEWBURY

CLONSHAUGH GREEN

PRIORSWOOD

MOATVIEW DRIVE
GROVE
GLIN PARK
FERRYCARRIG DRIVE
GLIN CRES.
GLIN DRIVE
GLIN GROVE
MACROOM ROAD

3

LARCH HILL
THE SQUARE
THE COURT
THE VIEW

AULDEN GRANGE

RIVERSIDE GROVE
RIVERSIDE AVENUE
RIVERSIDE PARK
RIVERSIDE DRIVE
RIVERSIDE GROVE
RIVERSIDE CRESCENT
RIVERSIDE

CLONSHAUGH ROAD

GLIN AVENUE
GLIN ROAD

St Joseph's
School

GREENCASTLE PARK
St Joseph's
Church

MACROOM AVENUE

COOLOCK LANE

OSCAR TRAYNOR ROAD

Santry River

Public Library

GREENCASTLE ROAD

BARRYSCOURT ROAD

Stardust
Memorial Park

CROMCASTLE ROAD

Northside
Shopping
Centre

ADARE ROAD

ADARE GREEN

4

CASTLETIMON DR.
CASTLETIMON ROAD
CASTLETIMON AVE.
CASTLETIMON GREEN

KILBARRON PARK
KILBARRON AVENUE
DUNDANEER DRIVE
CROMCASTLE GREEN

Scoil
Fhorsa

Daughters of
Charity Convent

Church of St Luke
the Evangelist

CROMCASTLE AVENUE
CROMCASTLE DRIVE
CROMCASTLE PARK
CROMCASTLE CT.
CROMCASTLE CT.

BUNRATTY AVENUE
ADARE PARK
EAGLE PARK
APOLLO WAY
TRANQUILITY GROVE
ARMSTRONG WALK
BUNRATTY ROAD

OSCAR TRAYNOR ROAD

BUNRATTY DRIVE
COOLOCK

AVENUE
LORCAN GREEN
LORCAN VILLAS
IVY COURT
BEAUMONT COURT
IVY COURT
THE CLOSE
LORCAN VILLAS

BALLYSHANNON ROAD

KILBARRON ROAD

KILMORE ROAD
KILMORE COURT

KILBARRON ROAD

CASTLEKEVIN ROAD

KILMORE AVENUE
KILMORE CRESCENT
BEECHLAWN GREEN
ADARE GREEN
TERRACE

KILMORE

Secondary Schools

Beaumont Hospital

28

29

A   B   C

1

Cemetery

BALGRIFFIN

MALAHIDE ROAD

Fingal Cemetery

BALGRIFFIN

ST. SAMSON

2

N32

Hilton Hotel

19

BELCAMP CRESCENT

BELCAMP GARDENS

MOATVIEW GARDENS

MOATVIEW COURT

TULIP CT

PRIMROSE ROAD

PRIMROSE GROVE

PRIMROSE GROVE

PRIMROSE GROVE

BELCAMP LANE

NEWTOWN COURT

N32

CLARE HALL

TEMPLEVIEW AVENUE

TEMPLE VIEW CRES

TEMPLE VIEW

TEMPLE VIEW GROVE

TEMPLE VIEW DOWNS

TEMPLE VIEW GREEN

RISE

WALK

PRIORSWOOD ROAD

BELCAMP GREEN

BELCAMP AVENUE

BELCAMP GROVE

DARNDALE

SNOWDROP ROAD

PRIMROSE DRIVE

MARIGOLD WALK

PANSY WALK

GREENWOOD

TEMPLE VIEW PARK

TEMPLE VIEW PLACE

SQUARE

GREENWOOD AVE

ELMFIELD

ELMFIELD WAY

AVENUE

3

FERRYCARRIG PARK

FERRYCARRIG ROAD

BELCAMP CRES 2

PARK AVENUE

COTTAGE

COURT

GROVE

BUTTERCUP PK

BUTTERCUP ROAD

BUTTERCUP ROAD

MARIGOLD ROAD

Park Hotel

GROVE

LANE

TEMPLE VIEW ROW

THE DOWNS

TEMPLE VIEW

WYTTLE AVE

DONAGHIES GRV

MANOR GRV

ARD NA GREINE

THE ORCHARD

THE ORCHARD

GREENWOOD DRIVE

GREENWOOD DRIVE

GREENWOOD COURT

GREENWOOD PARK

GREEN

FOXHILL

FOXHILL AVENUE

WYTTLE WAY

DONAGHIES CLOSE

BEECHBROOK GROVE

LENTISK LAWN

INVERMORE GRV

MACROOM AVE

FERRYCARRIG DRIVE

GREENCASTLE PARADE

GREENCASTLE CRESCENT

GREENCASTLE AVENUE

NEWTOWN COTTAGES

PARADE

GREENCASTLE AVENUE

NEWTOWN DRIVE

SLADEMORE DRIVE

BUNRATTY CLOSE

COURT

SLADEMORE PLACE

SLADEMORE AVENUE

BLUNDEN DRIVE

St Paul's Church Ayrefield

GLENROSE COURT

SLADEMORE AVE

ELTON PARK

ELTON WALK

ELTON COURT

FOXHILL DRIVE

FOXHILL LAWN

FOXHILL WAY

CEDAR PK

GLENTWORTH PARK

4

GREENCASTLE ROAD

MALAHIDE ROAD

AYREFIELD DRIVE

NEWTOWN DRIVE

AYREFIELD AVENUE

AYREFIELD COURT

AYREFIELD PARK

PARK

RATHVALE AVENUE

RATHVALE GROVE

RATHVALE GROVE

RATHVALE PARK

LIMEWOOD AVENUE

LIMEWOOD PARK

LIMEWOOD CLOSE

LIMEWOOD ROAD

ELTON COURT

MILLBROOK ROAD

MILLBROOK GROVE

MILLBROOK AVENUE

The Donaghies School

STREAMVILLE ROAD

LABBAGH GROVE

UCI Cinema

St John the Evangelist

29

MALAHIDE ROAD

OLD MALAHIDE ROAD

TONLEGEE ROAD

TONLEGEE DRIVE

WOODBINE ROAD

MILLWOOD VILLAS

MILLWOOD COURT

WOODBINE ROAD

WOODBINE CLOSE

Scoil Eithne

30

Portmarnock Station

1

COAST ROAD

DRUMNIGH WOODS

DRUMNIGH ROAD

MAYNE   ROAD

MAYNE   ROAD

2

Mayne River

11

THE HOLE IN THE WALL ROAD

ST. MICHAEL'S COTTAGES

PRIORY HALL

BEAU PARK ST

CASTLEROSE

CASTLEROSE

GRATTAN LODGE

GRATTAN WOOD

RANGE LODGE AVENUE

BEAU PARK PLACE

STAPOLIN LAWNS

GRANGE PARK DRIVE

CASTLEROSE VIEW

CLOSE

GRATTAN HALL

NEWGROVE ESTATE

Newgrove School

RANGE LODGE

AVENUE

STAPOLIN LAWNS

GRANGE PARK

3

Saint Columban's

OLD   GRANGE   ROAD

STAPOLIN LAWNS

GRANGE PARK

GRANGE PARK

BALDOYLE

GROVE

GREEN

ELMFIELD AVENUE

CT PARK

DRIVE

VALE

LAWN

GRANGE   ABBEY   DRIVE

ELMFIELD

GRANGEMORE DRIVE

GRANGEMORE

GRANGE

GRANGE   ROAD

Church

SEAGRANGE AVE

GRANGEMORE   ROAD

GRANGE ABBEY CRESCENT

Grange Abbey Grove

GRANGE AVENUE

GRANGE RISE

SEAGRANGE ROAD

SEAGRANGE DR

DONAGHMEDE

AVENUE

GRANGEMORE

GROVE

School

Donaghmede Park

GRANGE GREEN

GRANGE DRIVE

GRANGE

3

CLOSE

Holy Trinity Church

Donaghmede Shopping Centre

NEWBROOK AVENUE

NEWBROOK ROAD

CARNDONAGH PARK

GRANGE PARADE

CLOSE

GRANGE AVENUE

GRANGE DRIVE

ABBEY PARK

MARIAN PARK

SEACLIFF AVENUE

LABADOR CLOSE

GRANGE

TARA LAWN

FLUROWNY CL

KILLARY GR

WOODVIEW PARK

CARNDONAGH AVE

CARNDONAGH DR

CARNDONAGH LAWN

DONAGHMEDE AVE

DONAGHMEDE DR

SEACLIFF DRIVE

BALDOYLE INDUSTRIAL ESTATE

GRANGE AVENUE

SEACLIFF

HOWTH VIEW PARK

HOLYWELL CRESCENT

The Bizzie Kids Bungalow

DONAGHMEDE

GRANGE   WAY

ABBEY PARK

4

BEECHES

HOLYWELL ROAD

SAINT   DONAGH'S   ROAD

VERBENA LAWNS

BAYSIDE

BAYSIDE BOULEVARD

BAYSIDE WALK

ST DONAGH'S PK

KILBARRACK WAY

VERBENA PARK

VERBENA GROVE

BAYSIDE

KILBARRACK   ROAD

Howth Junction Station

Scoil Naisunta Muire agus Josef

GARTO LAWN

VERBENA AVE

ALLEN ROAD

BAYSIDE SQUARE NORTH

Secondary School

Kilbarrack Shopping Centre

MOUNT   OLIVE   ROAD

OLIVE GROVE

30

31

KILBARRACK

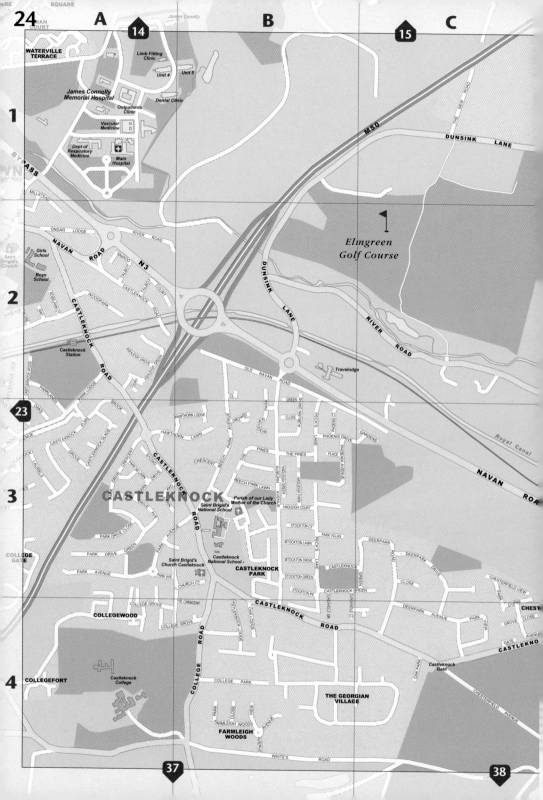

A **16** **B** **17** **C**

FINGLAS
FINGLAS EAST

MELLOWES ROAD
Jamestown Road Baptist Church
GLASNEVIN AVENUE

Social Welfare Office
SEAMUS ENNIS ROAD
BALLYGALL ROAD WEST
St Canice's National School
BENEAVIN PARK

CAPPAGH
Finglas Parochial School
Finglas Library
Finglas Main Centre
COLLINS
Beneavin College
BENEAVIN LODGE
BENEAVIN COURT

1

St Canice's Church
Convent of the Holy Faith
CHURCH ST
Church of St Canice
GLASAREE ROAD
De La Salle Brothers School
FERNDALE ROAD

Convent of the Holy Faith
Saint Fergal's Boys National School
ROAD

MAIN STREET
JAMESTOWN ROAD
FINGLAS ROAD
GLASANAON ROAD
BALLYGALL PARADE
Mother of Divine Grace School & College
BALLYGALL

WELLMOUNT ROAD
FINNEBER SQUARE
FINGLAS PLACE
GLENHILL
Johnstown Park

GLASANAON ROAD

FINGLAS SOUTH
SAINT HELENA'S ROAD
Janelle Shopping & Leisure Centre
FINGLAS
GRIFFITH DRIVE
GRIFFITH PARADE

2

Saint Malachy's School
St Oliver Plunkett Junior School
ST HELENA'S DRIVE
HAZELCROFT
PREMIER SQUARE
GLENHILL
FAIRWAYS GROVE
GLASNAMANA ROAD

Saint Oliver Plunkett's Church
GORTMORE ROAD
CLOONLARA
PROSPECT HILLS
GRIFFITH HEIGHTS
GLASNEVIN DOWNS
TOLKA ESTATE
GLASILAWN RD

KIPPURE PARK
GLASMEEN

GRIFFITH HEIGHTS
NORTHLAND DRIVE
CREMORE

25

TOLKA VALLEY ROAD
ROAD
OLD FINGL
CREMORE

Tolka Valley Park
GLASNEVIN WOODS
VIOLET HILL

BALLYBOGGAN ROAD
VIOLET HILL PARK

RIVERMOUNT COTTAGES

3

Royal Canal
LAGAN ROAD
FAS
BOYNE ROAD
NORE ROAD
BARROW ROAD
SLANEY ROAD

RATOATH ROAD
Marian School
RATOATH ESTATE
Broombridge Station
The Church of Jesus Christ of Latter Day Saints
Glasnevin (Cemet

Saint Mary's School & Clinic for the Deaf
MOYLE ROAD
LEE
BLACKWATER ROAD
SLANEY ROAD
THE WILLOWS
CLAREMONT

St Dominic's College
Dublin Corporation Water Division - North City Maintenance
CARNLOUGH ROAD
FAS Training Centre
CLAREMONT CRESCENT

VENTRY ROAD
BANNOW ROAD
CARNLOUGH ROAD

CABRA WEST
Saint Finbar's National School
KILKIERAN
Colaiste Eanna Cabra
CLAREVILLE

4

Pope John Paul II Park
Church of the Most Precious Blood
KILKIERAN ROAD
Glasnevin (Prospect) Cemetery

NEPHIN ROAD
RATOATH RD
FASSAUGH AVENUE
DINGLE ROAD
MULROY ROAD
SHANDON GARDENS

CBS St Declan's Secondary School
KILLALA
LISCANNOR ROAD

CBS Saint Joseph's School

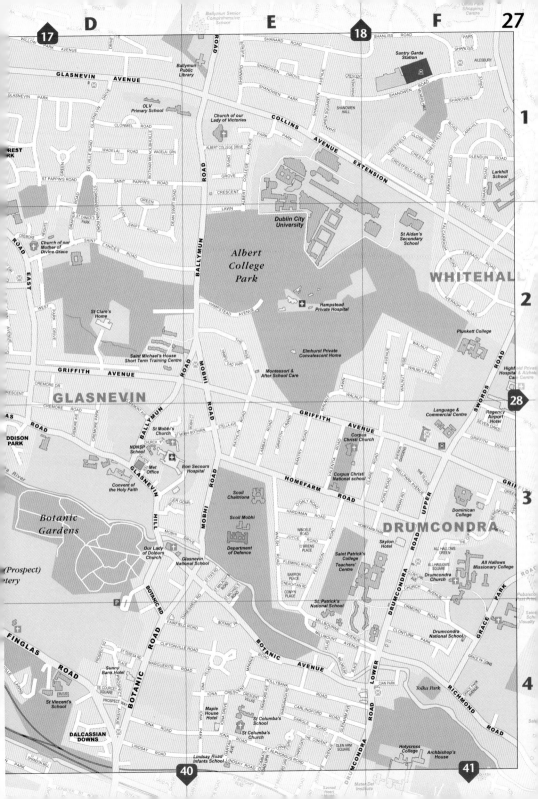

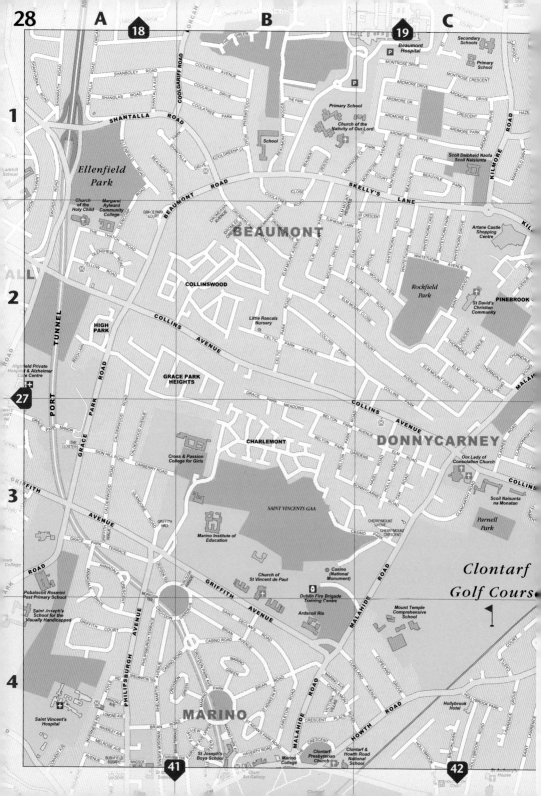

30

A · 20 · **B** · 21 · **C**

KILBARRACK

EDENMORE

Edenmore Park

Scoil Eithne

Millwood Park

Saint Malachy's Boys National School

St Monica's Church

Woodbine Close

Woodbine Park Drive

Woodbine Park

Secondary School

Kilbarrack Shopping Centre Crazy Prices

St Benedict's Church

MOUNT OLIVE GROVE

SWAN'S NEST

GRANGE PARK VIEW

Kilbarrack Station

SWAN'S WEST ROAD

BRIARFIELD GROVE

BRIARFIELD GROVE

THORNVILLE ROAD

THE BEER

KILBARRACK

KILBARR

1

RAHENY ROAD

GRANGE PARK AVENUE

GRANGE PARK DRIVE

GRANGE PARK WALK

GRANGE PARK GRN

GRANGE PARK RISE

GRANGE PARK

Special Needs School

Belmont

Capuchin Friary

BELMONT SQUARE

BELMONT PARK

GRANGE PARK CRESCENT

GRANGE PARK ROAD

BRIARFIELD VILLAS

Scoil Eoin

Greendale Community School

AVENUE

Greendale Shopping Centre

St John the Evangelist

Gael Scoil Mide

KILBARRACK GROVE

GREENDALE ROAD

KILBARRACK AVENUE

ROSEGLEN ROAD

FOXFIELD GREEN

FOXFIELD CRESCENT

FOXFIELD ST JOHN

GRANGE PARK CRESCENT

TUSCANY

DOWNS

FOXFIELD HEIGHTS

CEDAR WALK

FOXFIELD AVENUE

FOXFIELD GROVE

FOXFIELD DRIVE

FOXFIELD LAWN

FOXFIELD GROVE

FOXFIELD PARK

PRINGDALE

ROAD

LOUGH DERG

Raheny Station

Church of Our Lady Mother of Divine Grace Raheny

Raheny Shopping Centre

STATION ROAD

ASHCROFT

RATHMORE PARK

SAINT ASSAM'S ROAD WEST

SAINT ASSAM'S

SAINT ASSAM'S AVENUE

FOXFIELD ROAD

RAHENY

HOWTH ROAD

HOWTH ROAD

Fox's Lane

2

29

HOWTH ROAD

MAIN STREET

Public Library

All Saints Church Raheny - Church of Ireland

Naiscoil Ide Raheny

ALL SAINTS DRIVE

ALL SAINTS PARK

WATERMILL PARK

WATERMILL DRIVE

ST ANNE'S TERRACE

SAINT ANNE'S DRIVE

ST ANNE'S PARK

SAINT ANNE'S

WATERMILL AVENUE

WATERMILL ROAD

AVONDALE PARK

RAHENY PARK

MAYWOOD AVENUE

MAYWOOD PARK

MAYWOOD CRESCENT

MAYWOOD LAWN

MAYWOOD ROAD

MAYWOOD GROVE

MAYWOOD CLOSE

Shieling Hotel

BETTYGLEN

ORCHARD RD

THE GLEN

THE VILLAGE

THE COURT

JAMES LARKIN ROAD

St Anne's Park

3

CAUSEWAY ROAD

JAMES LARKIN ROAD

PARK LAWN

MOUNT PROSPECT AVENUE

THE GMS

BAYMOUNT PARK

4

Manresa House

DOLLYMOUNT AVENUE

CLONTARF ROAD

Gabriel's Church

Royal Dublin Golf Links

· 43 ·

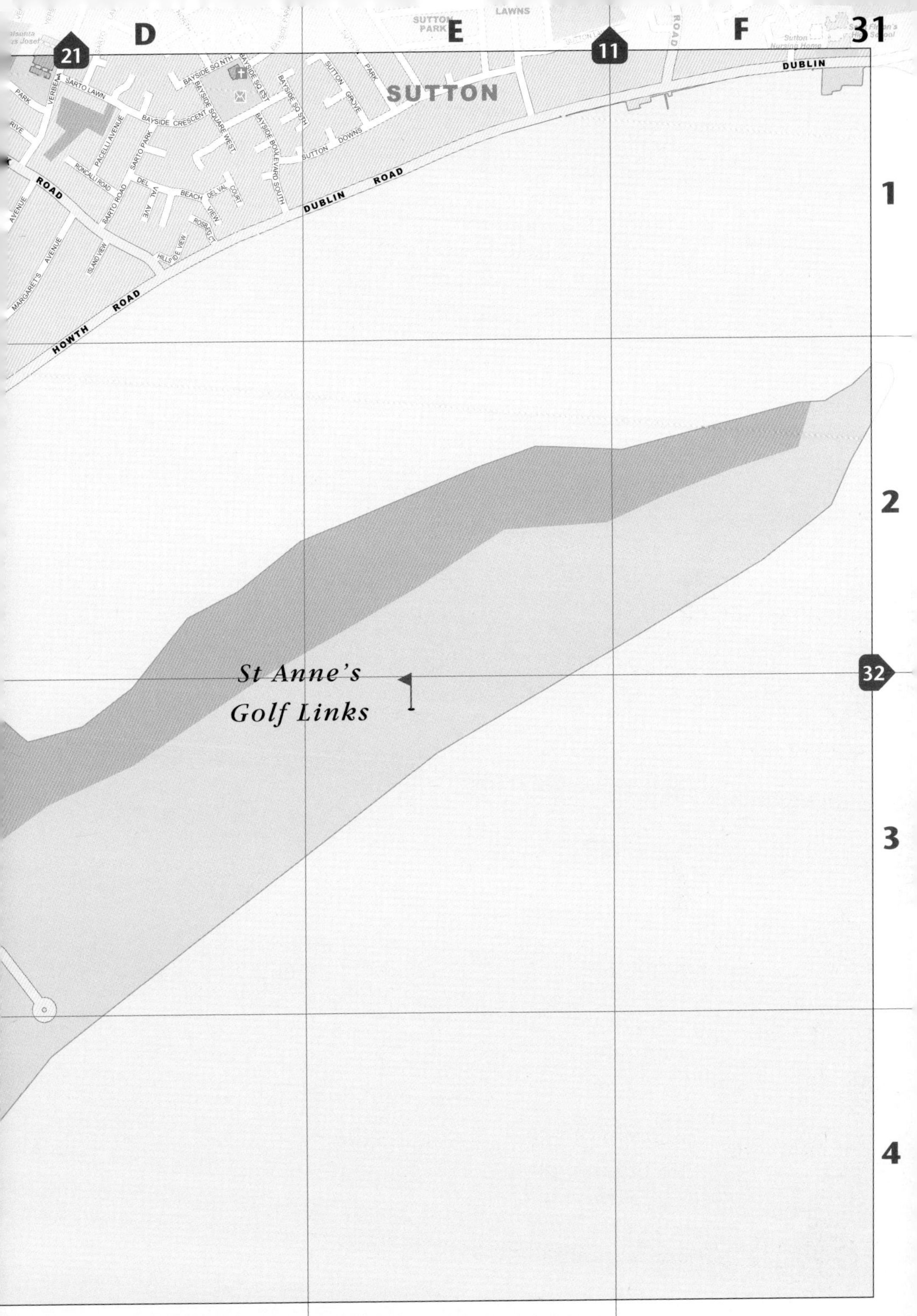

D
E
F

21

11

DUBLIN

SUTTON
PARK

LAWNS

Sutton
Nursing Home

SUTTON

BAYSIDE SQ NTH

BAYSIDE CRESCENT

BAYSIDE SQUARE WEST

BAYSIDE SQ STH

SUTTON GRVE

PARK

SUTTON DOWNS

SUTTON

AVENUE

VERNIER

SARTO LAWN

ROSCOLL ROAD

PACELLI AVENUE

SARTO PARK

SARTO ROAD

DEL VAL AVE

BEACH

DEL VAL
VIEW

ROSARY
CT

DUBLIN

ROAD

ROAD

ISLAND VIEW

HILL VIEW

MARGARET'S   AVENUE

AVENUE

HOWTH   ROAD

DUBLIN   ROAD

1

2

St Anne's
Golf Links

◄

32

3

4

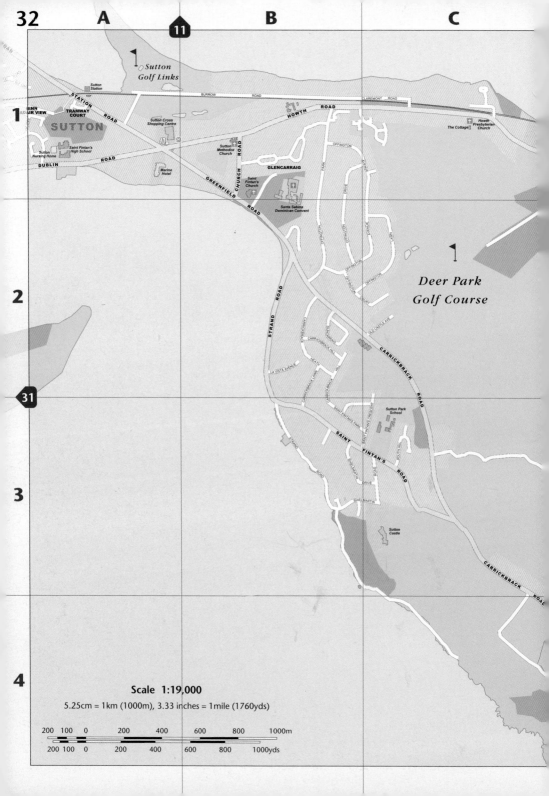

A **B** **C**

11

*Sutton
Golf Links*

Sutton
Station

Sutton
Station

1

INN
AIR VIEW

SUTTON

TRAMWAY
COURT

STATION ROAD

BURROW ROAD

HOWTH ROAD

CLAREMONT ROAD

Sutton Cross
Shopping Centre

Saint Fintan's
High School

Sutton
Nursing Home

DUBLIN ROAD

Marine
Hotel

GREENFIELD ROAD

CHURCH ROAD

Sutton
Methodist
Church

Saint
Fintan's
Church

GLENCARRAIG

Santa Sabina
Dominican Convent

OFFINGTON

The Cottage

Howth
Presbyterian
Church

*Deer Park
Golf Course*

STRAND ROAD

CARRICKBRACK ROAD

Sutton Park
School

LA VISTA AVENUE

SAINT FINTAN'S ROAD

Sutton
Castle

CARRICKBRACK ROAD

2

31

3

4

Scale 1:19,000

5.25cm = 1km (1000m), 3.33 inches = 1mile (1760yds)

| 200 | 100 | 0 | 200 | 400 | 600 | 800 | 1000m |

| 200 | 100 | 0 | 200 | 400 | 600 | 800 | 1000yds |

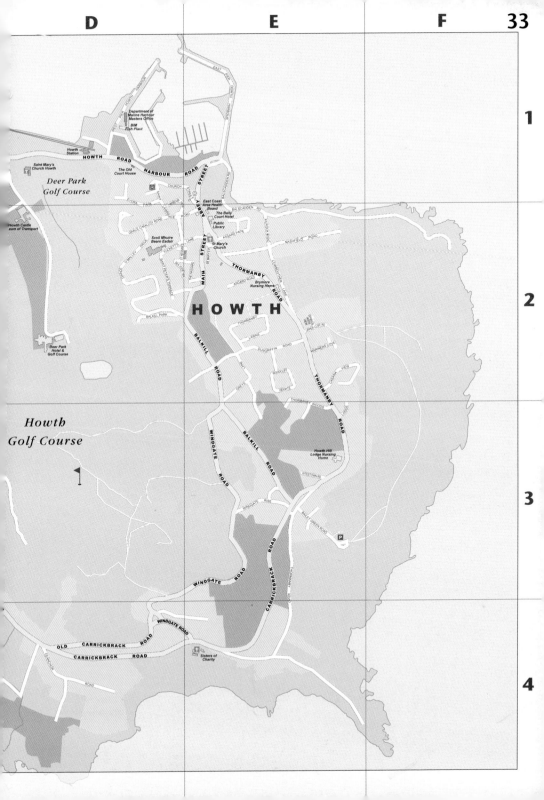

1

Department of
Marine Harbour
Masters Office

BIM
Fish Plant

Howth
Station

HOWTH ROAD

Saint Mary's
Church Howth

The Old
Court House

HARBOUR ROAD

*Deer Park
Golf Course*

CHURCH

Howth Castle
eum of Transport

East Coast
Area Health
Board

The Baily
Court Hotel

Public
Library

GRACE O'MALLO ROAD

ABBEY STREET

Scoil Mhuire
Bearn Eadair

NASHFIELD ROAD

St Mary's
Church

MAIN STREET

THORMANBY ROAD

Brymore
Nursing Home

H O W T H

2

BALKILL PARK

BALKILL ROAD

THORMANBY LANE

THORMANBY ROAD

*Howth
Golf Course*

Deer Park
Hotel &
Golf Course

WINDGATE ROAD

BALKILL ROAD

Howth Hill
Lodge Nursing
Home

3

WINDGATE RISE

BAILEY GREEN ROAD

P

WINDGATE ROAD

CARRICKBRACK ROAD

OLD CARRICKBRACK ROAD

WINDGATE ROAD

CARRICKBRACK ROAD

Sisters of
Charity

4

A   B   C

1

LARAGHCON

BARNHILL CROSS ROADS

LEIXLIP ROAD

2   N4

CELBRIDGE ROAD

WESTON CRESCENT
WESTON DRIVE
WESTON AVENUE
WESTON COURT
WESTON GREEN
WESTON WAY
WESTON HEIGHTS

KEW PARK CRESCENT
KEW PARK
KEW PARK AVE

MEADOW

CLOSE

Spa Hotel

CELBRIDGE ROAD

THE MALL
MAIN STREET
Depart
Social
Lucan
Studio
St Andrew's
Church of Ireland
Lucan
Presbyterian
Church
VESEY TER
Italian
Embassy
Methodist
Church
SARSFIEL
PARK

MAIN ROAD

THE ORCHARD
PRIMROSE LANE

LUCAN
NEWLANDS

WOODVIEW

ARDEER

ARDEEVIN DRIVE
JOESPH
AVENUE
ARDEEVIN COURT

WOODVIEW
HEIGHTS

Hillcrest
Shopping
Centre

DODSBORO ROAD

Dodsboro
Shopping
Centre

CHERRY LAWNS

GREEN

HILLCREST DRIVE

LUCAN BYPASS

ADAMSTOWN ROAD

LUCA

3   TUBBER LANE ROAD

DODSBORO ROAD

AIRLIE HEIGHTS

DODSBORO COTTAGES

DODSBORO
COTTAGES

HILLCREST CLOSE

WESTBROOK PARK

GREENPARK ROAD

MEADOW VIEW GROVE

HILLCREST WALK

HILLCREST VIEW

HILLCREST AVENUE

HILLCREST WAY

HILLCREST LAWNS

HILLCREST PARK

HILLCREST DRIVE

HILLCREST HEIGHTS

HILLCREST GROVE

HILLCREST ROAD

HILLCREST COURT

Esker
Church

Esker
School

CANNONBROOK

CANNONBROOK AVENU

Superquinn
Shopping
Centre

ESKER DR

NEWCASTLE ROAD

WESTBURY COURT

WESTBURY AVENUE

WESTBURY PARK

WESTBURY CLOSE

Lucan
Community
College

ESKER ROAD

FOXMORE
FOXWOOD
FOXPARK

REDBERRY

ELDERBERRY

BERRYFIELD

ROCKWOOD
ROCKFIELD
BROOKFIELD

SILVERBERRY
SILVERDALE
SILVERWOOD

WOODBERRY
WOODDALE

HAZEL

WINSTONHILL

THE GROVE

TANDY'S LANE

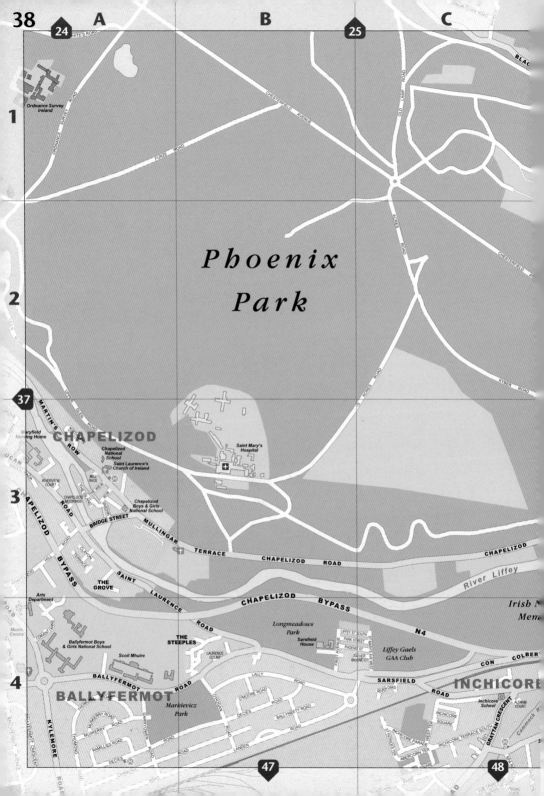

D   E   F

25   26

CBS St Declan's
Secondary School

CBS Saint
Joseph's School

NAVAN ROAD

RATOATH ROAD

DRUMCLIFFE

INVER ROAD

DRUMCLIFFE ROAD

CARNLOUGH

CARPLOUGH RD

SWILLY ROAD

FAUSSAGH ROAD

QUARRY ROAD

ERRIL ROAD

LEIX ROAD

NEPHIN ROAD

CROAGHPATRICK ROAD

ARDPATRICK ROAD

SKREEN ROAD

SLEMISH ROAD

PINE FLDS

HAMPTON
GREEN

CABRA

NEW   CABRA

ANNAMOE ROAD

ANNAMOE
TERRACE

1

Cabra
Gate

HORSE   AVENUE

VILLA PK GDNS

VILLA PARK AVENUE

NORTH ROAD

SPRINGFIELD

SKREEN ROAD

The Maple
Centre

Employment
Exchange

DUNARD COURT

DUNARD DRIVE

PARK VIEW

OLD CABRA ROAD

CARAGH   ROAD

CABRA DRIVE

CABRA PARK

ANNAMOE PARK

NORTH

NORTH ROAD

DUNARD AVENUE

DUNARD WALK

GLENBEIGH PARK

McKEE PARK

GLENMORE ROAD

GLENBEIGH ROAD

ELLESMERE   AVENUE

BLACKHORSE   AVENUE

PRUSSIA STREET

St JOSEPH'S PL

Church
of the
Holy
Family

2

SPA   ROAD

Dublin
Zoo

LORD'S ROAD

McKee
Barracks

MARLBOROUGH ROAD

BLACKHORSE   ROAD

RATHDOWN ROAD

OXMANTOWN

AUGHRIM   STREET

AUGHRIM LA

Garda
Headquarters

ZOO ROAD

NORTH   CIRCULAR   ROAD

CARNEW ST

ROSS ST

ASHFORD ST

OXMANTOWN RD

BEN EDAR ROAD

NIAL STREET

HALIDAY RD

MANOR STREET

40

People's
Garden

FOUNTAIN ROAD

PINDSTER ST

ABERDEEN ST

KINMAN ST

O'DEVANEY GDNS

O'DEVANEY GARDENS

PLACE

STANHOPE ST

ARBOUR HILL

MONTPELIER GARDENS

Saint Bricin's
Military Hospital

Arbour Hill
Prison

INFIRMARY   ROAD

CHESTERFIELD   AVENUE

Wellington
Monument

WELLINGTON ROAD

MONTPELIER PARK

MONTPELIER HILL

ST BRICIN'S PARK

DRIVE

MONTPELIER HILL

ARBOUR
HILL

National
Museum
(Collins Barracks)

Museum

3

Defence Forces
Headquarters

DEBIGH RD

Ashling
Hotel

PARKGATE

Sean
Heuston
Bridge

Frank
Sherwin
Bridge

WOLFE TONE QUAY

CONYNGHAM   ROAD

Computer
Services
Board

Dublin Bus

River Liffey

VICTORIA   QUAY

ISLANDBRIDGE

BRIDGEWATER QUAY

SOUTH

Heuston
Station

Heuston

Guinness
Brewery

BELLEVUE

ISLANDBRIDGE
COURT

CIRCULAR

Clancy
Barracks

SAINT   JOHN'S   ROAD   WEST

Saint Patrick's
Hospital

STEEVEN'S LANE

STREET

National War
morial Park

Gaelscoil
Inchicore

Royal Hospital
Kilmainham

Waverley
Ambulance
Station

MILITARY ROAD

BOW   LANE   WEST

JAMES'S

JAMES'S COURT

Guinness
Storehouse

4

INCHICORE   ROAD

Kilmainham
Congregational
Church

ROAD

Garda
Station

BRIDGE

James's

JAMES'S

PLACE

EGLIN ROW

METROPOLITAN
APARTMENTS

Kilmainham
Gaol
(Museum)

KEARN'S LANE

MOUNT   BROWN

DONNELLAN AVENUE

LEWINGTON LANE

School

BOND STREET

EMMET ROAD

St Michael's
Church

TURVEY AVE

Inchicore
Vocational School

BULFIN

ROAD

Kilmainham
Post Office

OLD   KILMAINHAM

ASHMOUNT
COURT

CAMERON
SQUARE

BROOMFIELD

ADELAIDE TERRACE

Saint James's
Hospital

School

NEWPORT STREET

FORBES LANE

MARROWBONE LANE

SOUTH   CIRCULAR   ROAD

Fatima

THE
MALTHOUSE

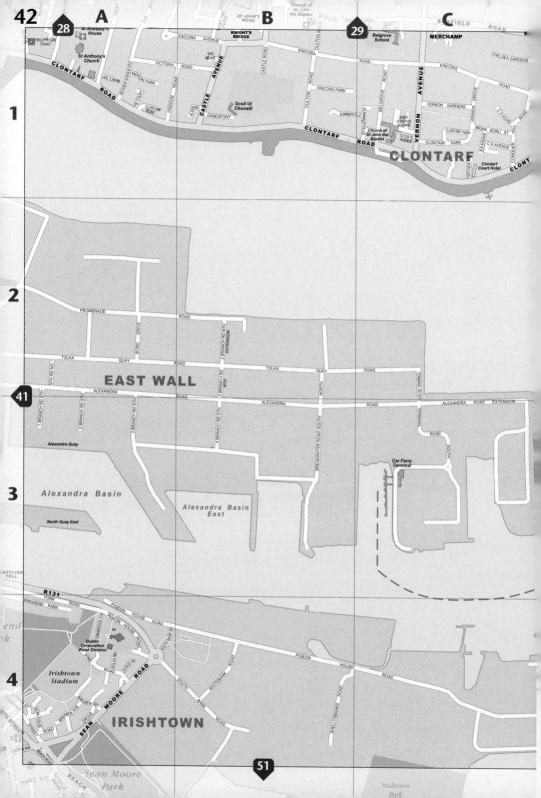

29

30

SEAFIELD ROAD EAST

SEAPARK DRIVE

COURT

CORA COURT

INCORA COURT

ROAD

Wooden
Bridge

1

*Royal Dublin
Golf Course*

2

D U B L I N

H A R B O U R

3

To Liverpool/Holyhead

4

44

A   B   C

34   **35**

1

2

3

4

LOCK

GRIFFEEN GLEN

GRIFFEEN GLEN

AVENUE

GRANGE MANOR

THE OLD FORGE

HAYDENS PARK

GRIFFEEN

ROSBERRY

OLDBRIDGE

GRIFFEEN AVENUE

FINNSTOWN GREEN

HANSTED

HANSTED DRIVE

TULLY HALL

HAYDEN'S LANE

GRANGECASTLE ROAD

LYNCHE'S   LANE

LYNCHE'S

KILCRONAN

CLUAININ CRONAN

DEANSRATH AVE

DEANSRATH ROAD

DEANSRATH PARK

GRANGE VIEW

CL

RATH GEAL

St Ronan's Church

WESTBOURN

School

INDUSTRIAL ESTATE

GRANGECASTLE   ROAD

CASTLEGRANGE

NANGOR   ROAD

KILCARBERY PARK

Round Tower School

GRANGECASTLE

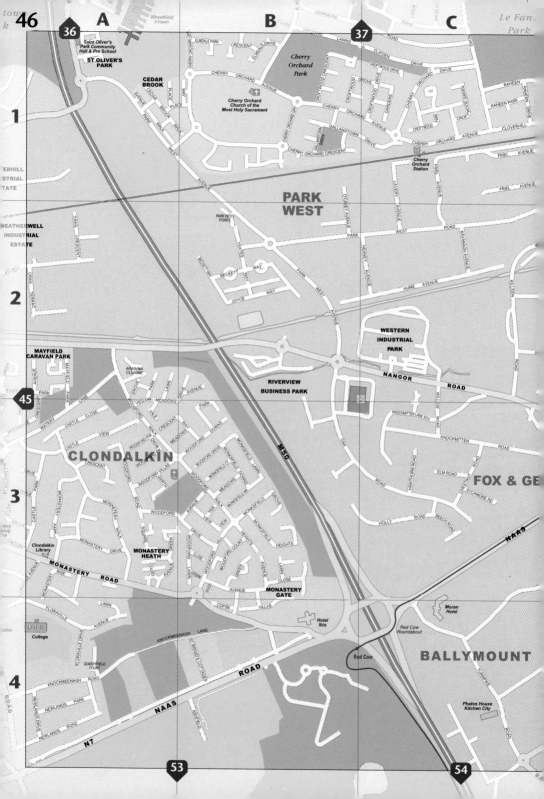

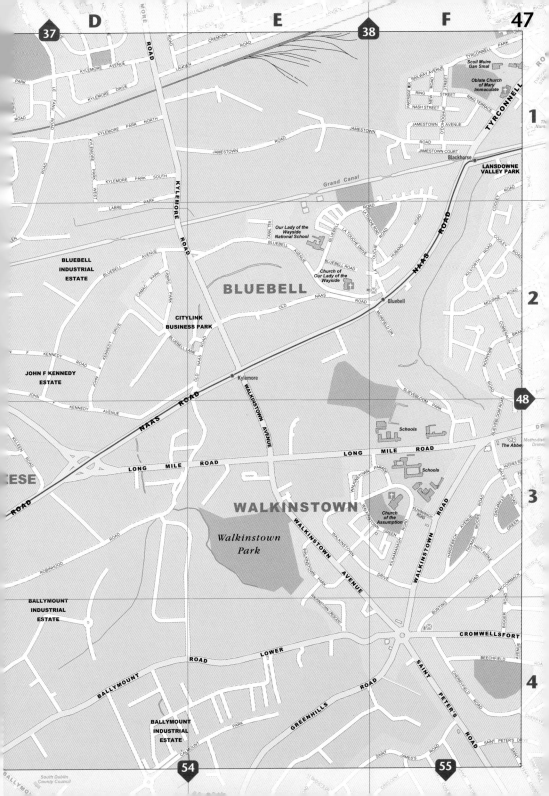

37 **38**

1

2

48

3

4

54 **55**

KYLEMORE AVENUE

KYLEMORE DRIVE

KYLEMORE PARK NORTH

KYLEMORE PARK SOUTH

KYLEMORE PARK WEST

LABRE PARK

CREMONA ROAD

LAHIEN

JAMESTOWN

JAMESTOWN

Grand Canal

RAILWAY AVENUE
TYRCONNELL PARK
PARTRIDGE
RING STREET
NASH STREET
NEW STREET
ODOHOGHUE

Scoil Muire
Gan Smal

Oblate Church
of Mary
Immaculate

JAMESTOWN AVENUE
JAMESTOWN
ROAD
JAMESTOWN COURT

Blackhorse

**LANSDOWNE
VALLEY PARK**

TYRCONNELL ROAD

The Nurs

KYLWORTH ROAD
MOURNE ROAD
COSBERGA
BRANDO

COOLEY ROAD

**BLUEBELL
INDUSTRIAL
ESTATE**

BLUEBELL AVENUE
CAMAC PARK
CAMAC PARK

BLUEBELL

OLD NAAS ROAD

Our Lady of the
Wayside
National School

CHALTER
BLUEBELL AVENUE
BLUEBELL
LA TOUCHE DRIVE
LA TOUCHE ROAD
RUBANO
BLUEBELL ROAD

Church of
Our Lady of the
Wayside

NAAS ROAD

Bluebell

MURFIELD DR

NAAS ROAD

**CITYLINK
BUSINESS PARK**

KENNEDY DRIVE

BLUEBELL LANE

OLD NAAS ROAD

KENNEDY ROAD

**JOHN F KENNEDY
ESTATE**

JOHN F KENNEDY AVENUE

NAAS ROAD

Kylemore

WALKINSTOWN AVENUE

ESE

ROAD

LONG MILE ROAD

SLIEVEBLOOM PARK

SLIEVEBLOOM ROAD

Schools

LONG MILE ROAD

WALKINSTOWN PARADE

Schools

The Abbe

Methodist
Drini

HUGHES RO

WALKINSTOWN

*Walkinstown
Park*

WALKINSTOWN AVENUE

WALKINSTOWN PARK

WALKINSTOWN GREEN

WALKINSTOWN DRIVE

KILNAMANAGH ROAD

Church
of the
Assumption

WALKINSTOWN ROAD

DRIMNAGH ROAD

MOORE GREEN

HARDEBECK AVENUE

THOMAS MOT AVENUE

ROBINHOOD

**BALLYMOUNT
INDUSTRIAL
ESTATE**

DAVITTOWN CRESCENT

SAINT PETER'S ROAD

CROMWELLSFORT

BUNTING

BIDGER ROAD

JOHN MCCORMACK

BEECHFIELD

CHERRYFIELD

SAINT PETER'S DRIVE

BALLYMOUNT

LOWER

ROAD

**BALLYMOUNT
INDUSTRIAL
ESTATE**

PARK

CALMOUNT

GREENHILLS ROAD

SAINT JAMES'S ROAD

SAINT

South Dublin
County Council

BALLYMQ

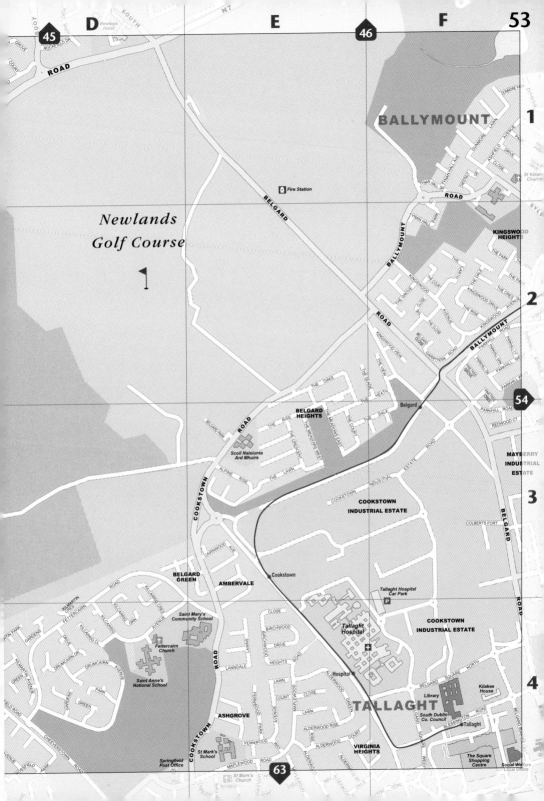

D   E   F

45

46

BALLYMOUNT

1

☐ Fire Station

Newlands
Golf Course

KINGSWOOD
HEIGHTS

2

54

Belgard

BELGARD
HEIGHTS

MAYBERRY
INDUSTRIAL
ESTATE

3

Scoil Naisiunta
Ard Mhuire

COOKSTOWN
INDUSTRIAL ESTATE

COLBERTS FORT

BELGARD
GREEN

AMBERVALE

Cookstown

Tallaght Hospital
Car Park

COOKSTOWN
INDUSTRIAL ESTATE

Kilakee
House

Saint Mary's
Community School

Tallaght
Hospital

Library

4

Fettercairn
Church

Saint Anne's
National School

Hospital

South Dublin
Co. Council

Tallaght

TALLAGHT

ASHGROVE

The Square
Shopping
Centre

Springfield
Post Office

St Mark's
School

VIRGINIA
HEIGHTS

Social Welfare
Local Office

63

St Mary's
Church

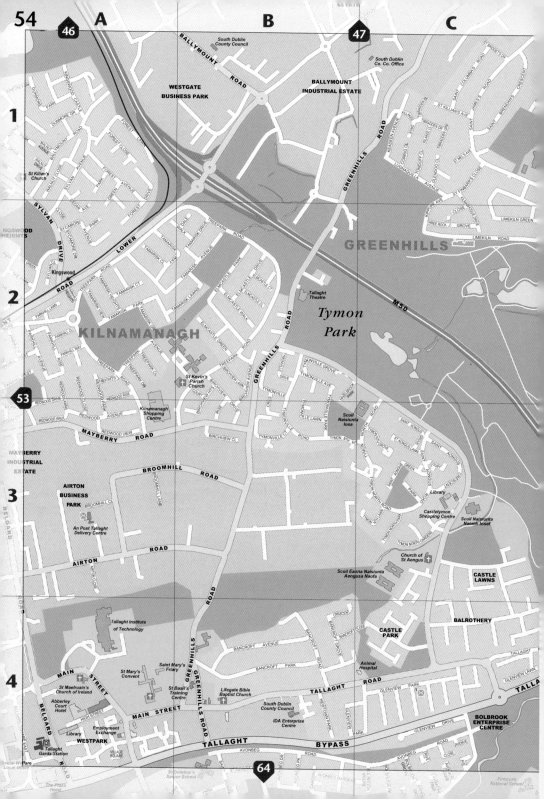

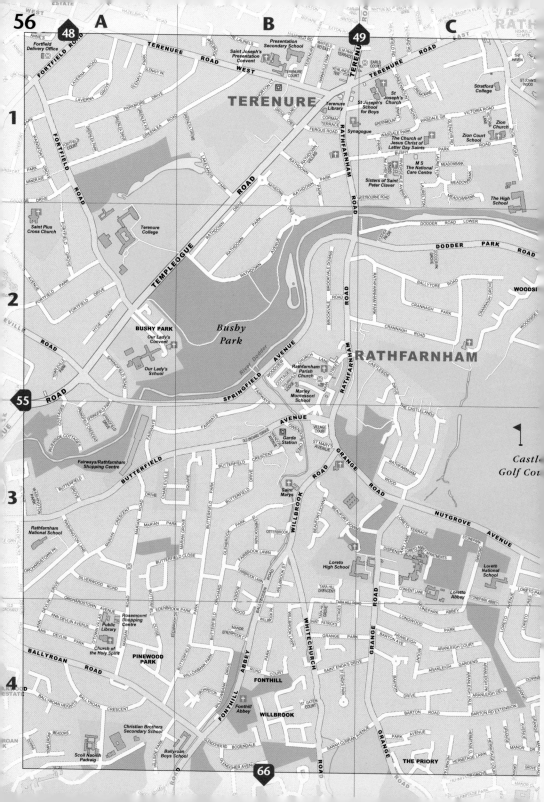

A   B   C

52   53

1

2

3

4

FORTUNESTOWN   LANE

FORTUNESTOWN   LANE

St Aidan's Community School

St Aidan's Primary School

Glenshane Grove

CARRAIGMORE

THE COTTAGES
DOWNES

FORTUNESTOWN

RUSSELL

SUNDALE PARADE

SUNDALE GROVE

SUNCROFT

VERSCHOYLE DRIVE

VERSCHOYLE VALE

VERSCHOYLE   AVENUE

GLEN

GREEN

PARK

VERSCHOYLE CLOSE

MAGNA   DRIVE

MAGNA DRIVE

WESTBROOK LAWNS

MAGNA

SUNDALE

SUNDALE RD

SUNDALE

RATHMINTIN CRESCENT

St Thomas's Church

Junior School

KILTALOWN WAY

KILTALOWN   ROAD

CITYWEST   ROAD

CORBALLY

BELFRY

FORTUNESTOWN

DE SELBY RISE

DE SELBY   LANE

DE SELBY   PARK

DE SELBY

KILTALOWN HEIGHTS

KILTALOWN VIEW

JOB

BELFRY DOWNS

BLESSINGTON   ROAD

BLESSINGTON   ROAD

BLESSINGTON   ROAD   N81

MOUNTSESKIN

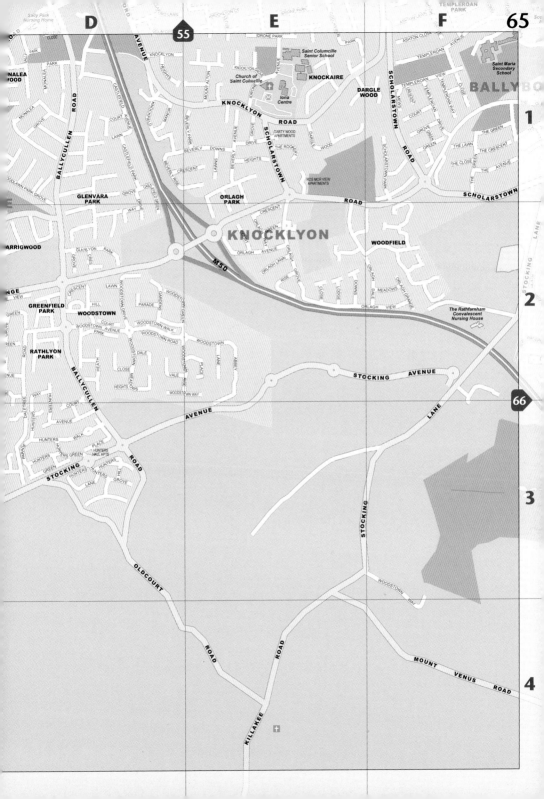

D
E
F
55

KNOCKLYON

M50

Saint Columcille
Senior School

Church of
Saint Columcille

Iona
Centre

KNOCKAIRE

DARGLE
WOOD

Saint Maria
Secondary
School

BALLYBO

TEMPLEROAN
PARK

Sally Park
Nursing Home

GULF

KNOCKTON CT

CROSS PARK

PARK

IDRONE PARK

ASHTON CLOSE

TEMPLEROAN AVENUE

TEMPLEROAN VIEW

TEMPLEROAN DRIVE

TEMPLEROAN WAY

CLOSE

THE GREEN

THE CRESCENT

THE CLOSE

THE LAWN

THE AVENUE

THE

BALLYCULLEN ROAD

MONALEA
WOOD

MONALEA
PARK

MONALEA
GROVE

CLOSE

HALL
PARK

WOODLAWN PARK GROVE

GLENVARA
PARK

CASTLEFIELD AVENUE

CASTLEFIELD PARK

MANOR

KNOCKLYON HEIGHTS

BEVERLY PARK

BEVERLY AVENUE

GROVE

DRIVE

BEVERLY DOWNS

BEVERLY RISE

CRESCENT

LAWN

GROVE

WAY

DRIVE

CASTLEFIELD GREEN

MONT ALTON

KNOCKLYON GREEN

KNOCKLYON DRIVE

KNOCKLYON
ROAD

SCHOLARSTOWN ROAD

DARGLE WOOD

CARTY WOOD
APARTMENTS

ORLAGH
PARK

SCHOLARSTOWN ROAD

THE ROOKERY

LAWNS

HEIGHTS

CRESCENT

ORLAGH AVENUE

ROS MOR VIEW
APARTMENTS

ROAD

SCHOLARSTOWN

SCHOLARSTOWN PARK

GROVE

GREEN

THE CRESCENT

WOODFIELD

ORLAGH LAWN

ORLAGH RISE

ORLAGH GROVE

CLOSE

LODGE

DOWNS

ORLAGH DALE

ORLAGH MEADOWS

ORLAGH GRANGE

ORLAGH VIEW

The Rathfarnham
Convalescent
Nursing House

ARRIGWOOD

GLENLYON PARK

GLENLYON CRES

GROVE

CRESCENT

VIEW

LAWN

WOODSTOWN DRIVE

GARDENS

WOODSTOWN GREEN

PARADE

WOODSTOWN WALK

WOODSTOWN ROAD

WOODSTOWN

HILL

COURT

WOODSTOWN AVENUE

WOODSTOWN PARK

DALE

CLOSE

MEADOWS

RISE

VALE

LANE

ABBEY

PLACE

WOODSTOWN WAY

GREENFIELD
PARK

WOODSTOWN

RATHLYON
PARK

BALLYCULLEN ROAD

HEIGHTS COPSE

HUNTERS WAY

HUNTERS

DALE TREE WAY

HUNTERS COURT

AVENUE

PARADE

HUNTERS GREEN

HUNTERS WALK

HUNTERS PLACE

HUNTERS HALL APTS

HUNTERS GREEN

STOCKING

HUNTERS LANE

HUNTERS GROVE

HUNTERS HILL

STOCKING AVENUE

STOCKING LANE

STOCKING LANE

AVENUE

66

OLDCOURT

ROAD

KILLAKEE

ROAD

WOODSTOWN WAY

MOUNT VENUS ROAD

STOCKING

1

2

3

4

A   **56**   B   THE PRIORY   C   **57**

Scoil Naomh
Pádraig

Ballyroan
Boys School

St Maria
Secondary
School

The Divine
Word School

LYBODEN

WHITECLIFF

St Enda's
Park

Pearse
Museum

1

THE GLEN

THE RISE

Whitechurch
Branch Library

TAYLOR'S   LANE

TAYLOR'S   LANE

GRANGE

PEARSE BROTHERS PARK

ROAD

BEECH
WALK

GLENMORE

Saint Mary's
School

MOYVILLE

Church of Our
Lady of Good
Counsel

Three Rock Rovers
Hockey Club

SPRINGVALE

WHITECHURCH

WHITECHURCH   ROAD

GREEN

EDMONDSTOWN COURT

CRESCENT

LAWN

EDMONDSTOWN
GREEN

2

PROSPECT AVENUE

PROSPECT

MANOR

PROSPECT VIEW

VIEW

DOWNS

COURT

HILL

EDMONDSTOWN   ROAD

WHITECHURCH   ROAD

Whitechurch
National School

65

EDMONDSTOWN

Whitechurch
Church of Ireland

3

Edmondstown
National School

M50

COLLEGE

ROAD

EDMONDSTOWN   ROAD

KILMASHOGUE   LANE

TIBRADDEN   ROAD

4

57

1

2

68

3

4

HILLVIEW GROVE

Ballinteer Community School

Saint Attracta's Junior National School Meadowbrook

LUDFORD DRIVE

BROADFORD

GRANGE WOOD

STONEMASONS WAY

BROADFORD WALK

BROADFORD HILL

BROADFORD DRIVE

BROADFORD CRESCENT

BROADFORD LAWN

BROADFORD PARK

BROADFORD CLOSE

AVENUE

BROADFORD RISE

LUDFORD PARK

LUDFORD ROAD

CHESTNUT GROVE

BALLINTEER GROVE

BALLINTEER CRESCENT

BALLINTEER C.

ROAD

BALLINTEER PARK

BALLINTEER AVENUE

MAYFIELD TER

BALLINTEER GDNS

ASHLAWN

WYCKHAM PLACE

Gort Muire

Wesley College

WYCKHAM

BALLINTEER ROAD

Dundrum Methodist Church

THE MEADOW

WOODPARK

THE COURT

THE GLADE

THE DRIVE

THE GREEN

DELBROOK PARK

GLON LEA

COLLEGE PARK

DELBROOK MANOR

Marley Park

Ballinteer Centre (Superquinn)

Scoil Maighdine Muire

St John's Church Ballinteer

MARLEY VIEW APARTMENTS

LA TOUCHE COURT

BALLINTEER

BALLINTEER

WOODS

WOODPARK

THE VIEW

THE LAWN

THE GROVE

THE WALK

THE CLOSE

THE GLEN

AVENUE

THE HILL

THE HEIGHTS

HEIGHTS

COLLEGE PARK

COLLEGE PARK WAY

BREHON

PINE VALLEY

PINE VALLEY GROVE

PINE VALLEY PARK

DOWNS

MEADOWS

HEATH

BALLINTYRE

FIELD

WALK

BALLINTYRE WALK

WOODPARK CRESCENT

THE

HEATH

ROAD

GRANGE ROAD

GRANGEFIELD

PINE VALLEY WAY

PARK

KINGSTON

VIEW

KINGSTON CRESCENT

KINGSTON CLOSE

KINGSTON AVENUE

KINGSTON DRIVE

KINGSTON HEIGHTS

NWOTSGNIK

KINGSTON GROVE

KINGSTON RISE

GREEN

THE HALL

KINGSTON

HAROLD'S GRANGE ROAD

ROAD

TICKNOCK

GROVE

HILL

DALE

WAY

TICKNOCK HILL

BLACKGLEN ROAD

ROCKVIEW

BRACKEN HILL

St Columba's College

BREHON'S CHAIR

KELLYSTOWN

ROAD

TICKNOCK ROAD

LYNWOOD

ARDGLAS ESTATE

BYPASS

ACORN ROAD

ACORN AVE

PINE COPSE RD

HAWTHORN DR

WYCKHAM PK RD

WYCKHAM

BALLINTEER

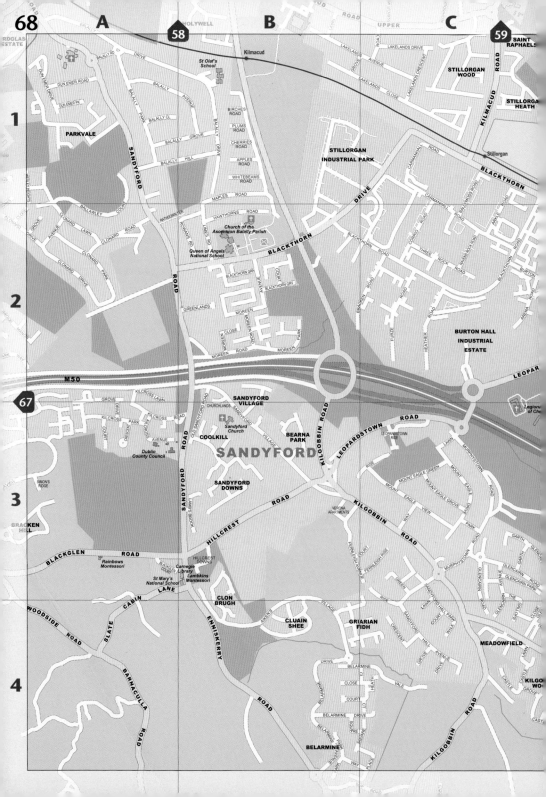

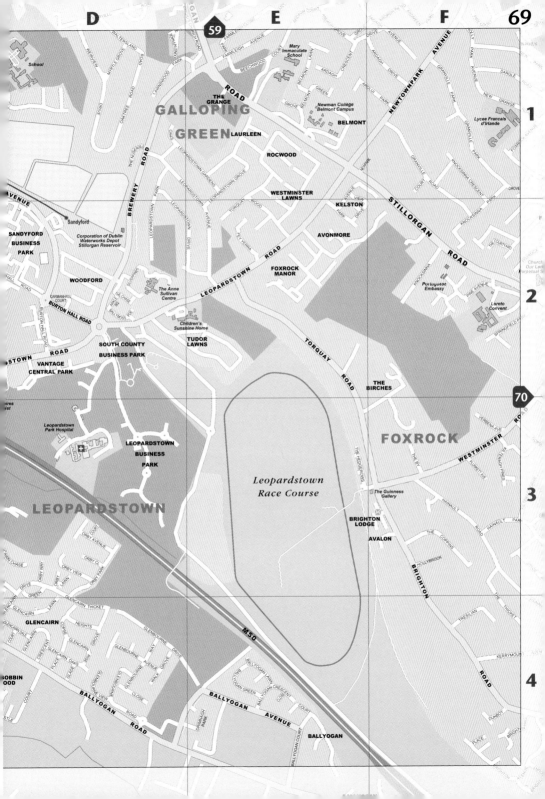

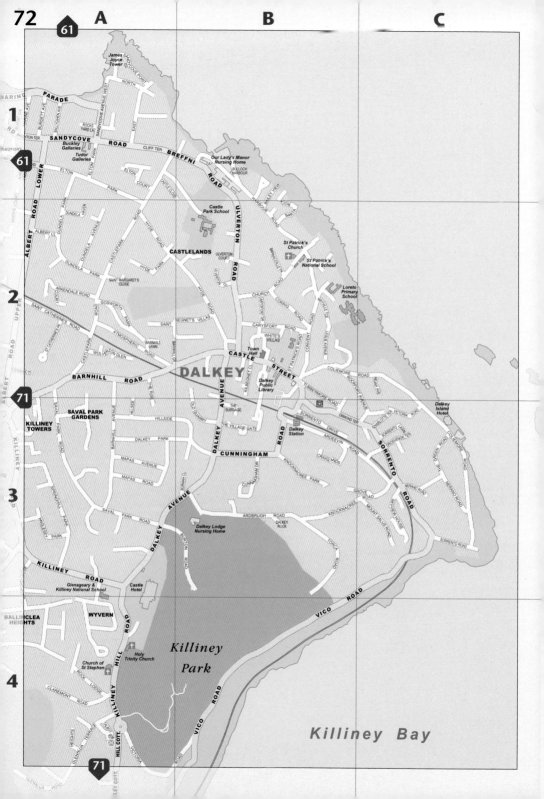

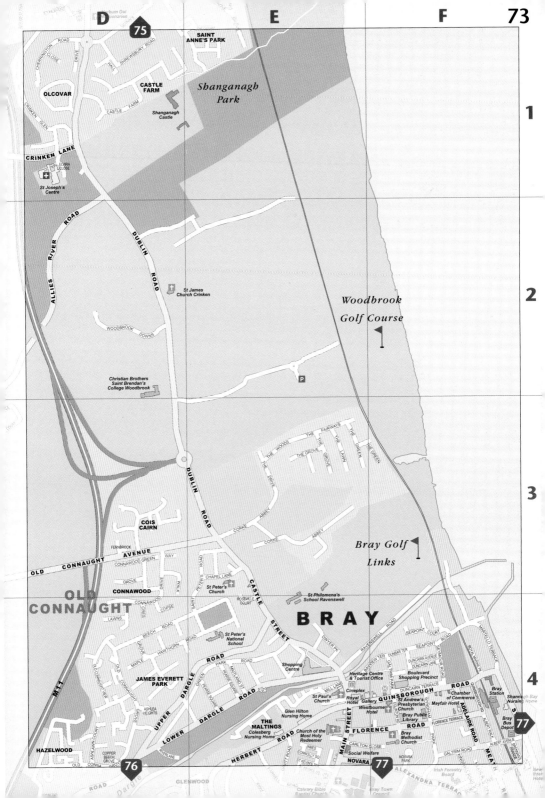

75

CHERRINGTON ROAD
CHERRINGTON CLOSE
SHREWSBURY ROAD
SAINT ANNE'S PARK

OLCOVAR

CASTLE FARM

CASTLE FARM

Shanganagh Castle

Shanganagh Park

CRINKEN GLEN

CRINKEN LANE
ELVIRA CLOSE
St Joseph's Centre

ALLIES RIVER ROAD

DUBLIN ROAD

St James Church Crinken

WOODBROOK DOWNS

Woodbrook Golf Course

Christian Brothers
Saint Brendan's
College Woodbrook

P

THE WOODS
THE FAIRWAYS
THE GROVE
THE GROVE
THE LAWN
THE GREEN
THE DRIVE

DUBLIN ROAD

COIS CAIRN

CORKE ABBEY

CORKE ABBEY

Bray Golf Links

FENNBROOK
OLD CONNAUGHT AVENUE
CONNAWOOD GREEN
WAY
GROVE
CONNAWOOD
CONNAWOOD CRES
LAWNS

SAINT PETER'S ROAD
CHAPEL LANE
St Peter's Church
ROSEVILLE COURT

St Philomena's
School Ravenswell

OLD CONNAUGHT

M 11

BEECH ROAD
HAWTHORN
MAPLE ROAD
GROVE

St Peter's National School

CASTLE STREET

B R A Y

SEAPOINT COURT
RAVENSWELL
DWYER PK
SEAPOINT
DUNBAR TER
DUNCAIRN AVENUE
DUNCAIRN LANE

MARTELLO TERRACE

JAMES EVERETT PARK

UPPER DARGLE ROAD

DARGLE ROAD

GREEN PARK ROAD
MALTINGS ROAD

Shopping Centre

Heritage Centre & Tourist Office
Cineplex
Royal Hotel
Gallery
MILL LANE

QUINSBOROUGH

St Andrew's Presbyterian Church
Boulevard Shopping Precinct
DUNCAIRN TERRACE
Chamber of Commerce
Mayfair Hotel

Bray Station

Shannagh Bay Nursing Home

ASHLEA HEIGHTS
OLD CONNAUGHT GROVE
OLD CONNAUGHT VIEW

HAZELWOOD

LOWER DARGLE ROAD

COPPER BEECH GROVE

THE MALTINGS

Glen Hilton Nursing Home
Colesberg Nursing Home
GREEN LANE

St Paul's Church
Westbourne Hotel
FLORENCE
Church of the Most Holy Redeemer
Social Welfare

Bray Public Library
Bray Methodist Church

ROAD
FLORENCE TERRACE
GALTRIM ROAD

ADELAIDE ROAD

ALBERT AVENUE

ROAD

Bray Bus Depot

77

76

HERBERT ROAD
WITT ROAD
ST KEVOR RD
CONNOLLY SQ
CARLTON CLOSE

NOVARA

MAIN STREET

77

NOVARA PARK

ALEXANDRA TERRACE

Irish Forestry Board

MEATH ROAD

OLD CONNA
GLENWOOD
Dargle
Calvary Bible Baptist Church
Bray Town Council

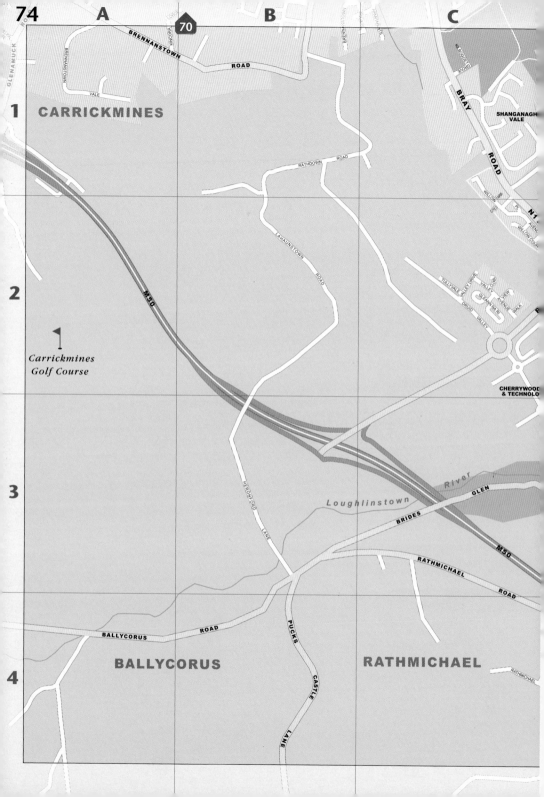

A **B** **C**

70

1 **CARRICKMINES**

BRENNANSTOWN ROAD

BRENNANSTOWN
VALE

GLENAMUCK

BRAY
ROAD

SHANGANAGH
VALE

N1

RATHDOWN ROAD

LAHAUNSTOWN ROAD

M50

2

TULLYVALE
VALLEY DRIVE
VALLEY CLOSE
VALLEY VIEW
VALLEY AVENUE
DRUID VALLEY
OCEAN WALK
OCEAN N2.BI

Carrickmines
Golf Course

CHERRYWOOD
& TECHNOLO

River

GLEN

3

HERONFORD LANE

Loughlinstown

BRIDES

M50

RATHMICHAEL ROAD

BALLYCORUS ROAD

PUCKS

CASTLE

LANE

RATHMICHAEL

4 **BALLYCORUS** **RATHMICHAEL**

73

1

2

3

4

Shopping
Centre

Heritage Centre
& Tourist Office

Boulevard
Shopping Precinct

St Paul's
Church

Royal
Hotel

Cineplex

Gallery

QUINSBOROUGH ROAD

St Andrew's
Presbyterian
Church

Chamber
of Commerce

Bray
Station

Shannagh Bay
Nursing Home

Glen Hilton
Nursing Home

Westbourne
Hotel

Mayfair Hotel

Bray Public
Library

THE
LTINGS
erg
Home

Church of the
Most Holy
Redeemer

FLORENCE

ROAD

Bray
Methodist
Church

Bray
Bus
Depot

STRAND

Carlton Close

Social Welfare

New International
Hotel

NOVARA AVE

ALEXANDRA TERRACE

Irish Forestry
Board

MEATH

Calvary Bible
Baptist Church

Bray Town
Council

MEATH ROAD

ROAD

Kinvara
House

Church of
Jesus Christ of
Latter Day Saints

Bray VEC/
Bray Senior
College

SIDMONTON ROAD

Esplanade
Hotel

Lucena
Clinic

San Remo
Nursing
Home

Annamoe
Nursing
Home

Strand
Lounge
Hotel

KILLARNEY VILLAS

Flos Feasa
Scoil Chronain
Naofa

St Cronan's

Garda
Station

Roseville
Nursing
Home

MT NORRIS
VILLAS

Registry of
Births Deaths
& Marriages

SIDMONTON
GARDENS

VEVAY ROAD

Marino
School

MOUNT
SOUCI WOOD

Loreto
Convent

Bray Head
Inn

ECROFT

Christ
Church

CHARNWOOD

Tara Nursing
Home

PUTLAND ROAD

B R A Y

LAUDERDALE
ESTATE

HEADLANDS

Our Lady Queen
of Peace Church

Presentation
School

GILTSPUR
BROOK

Scoil
Chualann

Kingdom Hall
of Jehovah's
Witnesses

Presentation
School

EATFIELD

VEVAY

St Andrew's
Newcourt
School

ROAD

BOGHALL ROAD

BRIARWOOD

Bray District
Court House

Woodland
Court Hotel

NEWCOURT

BELMONT

RIDDLESFORD

SOUTHERN CROSS

EARLSCROFT

Bray

SWANBROOK

Golf Course

RAY
INESS
ARK

HOLLYBROOK
PARK

VEVAY ROAD

IRISHTOWN

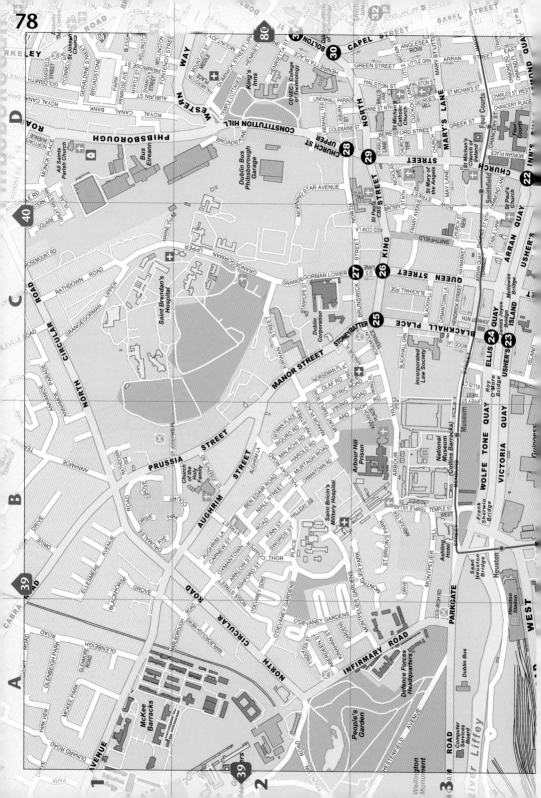

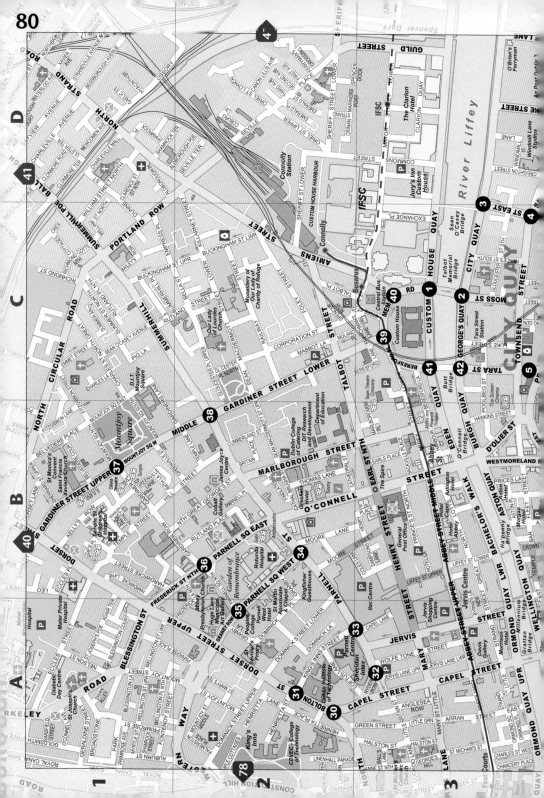

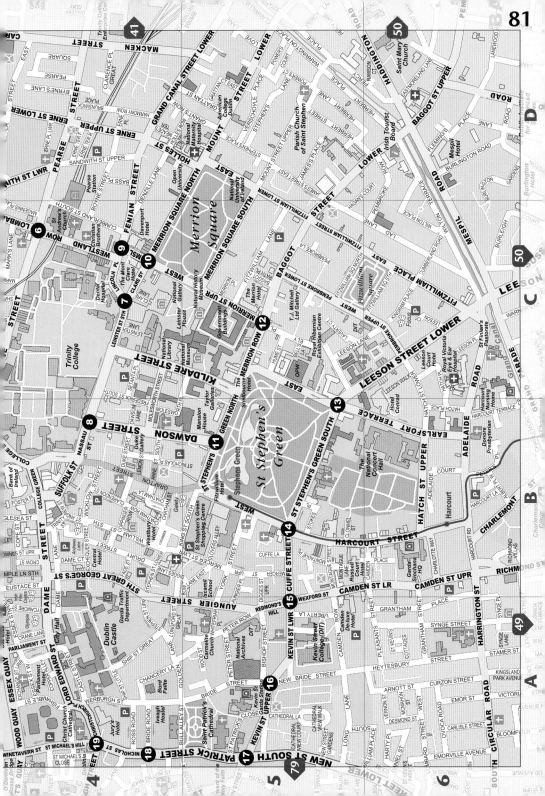

Index to Streets

General abbreviations used throughout the book:

Ave . . . . .Avenue	Gdn . . . . .Garden	Mdws . . . . .Meadows	St . . . . .Street
Apts . . . . .Apartments	Gdns . . . . .Gardens	Ms . . . . .Mews	Sth . . . . .South
Cl . . . . .Close	Gr . . . . .Grove	Mt . . . . .Mount	Ter . . . . .Terrace
Cott . . . . .Cottage	Grn . . . . .Green	Nth . . . . .North	Upr . . . . .Upper
Cotts . . . . .Cottages	Hse . . . . .House	Pde . . . . .Parade	Vw . . . . .View
Cres . . . . .Crescent	Hts . . . . .Heights	Pk . . . . .Park	W . . . . .West
Ct . . . . .Court	Ln . . . . .Lane	Pl . . . . .Place	Wk . . . . .Walk
Dr . . . . .Drive	Lwr . . . . .Lower	Rd . . . . .Road	Yd . . . . .Yard
E . . . . .East	Mdw . . . . .Meadow	Sq . . . . .Square	

A

1 Branch Road North	42	A2
1 Branch Road South	42	A3
15 Acres Road	38	C3
2 Branch Road North	42	B2
2 Branch Road North Extension	42	B2
2 Branch Road South	42	A3
3 Branch Road South	42	A3
4 Branch Road South	42	B3
Abbey Court	29	D2
Abbey Drive	25	F4
Abbey Park (Baldoyle)	21	F4
Abbey Park (Kill O' The Grange)	60	B4
Abbey Park (Killester)	29	D2
Abbey Road	60	B4
Abbey Street	33	E2
Abbey Street Lower	80	B3
Abbey Street Middle	80	B3
Abbey Street Upper	80	A3
Abbey View	70	B1
Abbeydale Close	35	F4
Abbeydale Crescent	35	F4
Abbeydale Park	35	F4
Abbeydale Rise	35	F4
Abbeydale Walk	35	F4
Abbeyfield (Killester)	29	D2
Abbeyfield (Milltown)	50	B4
Abbeylea Avenue	4	C2
Abbeylea Close	4	C2
Abbeylea Drive	4	C3
Abbeylea Green	4	C2
Abbeyvale Avenue	4	A3
Abbeyvale Close	4	A3
Abbeyvale Court	4	A3
Abbeyvale Crescent	4	A2
Abbeyvale Drive	4	A3
Abbeyvale Green	4	A3
Abbeyvale Grove	4	A2
Abbeyvale Lawn	4	A3
Abbeyvale Place	4	A3
Abbeyvale Rise	4	A3
Abbeyvale View	4	A3
Abbeyvale Way	4	A3
Abbeywood Avenue	35	E4
Abbeywood Close	35	F4
Abbeywood Court	35	E4
Abbeywood Crescent	35	F4
Abbeywood Way	35	F4
Abbotstown Avenue	25	F1
Abbotstown Drive	25	F1
Abbotstown Road	25	F1
Abbotts Hill	7	E3
Abercorn Road	41	E3
Abercorn Square	38	C4
Abercorn Terrace	38	C4
Aberdeen Street	78	A2
Abingdon Park	75	E3
Abington	6	B3
Achill Road (Drumcondra)	27	F3
Achill Road (Loughlinstown)	75	E2
Acorn Court	67	E1
Acorn Lane	67	E1
Acorn Road	67	E1
Acres Road	38	C2
Adair Terrace	80	A1
Adamstown Road	34	C3
Adare Avenue	19	F4
Adare Drive	19	F4
Adare Green	19	F4
Adare Park	19	F4
Adare Road	19	F3
Addison Park	27	D3
Addison Road	41	E1
Adelaide Court	81	B6
Adelaide Lane	61	E3
Adelaide Mews	51	E3
Adelaide Road (Bray)	77	E1
Adelaide Road (Central Dublin)	81	B6
Adelaide Road (Dún Laoghaire)	61	E3
Adelaide Street	61	E3
Adelaide Terrace	39	E4
Admiral Park	11	D3
Adrian Avenue	49	D3
Aideen Avenue	48	C4
Aideen Drive	49	D4
Aideen Place	48	D4
Aikenhead Terrace	41	F4
Aikens Village	68	B4
Ailesbury	27	F1
Ailesbury Drive	50	C3
Ailesbury Gardens	51	E3
Ailesbury Grove (Donnybrook)	51	D3
Ailesbury Grove (Dundrum)	57	F4
Ailesbury Lawn	57	F4
Ailesbury Mews	51	E3
Ailesbury Park	51	E3
Ailesbury Road	51	D3
Ailesbury Wood	51	D3
Airfield Court	51	D4
Airfield Park	51	D4
Airfield Road	49	E4
Airlie Heights	34	A3
Airton Close	54	A3
Airton Road	54	A3
Albany Avenue	60	B3
Albany Court	75	E1
Albany Road	50	A3
Albert Avenue	77	E1
Albert Close	72	A2
Albert College Avenue	27	E1
Albert College Crescent	27	E1
Albert College Drive	27	E1
Albert College Grove	27	E1
Albert College Lawn	27	E2
Albert College Park	27	E1
Albert Park	61	F4
Albert Place West	81	B6
Albert Road Lower	72	A2
Albert Road Upper	71	E1
Albert Walk	77	E1
Aldborough Parade	80	D2
Aldborough Place	80	D1
Aldemere Close	22	B2
Aldemere Drive	22	B1
Aldemere View	22	B2
Alden Drive	30	C1
Alden Park	30	C1
Alden Road	21	E4
Alderpark Court	63	E1
Alderwood Avenue	53	E4
Alderwood Close	53	E4
Alderwood Court	53	E4
Alderwood Drive	63	E1
Alderwood Green	53	E4
Alderwood Grove	53	E4
Alderwood Lawn	53	E4
Alderwood Park	63	E1
Alderwood Rise	53	E4
Alderwood Way	63	E1
Alexandra Road	42	A2
Alexandra Road Extension	42	C3
Alexandra Terrace (Bray)	77	D1
Alexandra Terrace (Churchtown)	57	F3
Alexandra Terrace (Rathgar)	49	E4
Alfie Byrne Road	41	E1
All Hallows Green	27	F3
All Hallows Square	27	F3
All Saints Drive	30	A2
All Saints Park	30	A2
All Saints Road	30	A3
Allen Park Drive	59	D4
Allen Park Road	59	D4
Allendale Close	22	B1
Allendale Copse	22	B1
Allendale Court	22	A1
Allendale Drive	22	B1
Allendale Elms	22	B1
Allendale Glade	22	A1
Allendale Glen	22	B1
Allendale Green	22	B1
Allendale Grove	12	C4
Allendale Heath	22	B1
Allendale Lawn	22	B1
Allendale Place	22	B1
Allendale Rise	22	B1
Allendale Square	22	A1
Allendale Terrace	22	B1
Allendale View	12	C4
Allendale Walk	22	B1
Allenton Avenue	64	B2
Allenton Crescent	64	B2
Allenton Drive	64	B3
Allenton Gardens	64	B3
Allenton Green	64	B3
Allenton Lawns	64	B2
Allenton Park	64	B2
Allenton Road	64	B2
Allenton Way	64	B3
Alley River Road	73	D2
Allingham Street	79	C5
Alma Road	60	B2
Alpine Heights	45	E3
Alpine Rise	53	E3
Altadore	71	E1
Altham Court	38	C4
Alverno	42	B1
Ambervale	53	E3
Amiens Street	80	C2
Anglesea Avenue	59	F2
Anglesea Lane	61	D3
Anglesea Road	50	C2
Anglesea Row	78	D3
Anglesea Street	81	B4
Anglesey Park	71	F2
Anley Court	35	E2
Ann Devlin Avenue	56	A4
Ann Devlin Drive	56	A4
Ann Devlin Park	56	A4
Ann Devlin Road	55	F3
Anna Villa	50	B3
Annabeg	75	D1
Annadale Avenue	28	A4
Annadale Crescent	28	A3
Annadale Drive	28	A3
Annagh Court	14	B4
Annaly Court	22	A1
Annaly Drive	22	A1
Annaly Road	39	F1
Annaly Terrace	22	A1
Annamoe Drive	39	F1
Annamoe Parade	78	B1
Annamoe Park	39	F1
Annamoe Road	39	F1
Annamoe Terrace	39	F2
Annaville Avenue	59	F4
Annaville Grove	57	F2
Annaville Park	57	F2
Annaville Terrace	57	F2
Anne Street North	78	D3
Anne Street South	81	B4
Anner Road	39	D4
Annesley Avenue	41	D1
Annesley Bridge Road	41	E1
Annesley Park	50	A3
Annesley Place	41	E1
Annfield Close	23	D3
Annfield Court	23	D3

Name	Page	Grid
Annfield Crescent	23	D3
Annfield Drive	23	D3
Annfield Lawn	23	D3
Annsbrook	58	A1
Annville Drive	58	C4
Apollo Way	19	E4
Appian Way	50	R2
Apples Road	68	B1
Applewood Avenue	4	C1
Applewood Avenue East	4	C1
Applewood Close	4	C1
Applewood Court	4	C1
Applewood Crescent	4	C1
Applewood Drive	4	C1
Applewood Lane	4	C1
Applewood Lawn	4	C1
Applewood Main Street	4	C1
Applewood Mews	4	C1
Applewood Place	4	C1
Applewood Square	4	C1
Aran Avenue	75	E2
Aran Court	14	C4
Aran Drive	75	E2
Aranleigh Court	56	C4
Aranleigh Dell	56	C4
Aranleigh Gardens	56	C4
Aranleigh Mount	56	C4
Aranleigh Park	56	C4
Aranleigh Vale	56	C4
Aras na Cluaine	46	A2
Aravon Court	77	E1
Arbour Hill	78	B3
Arbour Place	78	C3
Arbour Terrace	78	B3
Arbutus Avenue	49	D2
Arbutus Place	79	D6
Ard Lorcain Villas	59	E4
Ard Macha	63	F2
Ard na Greine	76	C4
Ard na Mara Crescent	6	B2
Ard na Meala	17	F3
Ard Righ Place	78	B3
Ard Righ Road	78	B2
Ardagh Avenue	59	F4
Ardagh Court	59	E4
Ardagh Crescent	69	E1
Ardagh Drive	69	F1
Ardagh Grove	59	E4
Ardagh Park	59	F4
Ardagh Park Road	59	F4
Ardagh Road	48	C2
Ardara Avenue	20	C3
Ardbeg Crescent	29	D1
Ardbeg Drive	29	D1
Ardbeg Park	29	D1
Ardbeg Road	29	D3
Ardbrugh Road	72	B3
Ardcian Park	4	B2
Ardcollum Avenue	29	D2
Ardee Court	79	C5
Ardee Road	49	F2
Ardee Street	79	C5
Ardeen	34	B2
Ardeevin Avenue	34	B2
Ardeevin Court	34	C3
Ardeevin Drive	34	C2
Ardeevin Road	72	B3
Ardenza	60	A2
Ardglas Estate	67	F1
Ardilaun	10	B3
Ardilaun Road	41	D1
Ardilea Downs	58	B3
Ardlea Road	29	D1
Ardlui Park	69	F1
Ardmeen Park	59	F4
Ardmore Avenue	52	B4
Ardmore Close (Beaumont)	28	C1
Ardmore Close (Tallaght)	52	B4
Ardmore Court	76	C2
Ardmore Crescent (Beaumont)	28	C1
Ardmore Crescent (Bray)	76	C2
Ardmore Drive	28	C1
Ardmore Grove	28	C1
Ardmore Park (Beaumont)	28	C1
Ardmore Park (Bray)	76	C2
Ardmore Park (Kill O' The Grange)	70	C1
Ardmore Park (Tallaght)	52	B4
Ardmore Walk	52	B4
Ardmore Wood	76	B2
Ardoyne House	50	C2
Ardpatrick Road	39	D1
Ardtona Avenue	57	E3
Arena Road	68	C2
Argyle Road	50	C2
Arkendale Court	71	F1
Arkendale Road	71	F1
Arkle Road	68	C2
Arkle Square	69	D2
Arklow Street	78	B2
Armagh Road	48	B3
Armstrong Walk	19	F4
Arnold Grove	71	E2
Arnold Park	71	D2
Arnott Street	81	A6
Arran Quay	78	C3
Arran Quay Terrace	78	C3
Arran Road	27	F3
Arran Street East	78	D3
Arranmore Avenue	40	B1
Arranmore Road	50	C2
Arthur Griffith Park	35	D4
Asgard Park	33	E2
Asgard Road	33	E2
Ash Hurst	75	F1
Ash Park Avenue	35	D4
Ash Park Court	35	D4
Ash Park Green	35	D4
Ash Park Heath	35	E4
Ashberry	34	C4
Ashbrook (Ashtown)	25	D3
Ashbrook (Donnycarney)	29	D4
Ashbury Park	77	E1
Ashcroft	30	A2
Ashdale Close	9	F1
Ashdale Park	49	D4
Ashdale Road (Swords)	9	F1
Ashfield (Ballymount)	46	B4
Ashfield (Templeogue)	55	F3
Ashfield Avenue (Ballymount)	53	F1
Ashfield Avenue (Ranelagh)	50	A3
Ashfield Close (Ballymount)	53	F1
Ashfield Close (Templeogue)	55	F3
Ashfield Court (Bray)	76	C3
Ashfield Court (Huntstown)	13	E3
Ashfield Drive	53	F1
Ashfield Gardens	13	E3
Ashfield Green	13	E3
Ashfield Grove	13	E3
Ashfield Lawn	13	E3
Ashfield Park (Booterstown)	58	C1
Ashfield Park (Clondalkin)	53	F1
Ashfield Park (Huntstown)	13	E3
Ashfield Park (Templeogue)	55	F3
Ashfield Park (Terenure)	49	D4
Ashfield Road	50	A3
Ashfield Way	13	E3
Ashford Street	78	B2
Ashgrove (Ashtown)	25	E4
Ashgrove (Kill O' The Grange)	60	C4
Ashgrove (Tallaght)	53	E4
Ashington Avenue	25	F4
Ashington Close	25	F3
Ashington Court	26	A3
Ashington Crescent	25	F3
Ashington Dale	25	F3
Ashington Gardens	25	F3
Ashington Green	25	F3
Ashington Grove	25	F4
Ashington Heath	25	F3
Ashington Park	25	F3
Ashington Rise	25	F3
Ashlawn	67	F1
Ashlawn Court	76	C1
Ashlawn Park	75	D1
Ashlea Heights	73	D4
Ashleigh Court	24	A2
Ashleigh Green	24	A2
Ashleigh Grove	24	A2
Ashleigh Lawn	7	D3
Ashley Avenue	5	E3
Ashley Drive	5	E4
Ashley Grove	5	E3
Ashley Rise	10	C1
Ashling Heights	14	B4
Ashmount Court	39	E4
Ashton Avenue (Ballyboden)	65	F1
Ashton Avenue (Swords)	4	B1
Ashton Avenue (Templeogue)	55	F4
Ashton Close (Ballyboden)	65	F1
Ashton Close (Swords)	4	B1
Ashton Court	4	B1
Ashton Drive	4	C1
Ashton Grove (Swords)	4	B1
Ashton Grove (Templeogue)	55	F4
Ashton Heights	4	B1
Ashton Lawn	55	F4
Ashton Park	60	B4
Ashton Rise	4	C1
Ashtown Gate	25	D3
Ashtown Grove	25	E4
Ashtown Road	25	D3
Ashtown Wood	76	B3
Ashville Close	35	E2
Ashwood Avenue	45	D3
Ashwood Close	45	D2
Ashwood Drive	45	E2
Ashwood Park	45	E2
Ashwood Road	45	E3
Ashwood Way	45	E2
Ashworth Place	49	E2
Aspen Avenue	22	C2
Aspen Drive	9	F1
Aspen Lawn	22	C2
Aspen Park	9	F1
Aspen Road	9	F1
Aspen Woods	22	C2
Assumpta Park	75	E4
Aston Place	80	B3
Aston Quay	80	B3
Athgoe Drive	75	E3
Athgoe Road	75	E4
Athlumney Villas	49	F2
Atmospheric Road	71	F1
Aubrey Grove	75	E4
Aubrey Park	75	E4
Auburn Avenue (Cabinteely)	71	D3
Auburn Avenue (Castleknock)	24	B3
Auburn Avenue (Donnybrook)	50	C3
Auburn Close (Cabinteely)	71	D3
Auburn Close (Castleknock)	24	B3
Auburn Drive (Cabinteely)	71	D4
Auburn Drive (Castleknock)	24	B3
Auburn Green	24	B2
Auburn Grove	6	B3
Auburn Road	71	D3
Auburn Street	78	D1
Auburn Villas	49	E4
Aughavannagh Road	49	D2
Aughrim Lane	78	B2
Aughrim Street	78	B2
Aulden Grange	18	C3
Aungier Place	81	B5
Aungier Street	81	A5
Avalon	69	F3
Ave Maria Road	79	B5
Avenue Road	49	E2
Avila Park	16	B4
Avoca Avenue (Bray)	77	D3
Avoca Avenue (Stillorgan)	59	E3
Avoca Park	59	E3
Avoca Place	59	F2
Avoca Road	59	E3
Avoca Woods	59	E3
Avonbeg Drive	64	B1
Avonbeg Gardens	64	B1
Avonbeg Park	64	B1
Avonbeg Road	54	B4
Avondale Avenue	40	A1
Avondale Crescent	71	E2
Avondale Lawn	59	F3
Avondale Lawn Court	60	A3
Avondale Park (Bray)	76	C2
Avondale Park (Dalkey)	71	E2
Avondale Park (Raheny)	30	A2
Avondale Road (Dalkey)	71	E2
Avondale Road (Phibsborough)	40	A1
Avondale Terrace	48	A4
Avonmore	69	E2
Avonmore Avenue	54	C4
Avonmore Close	54	C4
Avonmore Drive	64	C1
Avonmore Grove	64	C1
Avonmore Park	64	C1
Avonmore Road	64	B1
Ayrefield Avenue	20	B4
Ayrefield Court	20	B4
Ayrefield Drive	20	B4
Ayrefield Place	20	B4
Ayrefield Road	20	B4

B

Name	Page	Grid
Bachelor's Walk	80	B3
Back Lane (Baldoyle)	11	D3
Back Lane (Central Dublin)	79	D4
Back Road	6	C4
Baggot Court	50	B1
Baggot Lane	50	C1
Baggot Rath Place	81	C5
Baggot Road	25	F4
Baggot Street Lower	81	C5
Baggot Street Upper	81	D6
Bailey Green Road	33	E3
Bailey View	72	B1
Bailey's Row	80	C1
Baisley Lane	64	A4
Balally Avenue	68	A1
Balally Close	68	A1
Balally Drive (Clonskeagh)	58	A4
Balally Drive (Dundrum)	68	B1
Balally Grove	68	A1
Balally Hill	68	A1
Balally Park	68	A1
Balally Road	68	A1
Balbutcher Drive	17	E3
Balbutcher Way	17	E3
Balcurris Gardens	17	F3
Balcurris Road	17	F3
Baldoyle Road	11	E4
Balfe Avenue	48	A3
Balfe Road	47	F3
Balfe Road East	48	A3
Balgaddy Road	44	B1
Balgriffin Road	20	C2
Balheary Road	5	D2
Balkill Park	33	D2
Balkill Road	33	E2
Ball's Lane	78	D3

Name	Page	Grid
Ballawley Court	68	A2
Ballentree Close	14	A1
Ballentree Crescent	14	B1
Ballentree Drive	14	A1
Ballentree Grove	14	B1
Ballentree Lodge	14	A1
Ballentree Villas	14	A1
Ballinclea Heights	71	E3
Ballinclea Road	71	E3
Ballinclea Wood	71	E3
Ballinteer Avenue	67	E2
Ballinteer Close	67	E2
Ballinteer Court	67	E2
Ballinteer Crescent	67	E2
Ballinteer Drive	67	E2
Ballinteer Gardens	67	F1
Ballinteer Grove	67	E2
Ballinteer Park	67	E1
Ballinteer Road (Ballinteer)	67	F2
Ballinteer Road (Dundrum)	57	F4
Ballintrane Woods	4	C4
Ballintyre Apartments	67	E2
Ballintyre Downs	67	E2
Ballintyre Heath	67	E2
Ballintyre Meadows	67	E2
Ballintyre Walk	67	E2
Ballintyre Woods	67	E2
Ballsbridge Avenue	50	C2
Ballsbridge Court	51	D1
Ballsbridge Park	51	D2
Ballsbridge Wood	50	C1
Ballyboden Crescent	66	A1
Ballyboden Road	56	B4
Ballyboden Road	66	A1
Ballyboggan Road	26	A3
Ballybough Court	41	D1
Ballybough Road	41	D1
Ballybrack Road	75	E3
Ballybride Road	75	D4
Ballycoolin Road	14	B1
Ballycorus Road	74	A4
Ballycullen Avenue	64	C2
Ballycullen Drive	64	C2
Ballycullen Road	65	D1
Ballydowd Grove	35	E2
Ballyfermot Avenue	37	F4
Ballyfermot Crescent	38	A4
Ballyfermot Drive	37	F4
Ballyfermot Parade	37	F4
Ballyfermot Road	37	F4
Ballyfermot Road	38	A4
Ballygall Avenue	26	B1
Ballygall Crescent	26	B1
Ballygall Parade	26	B1
Ballygall Place	26	B1
Ballygall Road East	26	C1
Ballygall Road West	26	B1
Ballygihen Avenue	61	F4
Ballyhoy Avenue	29	F3
Ballymace Green	55	F3
Ballymorris	76	C3
Ballymoss Parade	69	D2
Ballymoss Road	68	C2
Ballymount Road	53	F2
Ballymount Road	54	A1
Ballymount Road Lower	47	D4
Ballymount Road Lower	53	F2
Ballymun Road (Ballymun)	18	A4
Ballymun Road (Glasnevin)	27	D3
Ballyneety Road	38	B4
Ballynoe Grove	76	C3
Ballyogan Avenue	69	E4
Ballyogan Court	69	E4
Ballyogan Crescent	69	E4
Ballyogan Green	69	E4
Ballyogan Lawn	69	E4
Ballyogan Road	68	D4
Ballyowen Avenue	35	F2
Ballyowen Crescent	35	F2
Ballyowen Drive	35	F2
Ballyowen Green	35	F2
Ballyowen Hall	35	F2
Ballyowen Lane	35	F3
Ballyowen Lawn	35	F2
Ballyowen Road	35	F2
Ballyowen View	35	F2
Ballyowen Way	35	F2
Ballyroan Crescent	56	A4
Ballyroan Heights	56	A4
Ballyroan Road	56	A4
Ballyshannon Road	19	D4
Ballytore Road	56	C2
Ballywaltrim Cottages	76	B3
Ballywaltrim Heights	76	B3
Ballywaltrim Lane	76	B4
Balnagowan	50	A4
Balrothery	54	C4
Balscadden Road	33	E1
Bancroft Avenue	54	B4
Bancroft Close	54	B4
Bancroft Crescent	54	B4
Bancroft Grove	54	B4
Bancroft Park	54	B4
Bancroft Road	54	B4
Bangor Road	48	C2
Bankside Cottages	57	F1
Bann Road	26	B3
Bannow Road	26	B4
Bantry Road	27	E3
Bantry Square	14	C4
Barclay Court	59	F2
Bargy Road	41	E2
Barnacoille Park	72	B2
Barnaculla Road	68	A4
Barnamore Crescent	26	A3
Barnamore Grove	26	A3
Barnamore Park	26	A2
Barnhill Avenue	71	F2
Barnhill Cross Roads	34	C2
Barnhill Grove	71	F1
Barnhill Lawn (Dalkey)	71	F1
Barnhill Lawn (Loughlinstown)	75	E3
Barnhill Road	71	F1
Barrett Street	61	D3
Barron Place	27	E3
Barrow Road	26	B3
Barrow Street	41	E4
Barry Avenue	16	B4
Barry Drive	16	B4
Barry Green	16	B4
Barry Park	16	B4
Barry Road	16	B4
Barryscourt Road	19	E4
Barta Rock	72	B2
Barton Avenue	56	C4
Barton Drive	56	C4
Barton Road	56	C4
Barton Road East	57	E4
Barton Road Extension	56	C4
Basin Street Lower	79	B4
Basin Street Upper	79	B4
Baskin Lane	9	E4
Bass Place	81	D4
Bath Avenue (Malahide)	7	E2
Bath Avenue (Sandymount)	50	C1
Bath Avenue Place	41	E4
Bath Lane	80	B1
Bath Place	59	F2
Bath Street	41	F4
Bawnlea Avenue	62	C1
Bawnlea Close	62	C1
Bawnlea Crescent	62	C1
Bawnlea Drive	62	C1
Bawnlea Green	62	C1
Bawnogue Road	45	D3
Bawnville Avenue	64	B1
Bawnville Close	64	B1
Bawnville Drive	64	B1
Bawnville Park	64	B1
Bawnville Road	64	B1
Baymount Park	30	A4
Bayshore Lane	75	F1
Bayside Boulevard North	21	F4
Bayside Boulevard South	31	D1
Bayside Crescent	31	D1
Bayside Park	21	F4
Bayside Square Estate	31	D1
Bayside Square North	31	D1
Bayside Square South	31	D1
Bayside Square West	31	D1
Bayside Walk	21	F4
Bayview Avenue	41	D1
Bayview Close	75	F2
Bayview Court	75	E2
Bayview Crescent	75	E2
Bayview Drive	75	E2
Bayview Green	75	E2
Bayview Lawns	75	E2
Bayview Park	75	E2
Bayview Terrace	73	E4
Beach Avenue	51	D1
Beach Drive	51	E1
Beach Road	51	D1
Beach View	31	D1
Bealing Avenue	14	A1
Bealing Close	14	A1
Bealing Crescent	14	A1
Bealing Grove	14	A1
Bealing Mews	14	A1
Bealing View	14	A1
Bealing Walk	14	A1
Bearna Park	68	B3
Beatty's Avenue	50	C2
Beau Park Place	21	E3
Beau Park Street	21	E3
Beaufield Park	59	D4
Beaufort Downs	56	B3
Beaumont Avenue	57	E3
Beaumont Close	57	E4
Beaumont Court	19	D4
Beaumont Crescent	28	B1
Beaumont Drive	57	E3
Beaumont Gardens	59	E2
Beaumont Grove	28	A1
Beaumont Road	28	A2
Beaumont Woods	28	B1
Beauvale Park	28	C1
Beaver Row	50	C3
Beckett Way	46	B2
Beech Court	71	D3
Beech Drive	57	E4
Beech Grove	35	D2
Beech Hill Avenue	50	C4
Beech Hill Crescent	50	C4
Beech Hill Drive	50	C4
Beech Hill Road	50	C4
Beech Hill Terrace	50	C4
Beech Lawn (Dundrum)	57	E4
Beech Lawn (Whitehall)	28	A2
Beech Park	35	D2
Beech Park Avenue (Castleknock)	24	B3
Beech Park Avenue (Dean's Grange)	70	A2
Beech Park Close	24	B2
Beech Park Crescent	24	B2
Beech Park Drive	70	A2
Beech Park Grove	70	B2
Beech Park Lawn	24	B3
Beech Park Orchard	24	B3
Beech Park Road	70	A2
Beech Road (Bray)	73	D4
Beech Road (Fox & Geese)	46	C3
Beech Walk	66	A1
Beechbrook Grove	20	C3
Beechdale Avenue	64	C3
Beechdale Close	64	C3
Beechdale Court	64	C3
Beechdale Crescent	64	C3
Beechdale Lawn	64	C3
Beechdale Park	64	C3
Beechdale Road	64	C3
Beechdale Way	64	C3
Beeches Park	71	E1
Beechfield Avenue	47	F4
Beechfield Close	12	B3
Beechfield Court	12	B3
Beechfield Drive	12	B3
Beechfield Green	12	C3
Beechfield Green	22	A1
Beechfield Haven	75	E4
Beechfield Heights	12	B3
Beechfield Lawn	12	C3
Beechfield Manor	75	E4
Beechfield Meadows	12	C3
Beechfield Place	12	C3
Beechfield Rise	12	C3
Beechfield Road (Huntstown)	12	C3
Beechfield Road (Walkinstown)	47	F4
Beechfield View	12	C3
Beechfield Way	12	C3
Beechlawn Avenue (Ballinteer)	57	E4
Beechlawn Avenue (Coolock)	29	D1
Beechlawn Close	29	D1
Beechlawn Drive	19	F4
Beechlawn Green	19	F4
Beechlawn Grove	29	D1
Beechmount Drive	57	F2
Beechpark Avenue	19	F4
Beechpark Court	29	E1
Beechurst	76	C2
Beechwood Avenue Lower	50	A3
Beechwood Avenue Upper	50	A3
Beechwood Close (Bray)	77	D3
Beechwood Close (Hartstown)	13	D4
Beechwood Court	69	E1
Beechwood Downs	13	D4
Beechwood Lawn	71	D2
Beechwood Park (Dún Laoghaire)	71	D2
Beechwood Park (Rathmines)	50	A3
Beechwood Road	50	A3
Beggars Bush	50	C1
Belarmine	68	B4
Belarmine Avenue	68	B4
Belarmine Close	68	B4
Belarmine Court	68	B4
Belarmine Drive	68	B4
Belarmine Heath	68	C4
Belarmine Park	68	B4
Belarmine Place	68	C4
Belarmine Square	68	B4
Belarmine Vale	68	C4
Belarmine Way	68	B4
Belcamp Avenue	20	A3
Belcamp Crescent	20	A2
Belcamp Gardens	20	A2
Belcamp Green	20	A3
Belcamp Grove	20	A3
Belcamp Lane	20	B3
Belcamp Road	20	A3
Belclare Avenue	17	E3
Belclare Crescent	17	E3
Belclare Drive	17	E3
Belclare Green	17	E3
Belclare Grove	17	E3
Belclare Park	17	E3
Belfield	58	B1
Belfield Close	58	A1
Belfield Court	51	D4
Belfield Downs	58	A3
Belfry Avenue	62	B2

Name	Page	Grid
Belfry Close	62	B2
Belfry Court	62	B2
Belfry Crescent	62	B2
Belfry Dale	62	B2
Belfry Downs	62	B2
Belfry Drive	62	B2
Belfry Gardens	62	B2
Belfry Green	62	B2
Belfry Grove	62	B2
Belfry Lawns	62	B2
Belfry Lodge	62	B2
Belfry Meadows	62	B2
Belfry Park	62	B2
Belfry Place	62	B2
Belfry Rise	62	B2
Belfry Road	62	B2
Belfry Square	62	B2
Belfry Terrace	62	B2
Belfry Walk	62	B2
Belfry Way	62	B2
Belgard Close	53	F2
Belgard Green	53	D3
Belgard Heights	53	E3
Belgard Park	53	E3
Belgard Road	45	E3
Belgard Road	53	F3
Belgard Square East	53	F4
Belgard Square North	53	F4
Belgard Square South	63	F1
Belgard Square West	53	F4
Belgrave Road (Monkstown)	60	B2
Belgrave Road (Rathmines)	50	A3
Belgrave Square East (Monkstown)	60	B3
Belgrave Square East (Rathmines)	50	A3
Belgrave Square North (Monkstown)	60	B3
Belgrave Square North (Rathmines)	49	F3
Belgrave Square South (Monkstown)	60	B3
Belgrave Square South (Rathmines)	50	A3
Belgrave Square West (Monkstown)	60	B3
Belgrave Square West (Rathmines)	49	F3
Belgrave View	50	A3
Belgrove Lawn	37	F3
Belgrove Park	37	F3
Belgrove Road	42	C1
Bell's Lane	81	C5
Bella Street	80	C2
Belle Ville Avenue	49	E4
Belleville	25	D4
Bellevue (Christchurch)	79	C4
Bellevue (Islandbridge)	39	D3
Bellevue Avenue (Dalkey)	71	E2
Bellevue Avenue (Merrion)	51	F4
Bellevue Copse	51	E4
Bellevue Court	51	F4
Bellevue Park	51	E4
Bellevue Park Avenue	51	E4
Bellevue Road	71	E2
Belmont (Bray)	77	D3
Belmont (Galloping Green)	69	E1
Belmont Avenue	50	B3
Belmont Gardens	50	B3
Belmont Green	69	E1
Belmont Grove	69	E1
Belmont Lawn	69	E1
Belmont Park (Donnybrook)	50	C3
Belmont Park (Edenmore)	30	A1
Belmont Square	30	A1
Belmont Villas	50	B3
Belton Park Avenue	28	B3
Belton Park Gardens	28	B3
Belton Park Road	28	B3
Belvedere Avenue	40	C1
Belvedere Court	80	B1
Belvedere Place	80	B1
Belvedere Road	40	C1
Ben Edair Road	79	B2
Benburb Road	48	B1
Benburb Street	78	B3
Beneavin Court	26	C1
Beneavin Drive	26	C1
Beneavin Lodge	26	C1
Beneavin Park	26	C1
Beneavin Road	26	C1
Benmadigan Road	48	B1
Benson Street	41	E3
Bentley Road	77	D3
Beresford Avenue	27	F3
Beresford Lane	80	C3
Beresford Place	80	C3
Beresford Street	78	D3
Berkeley Road	40	B1
Berryfield Crescent	25	F2
Berryfield Drive	25	F2
Berryfield Lane	76	A2
Berryfield Road	26	A2
Berwick Avenue	4	A3
Berwick Court	4	A3
Berwick Crescent	4	B2
Berwick Drive	4	A2
Berwick Grove	4	A2
Berwick Lawn	4	A3
Berwick Place	4	A3
Berwick Rise	4	A3
Berwick View	4	A3
Berwick Walk	4	A3
Berwick Way	4	A3
Berystede	50	A2
Bessborough Avenue	80	D1
Bessborough Parade	49	F2
Besser Drive	45	F2
Bettysglen	30	C2
Bettystown Avenue	29	F3
Beverly Avenue	65	E1
Beverly Crescent	65	D1
Beverly Downs	65	E1
Beverly Drive	65	E1
Beverly Grove	65	E1
Beverly Heights	65	E1
Beverly Lawns	65	E1
Beverly Park	65	E1
Beverly Rise	65	D1
Bewley Avenue	35	E3
Bewley Drive	35	E2
Bewley Grove	35	E3
Bewley Lawn	35	E2
Bigger Road	47	F4
Bilfe's Lane	23	D3
Binn Eadair View	11	E4
Birch Grove	60	C4
Birchdale Close	9	F1
Birchdale Drive	9	F1
Birchdale Road	9	F1
Birches Lane	58	A4
Birches Road	68	B1
Birchfield Avenue	58	A3
Birchfield Park	58	A4
Birchview Avenue	54	B3
Birchview Close	54	B3
Birchview Court	54	B3
Birchview Drive	54	B2
Birchview Heights	54	B2
Birchview Lawn	54	B2
Birchview Rise	54	B3
Birchwood Close	53	E4
Birchwood Drive	53	E4
Birchwood Heights	53	E4
Bird Avenue	57	F1
Biscayne	7	F3
Bishop Street	81	A5
Bishops Orchard	14	B1
Bisset's Strand	7	D2
Blackberry Lane (Portmarnock)	10	B3
Blackberry Lane (Rathmines)	49	F2
Blackberry Rise	10	B3
Blackcourt Road	14	B4
Blackditch Close	37	D4
Blackditch Drive	37	E4
Blackditch Road	37	D4
Blackglen Court	68	A3
Blackglen Road	67	F3
Blackhall Green	78	C3
Blackhall Parade	78	C3
Blackhall Place	40	A3
Blackhall Street	78	C3
Blackheath Avenue	29	E4
Blackheath Drive	29	E4
Blackheath Gardens	29	D4
Blackheath Grove	29	D4
Blackheath Park	29	E4
Blackhorse Avenue	25	D4
Blackhorse Grove	78	B1
Blackpitts	79	D6
Blackthorn Avenue	68	C1
Blackthorn Close	10	C2
Blackthorn Court	68	B2
Blackthorn Drive	68	B2
Blackthorn Green	68	B2
Blackthorn Grove	68	B2
Blackthorn Road	68	B2
Blackwater Road	26	B3
Blackwood Close	12	B4
Blackwood Crescent	12	B4
Blackwood Drive	12	B4
Blackwood Lane	10	A2
Blackwood Lawn	12	B4
Blackwood Mews	12	B4
Blackwood Park	12	B4
Blackwood Place	12	B4
Blakestown Drive	13	F4
Blakestown Road	13	E4
Blakestown Way	13	F4
Blanchardstown Bypass	13	E3
Blanchardstown Heath	14	A3
Blanchardstown Road North	14	A4
Blanchardstown Road South	23	D2
Blarney Park	48	C3
Blasket Square	14	B4
Blessington Court	80	A1
Blessington Lane	80	A1
Blessington Road	53	F4
Blessington Street	62	B2
Blessington Street	80	A1
Bloomfield Avenue	49	E2
Bloomfield Avenue	50	B2
Bloomfield Park	49	E2
Bluebell Avenue	47	D2
Bluebell Lane	47	D2
Bluebell Road	47	E2
Blunden Drive	20	B3
Blythe Avenue	41	E2
Boden Wood	56	B3
Bodendale	56	B4
Boeing Road	19	D2
Boghall Road	77	D3
Bolbrook Avenue	54	C4
Bolbrook Close	54	C4
Bolbrook Grove	54	C4
Bolbrook Villas	64	B1
Bolton Street	80	A2
Bond Drive	42	A2
Bond Road	41	F2
Bond Street	79	B5
Bonham Street	79	C4
Boolavogue Road	41	E2
Boot Road	45	F4
Boot Road Inner	45	F4
Booterstown Avenue	59	D2
Booterstown Grove	59	D1
Booterstown Park	59	D2
Boroimhe Alder	8	C1
Boroimhe Ash	8	B1
Boroimhe Aspen	8	B1
Boroimhe Beech	8	C1
Boroimhe Birches	8	C1
Boroimhe Blackthorn	8	B1
Boroimhe Cedars	8	C1
Boroimhe Cherry	8	C1
Boroimhe Hawthorns	8	C1
Boroimhe Laurels	8	C1
Boroimhe Oaks	8	C1
Boroimhe Poplars	8	C1
Boroimhe Rowan	8	B1
Botanic Avenue	27	E4
Botanic Park	27	E4
Botanic Road	27	D4
Bothar Mhaolbhuille	27	D1
Bothar na Life	36	C3
Bow Bridge	79	A4
Bow Lane East	81	B5
Bow Lane West	79	A4
Bow Street	78	D3
Boyne Road	26	B3
Boyne Street	81	C4
Bracken Drive	10	B2
Bracken Hill	67	F3
Bracken Road	68	B2
Brackenbush Park	71	D4
Brackenbush Road	71	D4
Brackenstown Avenue	4	C3
Brackenstown Road	4	B3
Braemor Avenue	57	D2
Braemor Drive	57	D2
Braemor Grove	57	D2
Braemor Park	57	D2
Braemor Road	57	D2
Braithwaite Street	79	C5
Bramblefield Crescent	13	E3
Bramblefield Drive	13	E3
Bramblefield Park	13	E3
Bramblefield View	13	E3
Bramblefield Walk	13	E3
Bramley Avenue	23	F3
Bramley Cottages	71	F4
Bramley Crescent	23	E3
Bramley Garth	23	E3
Bramley Green	23	E3
Bramley Grove	23	E3
Bramley Heath	23	E3
Bramley Park	23	E3
Bramley Walk	23	E3
Bramley Way	23	E3
Brandon Road	48	A2
Bray Road	70	A2
Bray Road	70	C4
Breakwater Road North	42	B2
Breakwater Road South	42	B3
Breffni Road	72	A1
Bregia Road	39	F1
Brehon's Chair	67	D3
Bremen Avenue	42	A4
Bremen Road	42	A4
Brendan Road	50	C3
Brennan's Parade	77	E1
Brennanstown Apartments	70	C4
Brennanstown Avenue	70	C4
Brennanstown Road	70	C4
Brennanstown Square	70	C4
Brennanstown Vale	74	A1
Brewery Road	69	D2
Brian Avenue	28	B4
Brian Boru Avenue	42	C1
Brian Boru Street	42	C1
Brian Road	28	B4
Brian Terrace	28	B4

Briar Walk	7	F4
Briarfield Grove	30	C1
Briarfield Road	30	B1
Briarfield Villas	30	C1
Briarly Court	57	E3
Briarwood	77	E3
Briarwood Avenue	13	E4
Briarwood Close	13	E3
Briarwood Lawn	13	E4
Briarwood Park	13	E4
Brickfield	76	C2
Brickfield Drive	48	C2
Brickfield Lane	79	C5
Bride Road	81	A4
Bride Street	81	A5
Brides Glen	74	C3
Brides Glen Avenue	4	B1
Brides Glen Park	4	B2
Bridge Street (Chapelizod)	38	A3
Bridge Street (Ringsend)	41	F4
Bridge Street Lower	79	D4
Bridge Street Upper	79	D4
Bridgefoot Street	40	A4
Bridgewater Quay	39	D3
Brighton Avenue (Monkstown)	60	B3
Brighton Avenue (Rathgar)	49	E4
Brighton Gardens	49	E4
Brighton Green	49	E4
Brighton Hall	69	F4
Brighton Lodge	69	E3
Brighton Mews	49	E4
Brighton Place	69	F4
Brighton Road (Foxrock)	69	F3
Brighton Road (Terenure)	49	E4
Brighton Square	49	E4
Brighton Terrace (Dún Laoghaire)	61	F4
Brighton Terrace (Monkstown)	60	B3
Brighton Vale	60	B2
Britain Place	80	B2
Britain Quay	41	E3
Broad Meadow	4	C2
Broadford Avenue	67	D2
Broadford Close	67	E2
Broadford Crescent	67	D1
Broadford Drive	67	D1
Broadford Hill	67	D1
Broadford Lawn	67	D2
Broadford Park	67	E2
Broadford Rise	67	D2
Broadford Road	67	E1
Broadford Walk	67	D1
Broadstone	78	D2
Broadstone Park	78	D1
Broadway Park	23	E2
Broadway Road	23	E2
Brompton Court	23	E2
Brompton Green	23	F2
Brompton Grove	23	F2
Brompton Lawn	23	F2
Brook Court	60	B3
Brook Vale	66	B2
Brook Wood	76	C2
Brookdale	64	A1
Brookdale Avenue	4	B4
Brookdale Close	4	A4
Brookdale Court	4	B4
Brookdale Drive	4	B4
Brookdale Green	4	A3
Brookdale Grove	4	A4
Brookdale Lawns	4	B4
Brookdale Park	4	B4
Brookdale Road	4	B4
Brookdale Walk	4	A4
Brookdale Way	4	B3
Brookdene	75	E2
Brookfield (Coolock)	29	E1
Brookfield (Donnybrook)	50	C3
Brookfield (Lucan)	34	C4
Brookfield Avenue (Blackrock)	59	F2
Brookfield Avenue (Bray)	77	E2
Brookfield Court	48	C4
Brookfield Estate	48	C4
Brookfield Green	48	C4
Brookfield Place	59	F2
Brookfield Road (Kilmainham)	39	E4
Brookfield Road (Tallaght)	52	C4
Brookfield Terrace	59	F2
Brookhaven Drive	14	B4
Brookhaven Grove	14	A4
Brookhaven Lawn	14	B4
Brookhaven Park	14	A4
Brookhaven Rise	14	A4
Brooklawn (Blackrock)	59	E2
Brooklawn (Clontarf)	28	C4
Brooklawn (Lucan)	34	C4
Brooklawn Avenue	60	A3
Brookmount Avenue	55	D4
Brookpark	34	C4
Brookstone Road	11	D3
Brookvale Downs	56	B2
Brookvale Road (Donnybrook)	50	C3
Brookvale Road (Rathfarnham)	56	B2
Brookview Avenue	52	C4
Brookview Close	62	C1
Brookview Crescent	52	C4
Brookview Drive	52	C4
Brookview Gardens	52	C4
Brookview Green	52	C4
Brookview Grove	62	C1
Brookview Lawns	52	C4
Brookview Park	52	C4
Brookview Rise	52	C4
Brookview Way	52	C4
Brookville	16	C4
Brookville Park (Artane)	29	D2
Brookville Park (Coolock)	29	E1
Brookville Park (Dean's Grange)	60	A4
Brookwood	66	A1
Brookwood Avenue	29	E2
Brookwood Crescent	29	E2
Brookwood Drive	29	D2
Brookwood Glen	29	E3
Brookwood Grove	29	E2
Brookwood Heights	29	E2
Brookwood Lawn	29	E2
Brookwood Meadow	29	E2
Brookwood Park	29	E2
Brookwood Road	29	D2
Broombridge Road	26	B3
Broomfield Court	75	E3
Broomhill Close	54	A3
Broomhill Lane	54	A3
Broomhill Road	54	A3
Brown Street North	78	C3
Brunswick Place	81	D4
Brunswick Street North	78	C3
Brusna Cottages	59	F2
Buckingham Street Lower	80	C2
Buckingham Street Upper	80	C1
Bulfin Gardens	39	D4
Bulfin Road	39	D4
Bull Alley Street	81	A4
Bulloch Harbour	72	B1
Bunbury Gate Avenue	4	B1
Bunratty Avenue	19	F4
Bunratty Drive	19	F4
Bunratty Road	19	F4
Bunting Road	47	F4
Burdett Avenue	61	F4
Burg an Rí Glen	45	D1
Burg an Rí Terrace	45	D1
Burg an Rí Walk	45	D1
Burgh Quay	80	B3
Burleigh Court	50	B1
Burlington Gardens	50	B1
Burlington Road	81	D6
Burmah Close	72	B3
Burn Side	18	C4
Burnell Park	23	E4
Burrow Court	10	C2
Burrow Road	32	B1
Burrowfield Road	11	E4
Burton Hall Road	69	D2
Burton Road	72	A3
Bushfield Avenue	50	B3
Bushfield Park	48	C1
Bushfield Square	28	A4
Bushfield Terrace	50	B3
Bushy Park	56	A2
Bushy Park Gardens	56	C1
Bushy Park Road	56	C1
Buttercup Park	20	B3
Buttercup Road	20	B3
Butterfield Avenue	56	A3
Butterfield Close	56	A3
Butterfield Crescent	56	B3
Butterfield Drive	56	B3
Butterfield Grove	56	A3
Butterfield Orchard	56	B4
Butterfield Park	56	B3
Byrne's Lane	81	D4
Byrne's Lane New	80	A3

C

Cabinteely Avenue	70	C3
Cabinteely Bypass	70	B3
Cabinteely Close	70	B3
Cabinteely Crescent	70	C3
Cabinteely Drive	70	C3
Cabinteely Green	70	C3
Cabinteely Way	70	B3
Cabra Drive	39	F1
Cabra Grove	39	F1
Cabra Park	40	A1
Caddell	10	A4
Cadogan Road	41	E1
Cairn Court	17	F3
Cairn Hill	70	A2
Cairnwood Avenue	53	E3
Calderwood Avenue	28	A3
Calderwood Road	28	A3
Caledon Road	41	E2
Callary Road	58	C2
Calmount Park	47	D4
Camac Park	47	D2
Camaderry Road	77	E2
Camberly Oaks	57	E3
Cambridge Avenue	42	A4
Cambridge Road (Rathmines)	49	F3
Cambridge Road (Ringsend)	41	F4
Cambridge Square	41	F4
Cambridge Terrace	50	A2
Camden Lock	41	F4
Camden Place	81	B6
Camden Row	81	A5
Camden Street Lower	81	B5
Camden Street Upper	81	B6
Cameron Square	79	A5
Cameron Street	79	B5
Canal Road	49	F2
Canal Terrace	47	E2
Cannon Rock View	33	E2
Cannonbrook Avenue	34	C3
Cannonbrook Court	34	C3
Cannonbrook Park	35	D3
Canon Lillis Avenue	80	D2
Capel Lane	80	A3
Capel Street	80	A3
Cappagh Avenue	16	B4
Cappagh Drive	25	F1
Cappagh Green	16	B4
Cappagh Road	15	E2
Cappaghmore	45	E2
Captain's Avenue	48	B4
Captain's Drive	48	B4
Captain's Road	48	B3
Caragh Road	39	E1
Carberry Road	28	A3
Cardiff Lane	41	E3
Cardiffsbridge Avenue	25	F1
Cardiffsbridge Road	25	F2
Cardiffscastle Road	26	A1
Carey's Lane	6	B3
Carleton Road	28	B4
Carley Street	49	E2
Carlingford Road	27	E4
Carlisle Avenue	50	B3
Carlisle Street	79	D6
Carlton Close	77	D1
Carlton Court	5	D4
Carlton Road	42	A1
Carman's Hall	79	D5
Carmanhall Court	69	D2
Carmanhall Road	68	C1
Carna Road	37	E4
Carndonagh Drive	21	E4
Carndonagh Lawn	21	E4
Carndonagh Park	21	E4
Carndonagh Road	21	E4
Carne Court	13	D3
Carnew Street	78	B2
Carnlough Road	26	B4
Carpenterstown Avenue	23	F3
Carpenterstown Park East	23	E3
Carpenterstown Road	23	E4
Carraig Grennane	71	E4
Carraigmore Avenue	62	A1
Carraigmore Close	62	A1
Carraigmore Dale	62	A1
Carraigmore Downes	62	A1
Carraigmore Green	62	A1
Carraigmore Grove	62	A1
Carraigmore Lawns	62	A1
Carraigmore Place	62	A1
Carrarroe Avenue	21	D4
Carrick Court	10	B3
Carrick Terrace	79	B6
Carrickbrack Heath	32	B2
Carrickbrack Hill	32	B2
Carrickbrack Lawn	32	B2
Carrickbrack Road	33	D4
Carrickbrennan Lawn	60	C3
Carrickbrennan Road	60	C3
Carrickhill Close	10	B2
Carrickhill Drive	10	B3
Carrickhill Heights	10	B2
Carrickhill Rise	10	B2
Carrickhill Road	10	B3
Carrickhill Walk	10	C2
Carrickmines Avenue	70	B4
Carrickmines Chase	70	A4
Carrickmines Garth	70	B4
Carrickmines Oaks	70	A4
Carrickmount Avenue	57	E4
Carrickmount Drive	57	E4
Carrig Road	17	E3
Carrigallen Drive	26	A2
Carrigallen Park	26	A2
Carrigallen Road	26	A2
Carriglawn	58	B4
Carriglea Avenue (Firhouse)	64	C2
Carriglea Avenue (Kill O' The Grange)	70	C1
Carriglea Court	64	C2
Carriglea Downs	64	C2
Carriglea Drive	64	C2
Carriglea Gardens	70	C1
Carriglea Grove	64	C1

Name	Page	Grid	Name	Page	Grid	Name	Page	Grid	Name	Page	Grid
Carriglea Rise	64	C2	Castlecurragh Park	14	A3	Cathal Brugha Street	80	B2	Charlotte Terrace	72	C3
Carriglea View	64	C2	Castlefarm	4	C2	Cathedral Lane	81	A5	Charlotte Way	81	B6
Carriglea Walk	64	C2	Castlefield Avenue	65	D1	Cathedral Street	80	B2	Charnwood	77	D2
Carrigmore Drive	63	F2	Castlefield Court (Clonsilla)	22	B2	Cathedral View Court	81	A5	Charnwood Avenue	22	C2
Carrigmore Grove	63	F3	Castlefield Court (Firhouse)	65	D1	Cathedral View Walk	81	A5	Charnwood Dale	22	C2
Carrigmore Park	63	F2	Castlefield Drive	65	D1	Catherine's Lane West	79	C4	Charnwood Gardens	22	C2
Carrigmore Road	63	F2	Castlefield Green	65	D1	Causeway Road	30	C3	Charnwood Green	22	C2
Carrigwood	65	D2	Castlefield Grove	65	D1	Cave's Strand	6	C1	Charnwood Heath	22	C2
Carrow Road	48	A2	Castlefield Lawn	65	D1	Ceanchor Road	33	D4	Charnwood Lawns	22	C2
Carysfort Avenue	59	F3	Castlefield Manor	7	D3	Cedar Avenue	54	A1	Charnwood Meadows	22	C2
Carysfort Downs	59	F4	Castlefield Park (Clonsilla)	22	C2	Cedar Brook Avenue	46	A1	Charnwood Park	22	C2
Carysfort Drive	72	B2	Castlefield Park (Firhouse)	65	D1	Cedar Brook Place	46	A1	Chatham Lane	81	B4
Carysfort Grove	59	F4	Castlefield Way	65	D2	Cedar Brook Walk	46	A1	Chatham Row	81	B4
Carysfort Hall	59	F3	Castlefield Woods	22	C2	Cedar Brook Way	46	B1	Chatham Street	81	B4
Carysfort Park	59	F3	Castleforbes Road	41	E3	Cedar Court (Loughlinstown)	75	D1	Cheeverstown Road	63	D1
Carysfort Road	72	B2	Castlegrange Avenue	5	D2	Cedar Court (Terenure)	49	D4	Chelmsford Avenue	50	A2
Carysfort Woods	59	F4	Castlegrange Close	44	C3	Cedar Drive	36	C2	Chelmsford Mews	50	A2
Casana View	33	E2	Castlegrange Court	44	C3	Cedar Park	20	C4	Chelmsford Road	50	A2
Casement Drive	16	B4	Castlegrange Drive	44	C3	Cedar Square	59	E3	Chelsea Gardens	42	C1
Casement Green	16	C4	Castlegrange Green	44	C3	Cedar Walk	30	B2	Cherbury Court	59	D2
Casement Grove	16	B4	Castlegrange Heights	5	D2	Cedarmount Road	58	C3	Cherbury Gardens	59	D2
Casement Park	16	B4	Castlegrange Lawn	44	C3	Cedarwood Avenue	17	D4	Cherbury Park Avenue	35	D3
Casement Road	16	C4	Castlegrange Road (Clondalkin)	44	C3	Cedarwood Green	17	E4	Cherbury Park Road	35	D3
Casement Villas	70	B1	Castlegrange Road (Swords)	5	D2	Cedarwood Grove	17	E4	Cherries Road	68	B1
Cashel Avenue	48	C4	Castlegrange Square	44	C3	Cedarwood Park	17	E4	Cherrington Close	73	D1
Cashel Road	48	B3	Castleheath	6	B3	Cedarwood Rise	17	E4	Cherrington Drive	73	D1
Casimir Avenue	49	E3	Castlekevin Road	19	E4	Cedarwood Road	17	E4	Cherrington Road	73	D1
Casimir Road	49	D3	Castleknock Avenue	23	F3	Celbridge Road	34	A2	Cherry Avenue	23	E3
Casino Park	28	C3	Castleknock Brook	24	A3	Celestine Avenue	41	F4	Cherry Avenue (Swords)	4	C4
Casino Road	28	B4	Castleknock Close	23	F3	Celtic Park Avenue	28	B2	Cherry Court (Loughlinstown)	75	D2
Castaheany	12	C3	Castleknock Crescent	23	F3	Celtic Park Road	28	B2	Cherry Court (Terenure)	49	D4
Castilla Park	29	E4	Castleknock Downs	23	F3	Chalet Gardens	35	D2	Cherry Drive	23	E3
Castle Avenue (Clondalkin)	45	F3	Castleknock Drive	23	F2	Chalfont Avenue	6	C2	Cherry Garth (Mount Merrion)	59	D3
Castle Avenue (Clontarf)	29	D4	Castleknock Elms	24	A3	Chalfont Park	6	C2	Cherry Garth (Swords)	4	B4
Castle Avenue (Swords)	5	D3	Castleknock Gate	24	A4	Chalfont Place	6	C2	Cherry Grove	48	A4
Castle Byrne Park	60	A3	Castleknock Glade	24	A3	Chalfont Road	6	C2	Cherry Lawn	23	E3
Castle Close (Clondalkin)	46	A3	Castleknock Grange	23	F3	Chamber Street	79	C5	Cherry Lawns	34	B3
Castle Close (Dalkey)	72	A1	Castleknock Green	24	B3	Chamley Park	6	A2	Cherry Orchard Avenue	46	B1
Castle Court (Ballybrack)	75	E2	Castleknock Grove	24	A3	Chancel Mews	25	F4	Cherry Orchard Crescent	46	B1
Castle Court (Booterstown)	59	D1	Castleknock Laurels	23	F3	Chancery Lane	81	A4	Cherry Orchard Drive	46	C1
Castle Court (Clontarf)	28	C4	Castleknock Lodge	24	A4	Chancery Place	78	D3	Cherry Orchard Green	46	B1
Castle Court (Leopardstown)	68	C4	Castleknock Meadows	23	F2	Chancery Street	78	D3	Cherry Orchard Grove	46	B1
Castle Cove	6	B2	Castleknock Oaks	24	A3	Chanel Avenue	29	D1	Cherry Park	8	B1
Castle Crescent	45	F3	Castleknock Park	24	B3	Chanel Grove	29	D1	Cherryfield Avenue	48	A4
Castle Down Croft	6	B2	Castleknock Rise	23	F3	Chanel Road	29	D1	Cherryfield Avenue Lower	50	A3
Castle Down Grove	6	B2	Castleknock Road	24	B4	Chapel Crescent	25	F3	Cherryfield Avenue Upper	50	A3
Castle Down Road	6	B2	Castleknock Vale	23	F3	Chapel Lane (Bray)	73	E3	Cherryfield Close	13	D4
Castle Drive (Clondalkin)	46	A3	Castleknock View	23	F2	Chapel Lane (Swords)	5	E3	Cherryfield Court	13	D4
Castle Drive (Swords)	5	D3	Castleknock Walk	23	F3	Chapelgate	27	E4	Cherryfield Drive	48	A4
Castle Farm	73	D1	Castleknock Way	23	F3	Chapelgate The Convent	27	E4	Cherryfield Lawn	22	B1
Castle Grove (Clondalkin)	45	F3	Castleknock Wood	24	A2	Chapelizod Hill Road	37	F3	Cherryfield Park	13	D4
Castle Grove (Clontarf)	29	D4	Castlelands	72	B2	Chapelizod Moorings	38	A3	Cherryfield Road	47	F4
Castle Grove (Leopardstown)	68	C4	Castlemoyne	20	C2	Chapelizod Road	38	C3	Cherryfield View	22	B1
Castle Grove (Swords)	5	D3	Castlepark Road	71	F1	Chaplins Terrace	36	B4	Cherryfield Walk	13	D4
Castle Lawn	68	C4	Castlerose Close	21	F3	Charlemont	28	B3	Cherryfield Way	55	E3
Castle Lawns (Malahide)	6	A2	Castlerose Drive	21	F3	Charlemont Avenue	61	D3	Cherrymount Crescent	28	C3
Castle Lawns (Tallaght)	54	C3	Castlerose View	21	F3	Charlemont Mall	49	F2	Cherrymount Grove	28	C3
Castle Park (Clondalkin)	46	A3	Castleside Drive	56	C2	Charlemont Place	50	A2	Cherrymount Park	40	A1
Castle Park (Monkstown)	60	C4	Castletimon Avenue	19	D4	Charlemont Road	28	B4	Cherrywood	75	D2
Castle Park (Swords)	5	E3	Castletimon Drive	19	D4	Charlemont Street	49	F1	Cherrywood Avenue	45	E3
Castle Park (Tallaght)	54	C4	Castletimon Gardens	18	C4	Charles Lane	80	C1	Cherrywood Crescent	45	D4
Castle Riada Avenue	35	E3	Castletimon Green	19	D4	Charles Street North Great	80	C1	Cherrywood Drive	45	D3
Castle Riada Crescent	35	E3	Castletimon Park	19	D4	Charles Street West	78	D3	Cherrywood Grove	45	E3
Castle Riada Drive	35	E4	Castletimon Road	19	D4	Charleston Avenue	50	A3	Cherrywood Lawn	45	D4
Castle Riada Grove	35	E3	Castleview Close	4	B1	Charleston Road	50	A3	Cherrywood Park	75	D2
Castle Road (Clontarf)	42	B1	Castleview Court	4	B1	Charlestown	16	C3	Cherrywood Road	75	D3
Castle Road (Lucan)	35	F3	Castleview Crescent	4	C1	Charlestown Avenue	17	D3	Cherrywood Villas	45	D4
Castle Street (Bray)	73	E3	Castleview Drive	4	C1	Charlestown Court	16	C3	Chester Road	50	A2
Castle Street (Central Dublin)	81	A4	Castleview Grove	4	C1	Charlestown Drive	16	C3	Chesterfield Avenue	24	C4
Castle Street (Dalkey)	72	B2	Castleview Heath	4	B1	Charlestown Park	16	C3	Chesterfield Avenue	38	C2
Castle View (Artane)	29	D2	Castleview Heights	4	B1	Charlestown Way	16	C3	Chesterfield Close	24	C4
Castle View (Clondalkin)	46	A3	Castleview Lawns	4	B1	Charleville	57	E3	Chesterfield Copse	24	C4
Castle View (Dundrum)	57	F4	Castleview Place	4	C1	Charleville Avenue	80	D1	Chesterfield Grove	24	C4
Castle View Drive	44	C3	Castleview Way	4	B1	Charleville Close	49	F3	Chesterfield Park	24	C3
Castle Way	51	D2	Castlewood	13	D4	Charleville Mall	80	D1	Chesterfield View	24	C3
Castlebrook	57	F4	Castlewood Avenue	49	F3	Charleville Road (Phibsborough)	40	A1	Chestnut Grove (Ballinteer)	67	E1
Castlecurragh	14	A3	Castlewood Park	49	F3	Charleville Road (Rathmines)	49	F3	Chestnut Grove (Ballymount)	53	F1
Castlecurragh Heath	14	A3	Castlewood Terrace	49	F3	Charleville Square	56	A3	Chestnut Road (Fox & Geese)	46	C3

Entry	Page	Grid
Chestnut Road (Mount Mernion)	58	C2
Chipping Row	12	B4
Chipping Terrace	12	B4
Christchurch Place	81	A4
Church Avenue (Blanchardstown)	23	F2
Church Avenue (Central Dublin)	78	D3
Church Avenue (Glasnevin)	27	D3
Church Avenue (Irishtown)	41	F4
Church Avenue (Killiney)	75	E1
Church Avenue (Portmarnock)	10	B4
Church Avenue (Rathmines)	49	F3
Church Avenue South	79	A6
Church Court	24	B3
Church Gardens	49	F3
Church Grove	63	F2
Church Lane	56	B2
Church Park Court	49	D3
Church Road (Blanchardstown)	14	A2
Church Road (Bray)	77	D2
Church Road (Dalkey)	72	B2
Church Road (East Wall)	41	E2
Church Road (Finglas)	26	A1
Church Road (Killiney)	71	E3
Church Road (Killiney)	75	E1
Church Road (Malahide)	7	D2
Church Road (Sutton)	32	B1
Church Road (Swords)	5	D3
Church Street (Central Dublin)	40	B3
Church Street (Finglas)	26	A1
Church Street (Howth)	33	D1
Church Street East	41	E2
Church Street New	78	C3
Church Street Upper	78	D2
Church Terrace	78	D3
Church View	45	E4
Church Walk	25	F4
Churchfields	57	F1
Churchgate Avenue	42	C1
Churchill Terrace	51	D2
Churchlands	68	B3
Churchtown Avenue	57	E1
Churchtown Close	57	E1
Churchtown Drive	57	E1
Churchtown Road	57	D3
Churchtown Road Lower	57	E1
Churchtown Road Upper	57	E3
Churchview Avenue	71	D4
Churchview Drive	71	D3
Churchview Park	71	D4
Churchview Road	71	D4
Cianlea	4	B2
Cill Cais	63	F2
Cill Eana	29	F2
Cill Sarain	76	B3
City Quay	80	C3
Citywest Avenue	52	B4
Citywest Road	62	B2
Claddagh Road	37	E4
Clanawley Road	29	D3
Clanboy Road	29	D3
Clanbrassil Street Lower	79	D6
Clanbrassil Street Upper	49	E2
Clanbrassil Terrace	79	D6
Clancarthy Road	28	C3
Clancy Avenue	17	D4
Clancy Road	17	D4
Clandonagh Road	28	C3
Clanhugh Road	29	D3
Clanmahon Road	29	D3
Clanmaurice Road	28	D3
Clanmawr	75	F3
Clanmoyle Road	29	C3
Clanranald Road	28	C3
Clanree Road	28	C3
Clanwilliam Place	41	E4
Clanwilliam Square	41	E4
Clanwilliam Terrace	41	E4
Clare Hall	20	C3
Clare Lane	81	C4
Clare Road	27	F3
Clare Street	81	C4
Claremont Avenue	27	D2
Claremont Court	26	C3
Claremont Crescent	26	C3
Claremont Drive	26	C2
Claremont Park	51	D1
Claremont Road (Howth)	32	C1
Claremont Road (Killiney)	71	F3
Claremont Road (Sandymount)	51	D1
Claremont Villas	61	E4
Claremount Pines	70	A4
Clarence Mangan Road	79	C5
Clarence Place Great	81	D4
Clarence Street	61	D3
Clarence Street Great North	80	D1
Clarendon Street	81	B4
Clareville Lawns	26	C4
Clareville Road	49	D4
Clarinda Park East	61	E4
Clarinda Park North	61	E3
Clarinda Park West	61	D4
Clarion Quay	80	D3
Claude Road	40	B1
Clayon Terrace	38	A3
Cleggan Avenue	37	E4
Cleggan Park	37	E4
Cleggan Road	37	E4
Clifden Drive	46	C1
Clifden Road	37	E4
Cliff Terrace	72	A1
Clifton Avenue	60	C3
Clifton Park	75	E3
Clifton Terrace	60	B3
Cliftonville Road	27	D4
Clogher Road	49	D2
Cloister Avenue	59	F3
Cloister Close	59	E3
Cloister Court	26	A3
Cloister Green	59	F3
Cloister Grove	59	F3
Cloister Park	59	E3
Cloister Square	59	F3
Cloister Way	59	F3
Clon Brugh	68	B3
Clonard Avenue	68	A2
Clonard Close	67	F2
Clonard Drive	68	A2
Clonard Grove	68	A2
Clonard Lawn	68	A2
Clonard Park	68	A2
Clonard Road (Crumlin)	48	A3
Clonard Road (Dundrum)	68	A2
Cloncourt	12	B2
Clonee Bypass	12	C2
Clonfadda Wood	59	D2
Clonfert Road	48	C3
Clonkeen Court	70	B3
Clonkeen Crescent	70	B2
Clonkeen Drive	70	B2
Clonkeen Grove	70	B1
Clonkeen Road	70	B2
Clonlea	67	F2
Clonliffe Avenue	41	D1
Clonliffe Gardens	41	D1
Clonliffe Road	40	C1
Clonmacnoise Road	48	C3
Clonmel Road	27	D1
Clonmel Street	81	B5
Clonmellon Grove	20	C3
Clonmore Road (Ballybough)	80	D1
Clonmore Road (Goatstown)	58	C3
Clonmore Terrace	80	D1
Clonrosse Court	20	B4
Clonrosse Drive	20	B4
Clonrosse Park	20	B4
Clonshaugh Avenue	19	E3
Clonshaugh Close	19	F2
Clonshaugh Crescent	19	E3
Clonshaugh Drive	19	F2
Clonshaugh Green	19	F3
Clonshaugh Grove	19	F3
Clonshaugh Heights	19	E3
Clonshaugh Meadow	19	E2
Clonshaugh Park	19	F2
Clonshaugh Road	19	E2
Clonshaugh Walk	19	F2
Clonsilla Close	23	F1
Clonsilla Park	23	F2
Clonsilla Road	22	C2
Clonskeagh Drive	50	C4
Clonskeagh Road	58	A1
Clonskeagh Square	58	A1
Clonskeagh Terrace	50	C4
Clontarf Park	42	C1
Clontarf Road	42	A1
Clonturk Avenue	27	F3
Clonturk Park	27	F4
Cloonlara Crescent	26	B2
Cloonlara Drive	26	B2
Cloonlara Road	26	B2
Cloonmore Avenue	63	D2
Cloonmore Close	63	D2
Cloonmore Crescent	63	D2
Cloonmore Drive	62	C2
Cloonmore Gardens	63	D2
Cloonmore Green	62	C1
Cloonmore Grove	62	C2
Cloonmore Lawns	62	C2
Cloonmore Park	62	C2
Cloonmore Road	62	C2
Clover Hill	76	B3
Cloverhill Drive	46	C1
Cloverhill Road	45	F2
Cluain Mhuire	71	D1
Cluain na Greine Court	75	E4
Cluain Shee	68	B4
Cluainin Cronan	44	C2
Cluainn Rí	35	F3
Clune Road	26	B1
Cluny Grove	71	E2
Clyde Lane	50	C3
Clyde Road	50	C2
Coast Road (Baldoyle)	11	D2
Coast Road (Malahide)	7	A2
Coburg Place	80	D2
Cois Cairn	73	D3
Cois Culainn	75	E2
Cois na Habhann	63	F1
Cois Sleibh	76	C4
Colberts Fort	53	F3
Coldcut Road	36	C3
Coldwell Street	61	E4
Colepark Avenue	37	F4
Colepark Drive	37	F4
Colepark Green	37	F4
Colepark Road	37	F4
Coleraine Street	78	D2
Coles Lane	80	B3
Coliemore Road	72	C3
College Crescent	55	F2
College Drive	55	F1
College Gate	23	F3
College Green	81	B4
College Grove	24	A4
College Park (Castleknock)	24	B4
College Park (Kimmage)	55	F2
College Park Avenue	67	F2
College Park Close	67	F2
College Park Grove	67	F2
College Park Way	67	F2
College Road	66	C3
College Road (Castleknock)	24	B4
College Street (Baldoyle)	11	D3
College Street (Central Dublin)	81	B4
Collegefort	19	E2
Collegefort (Castleknock)	24	A4
Collegewood	24	A4
Collier's Avenue	50	B3
Collin's Court	59	F2
Collins Avenue	28	A2
Collins Avenue East	28	C3
Collins Avenue Extension	27	E1
Collins Drive	26	C1
Collins Green	26	B1
Collins Park	28	B2
Collins Place	26	B1
Collins Row	26	B1
Collinstown Grove	45	F1
Collinstown Road	36	B4
Collinswood	28	B2
Colthurst Close	35	F3
Colthurst Cresent	35	F3
Colthurst Gardens	35	F3
Colthurst Green	35	F3
Colthurst Mews	35	F3
Colthurst Park	35	F3
Colthurst Rise	35	F3
Colthurst Road	35	F3
Colthurst Way	35	F3
Comeragh Road	47	F2
Commons East	5	E4
Commons Road (Clondalkin)	45	E4
Commons Road (Loughlinstown)	75	D2
Commons Street	80	D3
Comyn Place	27	E3
Con Colbert Road	38	C4
Congress Gardens	61	E4
Connaught Parade	40	A1
Connaught Street	40	A1
Connawood Copse	73	D4
Connawood Crescent	73	D4
Connawood Drive	73	D4
Connawood Green	73	D3
Connawood Grove	73	D3
Connawood Lawns	73	D4
Connawood Walk	73	D3
Connawood Way	73	D3
Connolly Avenue (Inchicore)	48	B1
Connolly Avenue (Malahide)	6	C4
Connolly Gardens	48	B1
Conor Clune Road	25	E4
Conquer Hill Avenue	42	C1
Conquer Hill Road	42	C1
Constellation Road	18	C3
Constitution Hill	78	D2
Convent Avenue (Bray)	77	E2
Convent Avenue (Marino)	28	A4
Convent Hall	50	B4
Convent Lane	56	C3
Convent Lawns	38	A4
Convent Road (Blackrock)	59	F2
Convent Road (Clondalkin)	45	F2
Convent Road (Dalkey)	72	B2
Convent Road (Dún Laoghaire)	61	D3
Convent Way	25	F4
Conyngham Road	39	D3
Cook Street	79	D4
Cookstown Industrial Estate Road	53	E3
Cookstown Road	53	E3
Coolamber Court	55	F4
Coolamber Park	55	F4
Coolatree Close	28	B1
Coolatree Park	28	B1
Coolatree Road	28	B1
Cooleen Avenue	28	B1
Coolevin	75	D1
Cooley Road	48	A2
Coolgariff Road	28	B1

Name	Page	Grid
Coolgreena Close	28	B1
Coolgreena Road	28	B1
Coolkill	68	B3
Coolmine Boulevard	23	E2
Coolmine Close	23	E2
Coolmine Court	23	E2
Coolmine Green	23	E2
Coolmine Lawn	23	E2
Coolmine Park	23	E2
Coolmine Road	23	E2
Coolmine Woods	23	E2
Coolnevaun	59	D4
Coolock Drive	19	F4
Coolock Lane	19	D3
Coolock Village	29	E1
Coolrua Drive	28	B1
Cope Street	81	B4
Copeland Avenue	28	C4
Copeland Grove	28	C4
Copper Alley	81	A4
Copper Beech Grove	73	D4
Coppinger Close	59	E4
Coppinger Glade	59	E4
Coppinger Row	81	D4
Corbally Avenue	62	A2
Corbally Close	62	A2
Corbally Downs	62	A2
Corbally Drive	62	A2
Corbally Glade	62	A2
Corbally Lawn	62	A2
Corbally Park	62	A2
Corbally Rise	62	A2
Corbally Square	62	A2
Corbally Vale	62	A2
Corbally Way	62	A2
Corbawn Avenue	75	F3
Corbawn Close	75	F4
Corbawn Court	75	F3
Corbawn Drive	75	F4
Corbawn Grove	75	F3
Corbawn Lane	75	E4
Corbawn Wood	75	F3
Corduff Avenue	14	B4
Corduff Close	14	B4
Corduff Cottages	14	B4
Corduff Crescent	14	B4
Corduff Gardens	14	C4
Corduff Green	14	B4
Corduff Grove	14	B3
Corduff Park	14	B3
Corduff Place	14	B4
Corduff Way	14	C4
Cork Street	79	C5
Corkagh View	45	E4
Corke Abbey	73	E3
Cormac Terrace	56	B1
Cornelscourt Hill Road	70	A4
Cornmarket	79	C4
Corporation Street	80	C2
Corrib Gardens	49	D4
Corrib Road	49	D4
Corrig Avenue	61	D4
Corrig Close	54	C1
Corrig Court	61	D3
Corrig Park	61	D4
Corrig Road (Dalkey)	72	B2
Corrig Road (Dún Laoghaire)	61	D4
Corrig Road (Sandyford)	68	C2
Corrybeg	55	F3
Coulson Avenue	49	E4
Coultry Avenue	18	B4
Coultry Close	18	A4
Coultry Crescent	18	A3
Coultry Drive	18	A3
Coultry Gardens	18	A3
Coultry Grove	18	B3
Coultry Lawn	18	B3
Coultry Park	18	B3
Coultry Road	18	A3
Coultry Way	18	B4
Coundon Court	71	E4
Courtney Place	41	D1
Cowboother Lane	33	E2
Cowper Drive	50	A4
Cowper Gardens	49	F4
Cowper Road	49	F4
Cowper Road	50	A4
Cowper Street	78	B2
Cowper Village	49	F4
Crag Avenue	45	F2
Crag Crescent	46	A3
Crag Terrace	46	A3
Craigford Avenue	29	D2
Craigford Road	29	D2
Craiglands	72	B3
Craigmore Gardens	60	A2
Cramer Lane	50	C1
Crane Lane	81	A4
Crane Street	79	C4
Cranfield Place	51	D1
Cranford Court	58	C1
Crannagh Grove	56	C2
Crannagh Park	56	C2
Crannagh Road	56	C2
Crannoge Close	17	E3
Crannoge Road	17	E3
Crawford Avenue	27	E4
Creevagh House Apartments	57	F3
Creighton Street	80	D3
Cremona Road	47	E1
Cremore Avenue	27	D3
Cremore Crescent	26	C2
Cremore Drive	27	D2
Cremore Heights	27	D2
Cremore Lawn	26	C3
Cremore Park	27	D3
Cremore Road	27	D3
Cremorne (Templeogue)	55	E4
Cremorne (Terenure)	56	C1
Crescent Place	28	B4
Crescent Villas	27	E4
Crestfield Avenue	27	F1
Crestfield Close	27	F1
Crestfield Drive	27	F1
Crestfield Road	27	F1
Crinan Strand	80	D2
Crinken Glen	73	D1
Crinken Lane	73	D1
Croaghpatrick Road	39	D1
Crofton Avenue	61	D3
Crofton Road	61	D2
Croftwood Crescent	46	B1
Croftwood Drive	46	C1
Croftwood Gardens	46	B1
Croftwood Green	46	C1
Croftwood Grove	46	B1
Croftwood Park	46	C1
Cromcastle Avenue	19	E4
Cromcastle Court	19	E4
Cromcastle Drive	19	E4
Cromcastle Green	19	E4
Cromcastle Park	19	E4
Cromcastle Road	19	E4
Cromlech Fields	75	E2
Cromwellsfort Road	47	F4
Cross Avenue (Booterstown)	59	E2
Cross Avenue (Dún Laoghaire)	61	D3
Crosthwaite Park East	61	D4
Crosthwaite Park South	61	D4
Crosthwaite Park West	61	D4
Crotty Avenue	48	A3
Crow Street	81	B4
Crown Alley	81	B4
Croydon Gardens	28	A4
Croydon Green	28	A4
Croydon Park Avenue	28	B4
Croydon Terrace	28	A3
Crumlin Park	48	B2
Crumlin Road	48	B2
Cuala Road (Bray)	77	E2
Cuala Road (Phibsborough)	40	A1
Cuckoo Lane	78	D3
Cuffe Lane	81	B5
Cuffe Street	81	B5
Cuilenn Park	17	E4
Cul na Greine	63	F2
Cullenswood Gardens	50	B3
Cullenswood Park	50	B3
Culmore Park	37	E3
Culmore Road	37	E3
Cumberland Road	81	C6
Cumberland Street (Central Dublin)	80	B2
Cumberland Street (Dún Laoghaire)	60	C3
Cumberland Street South	81	C4
Cunningham Drive	72	B3
Cunningham Road	72	B3
Curlew Road	48	A2
Curragh Hall Avenue	14	A1
Curragh Hall Court	14	A1
Curragh Hall Crescent	14	A1
Curragh Hall Drive	14	A1
Curragh Hall Gate	14	A1
Curragh Hall Green	14	A1
Curragh Hall House	14	A1
Curragh Hall Road	14	A1
Curragh Hall View	14	A1
Curzon Street	81	A6
Cushlawn Avenue	63	F2
Cushlawn Close	63	F3
Cushlawn Dale	63	E3
Cushlawn Drive	63	F2
Cushlawn Grove	63	F2
Cushlawn Park	63	E2
Cushlawn Walk	63	F3
Cushlawn Way	63	F3
Custom House Quay	80	C3
Cypress Court	75	E1
Cypress Drive	55	E2
Cypress Garth	55	F3
Cypress Grove North	55	F2
Cypress Grove Road	55	F2
Cypress Grove South	55	F3
Cypress Lawn	55	F3
Cypress Park	55	F2
Cypress Road	58	C2

D

Name	Page	Grid
D'Olier Street	80	B3
Dakota Avenue	18	C2
Dal Riada	7	F4
Dalcassian Downs	27	D4
Dale Drive	58	C4
Dale Road	58	C4
Dale View Park	75	E1
Dalepark Road	64	A2
Daletree Crescent	64	C2
Daletree Park	64	C3
Daletree Road	65	D3
Daletree View	64	C2
Daleview Road	4	B2
Dalkey Avenue	72	A3
Dalkey Park	72	A3
Dalkey Rock	72	B3
Dalton Mews	7	D3
Daltree Avenue	64	C2
Daltree Close	64	C2
Damastown Avenue	13	E1
Damastown Close	13	E2
Damastown Court	13	E2
Damastown Drive	13	D2
Damastown Green	13	D2
Damastown Road	13	D2
Dame Court	81	B4
Dame Lane	81	A4
Dame Street	81	A4
Dane Road	17	F3
Danes Court	43	D1
Danesfort	42	B1
Daneswell Road	27	D4
Dangan Avenue	48	A4
Dangan Drive	48	B4
Dangan Park	48	B4
Daniel Court	79	D6
Daniel Street	79	D6
Danieli Drive	29	D2
Danieli Road	29	D2
Dargle Drive	57	D4
Dargle Lane	76	B3
Dargle Road (Dean's Grange)	69	F1
Dargle Road (Drumcondra)	27	E4
Dargle View	67	D1
Dargle Wood	65	E1
Darley Street	49	E2
Darling Estate	25	E4
Dartmouth Lane	50	A2
Dartmouth Place	50	A2
Dartmouth Road	50	A2
Dartmouth Square East	50	A2
Dartmouth Square North	50	A2
Dartmouth Square South	50	A2
Dartmouth Square West	50	A2
Dartmouth Terrace	50	A2
Dartry Cottages	57	E1
Dartry Park	57	E1
Dartry Road	49	F4
David Park	40	B1
David Road	40	B1
David's Terrace	27	D3
Davis Court	48	A1
Davitt Park	75	D1
Davitt Road (Bray)	77	D1
Davitt Road (Drimnagh)	48	B1
Dawson Lane	81	B4
Dawson Street	81	B5
De Courcey Square	27	D4
De Selby Lane	62	C2
De Selby Park	62	B2
De Selby Rise	62	C2
De Vesci Terrace	60	C3
Dean Street	79	D5
Dean Swift Green	27	D1
Dean Swift Road	27	D2
Dean Swift Square	79	D4
Dean's Court	70	B1
Dean's Grange Road	70	A1
Deansrath Avenue	44	C2
Deansrath Grove	44	C2
Deansrath Lawn	44	C2
Deansrath Park	44	C2
Deansrath Road	44	C3
Deanstown Avenue	25	F2
Deanstown Drive	25	F2
Deanstown Green	25	F2
Deanstown Park	25	F2
Deanstown Road	25	F2
Deburgh Road	78	A3
Decies Road	38	B4
Deepdales	76	C4
Deer Haven Avenue	13	D3
Deer Haven Close	13	D3
Deer Haven View	13	D3
Deer Haven Walk	13	D3
Deer Park	76	C3
Deerpark Avenue (Castleknock)	24	C4
Deerpark Avenue (Killinarden)	63	F3
Deerpark Close (Castleknock)	24	C3
Deerpark Close (Killinarden)	63	E3

Deerpark Downs	63	E3
Deerpark Drive (Castleknock)	24	C3
Deerpark Drive (Killinarden)	63	F3
Deerpark Green	63	F3
Deerpark Place	63	F3
Deerpark Road (Castleknock)	24	C3
Deerpark Road (Killinarden)	63	F3
Deerpark Road (Mount Merrion)	58	C3
Deerpark Square	63	E3
Del Val Avenue	31	D1
Del Val Court	31	D1
Delaford Avenue	55	D4
Delaford Drive	55	D4
Delaford Grove	55	D4
Delaford Lawn	55	E4
Delaford Park	55	D4
Delbrook Manor	67	F2
Delbrook Park	67	F2
Delhurst Avenue	22	A1
Delhurst Close	22	A1
Delhurst Court	22	A1
Delhurst Mews	22	A1
Delville Road	27	D1
Delwood Close	23	E2
Delwood Drive	23	E2
Delwood Grove	23	E3
Delwood Park	23	E3
Delwood Road	23	E2
Delwood Walk	23	E2
Demesne	29	D3
Denville Court	71	E4
Denzille Lane	81	D4
Dermot O'Hurley Avenue	41	F4
Derravaragh Road	49	D4
Derry Drive	48	B3
Derry Park	48	B3
Derry Road	48	B3
Derrynane Gardens	41	F4
Derrynane Parade	40	C1
Desmond Avenue	61	D3
Desmond Street	81	A6
Devenish Road	48	C3
Devery's Lane	40	B1
Devitt Villas	61	E4
Devoy Road	48	B1
Dewberry Park	10	C2
Diamond Valley Apartments	76	B1
Digges Lane	81	B4
Digges Street Upper	81	B5
Dingle Road	26	B4
Dispensary Lane	56	C3
Distillery Loft	41	D1
Distillery Road	41	D1
Diswellstown Road	23	D3
Diswelltown Cottages	23	F4
Dodder Avenue	64	B2
Dodder Crescent	64	B2
Dodder Park Drive	56	C2
Dodder Park Grove	56	C2
Dodder Park Road	56	C2
Dodder Road Lower	56	C2
Dodsboro Cottages	34	B3
Dodsboro Road	34	B3
Dollymount Avenue	30	A4
Dollymount Grove	29	F4
Dollymount Park	29	F4
Dollymount Rise	30	A4
Dolmen Court	17	F3
Dolphin Avenue	49	D2
Dolphin House	79	A6
Dolphin Park	79	A6
Dolphin Road	79	A6
Dolphin's Barn Street	79	B6
Dominick Lane	80	A2
Dominick Place	80	A2
Dominick Street	61	D3
Dominick Street Lower	80	A2
Dominick Street Upper	80	A2
Domville Drive	55	E2
Domville Grove	75	E1
Domville Road	55	E2
Donaghmede Avenue	21	D4
Donaghmede Drive	21	E4
Donaghmede Park	21	D4
Donaghmede Road	21	D4
Donnellan Avenue	79	A5
Donnybrook Castle	50	C4
Donnybrook Close	50	C4
Donnybrook Manor	50	C3
Donnybrook Road	50	C3
Donnycarney Road	28	C3
Donomore Avenue	63	D2
Donomore Crescent	63	E2
Donomore Green	63	D2
Donomore Park	63	E2
Donore Avenue	79	C5
Donore Road	79	C6
Donore Terrace	79	C5
Donovan Lane	79	D6
Doon Court	17	E3
Doonamana Road	71	D3
Doonanore Park	71	D4
Doonsalla Drive	71	D3
Doonsalla Park	71	D3
Doris Street	41	E4
Dornden Park	51	F4
Dorney Court	75	E4
Dorset Lane	40	C1
Dorset Street Lower	40	C2
Dorset Street Upper	80	A2
Dowland Road	48	A4
Downpatrick Road	48	C2
Dowth Avenue	40	A1
Drapier Road	27	D2
Drimnagh Park	69	E4
Drimnagh Road	48	A1
Droim na Coille Avenue	35	F3
Droim na Coille Court	35	F3
Droim na Coille Drive	35	F3
Droim na Coille Place	35	F3
Dromard Avenue	51	E1
Dromard Road	48	A2
Dromawling Road	28	B2
Dromcarra Avenue	63	D1
Dromcarra Drive	63	D1
Dromcarra Green	63	D1
Dromcarra Grove	63	D1
Dromdawn Avenue	28	B2
Dromeen Avenue	28	B2
Dromheath Avenue	14	A2
Dromheath Drive	14	A3
Dromheath Gardens	14	A3
Dromheath Grove	14	A3
Dromheath Park	14	A3
Dromlee Crescent	28	B2
Dromnanane Road	28	B2
Dromore Road	48	B2
Druid Court	17	F3
Druid Valley	74	C2
Drumahill	58	B4
Drumalee Avenue	78	B1
Drumalee Court	78	B1
Drumalee Drive	78	B1
Drumalee Grove	78	B1
Drumalee Park	78	B1
Drumalee Road	78	B1
Drumcairn Avenue	53	D4
Drumcairn Drive	53	D4
Drumcairn Gardens	53	D4
Drumcairn Green	53	D4
Drumcairn Park	53	D4
Drumcliffe Drive	39	E1
Drumcliffe Road	39	E1
Drumcondra Park	40	C1
Drumcondra Road Lower	40	C1
Drumcondra Road Upper	27	F4
Drumfinn Avenue	37	E3
Drumfinn Road	37	E4
Drumkeen Manor	71	D3
Drummartin Close	58	B4
Drummartin Park	58	B4
Drummartin Road	58	B3
Drummartin Terrace	58	B3
Drummond Place	49	E2
Drumnigh Road	21	D1
Drumnigh Woods	21	E1
Drury Street	81	B4
Drynam Close	9	F2
Drynam Court	5	E4
Drynam Crescent	9	F1
Drynam Drive	9	F1
Drynam Glen	9	F2
Drynam Grove	9	F1
Drynam Lane	5	E4
Drynam Place	9	F2
Drynam Rise	9	F2
Drynam Road (Swords, east of M1)	9	F1
Drynam Road (Swords, west of M1)	5	E4
Drynam View	9	F1
Drynam Walk	9	F1
Drynam Way	9	F2
Drysdale Close	64	A2
Dubber Cross	16	C2
Dublin Road (Bray)	73	E3
Dublin Road (Malahide)	6	C2
Dublin Road (Shankill)	75	E4
Dublin Road (Stillorgan)	59	D3
Dublin Road (Sutton)	31	E1
Dublin Road (Sutton)	32	A1
Dublin Road (Swords)	5	D4
Dublin Road (Swords)	8	C1
Dublin Street	11	D3
Dufferin Avenue	79	C6
Duke Street	81	B4
Dun an Oir	63	F1
Dun Emer Drive	68	A1
Dun Emer Park	68	A1
Dun Emer Road	68	A1
Dunard Avenue	39	E1
Dunard Court	39	E1
Dunard Drive	39	E1
Dunard Park	39	E2
Dunard Road	78	A1
Dunard Walk	39	E2
Dunawley Avenue	45	E3
Dunawley Drive	45	E3
Dunawley Grove	45	E3
Dunawley Way	45	E3
Dunbar Terrace	73	F4
Dunboy	69	F4
Duncairn Avenue	73	F4
Duncairn Lane	73	F4
Duncairn Terrace	73	F4
Duncarraig	32	B2
Dundaniel Road	19	D4
Dundela Avenue	72	A2
Dundela Haven	61	F4
Dundela Park	72	A2
Dundrum Gate	57	F4
Dundrum Road	57	F1
Dundrum Wood	57	F4
Dunedin Drive	60	C4
Dunedin Terrace	60	C4
Dungriffan Road	33	E2
Dunleary Road	60	C3
Dunluce Road	29	E3
Dunmanus Road	26	B4
Dunmore Grove	54	A1
Dunmore Lawn	53	F1
Dunmore Park	54	A1
Dunne Street	80	C1
Dunree Park	29	E1
Dunsandle Court	24	B3
Dunsandle Grove	24	B3
Dunseverick Road	29	D4
Dunsink Avenue	26	A2
Dunsink Drive	26	A2
Dunsink Gardens	26	A2
Dunsink Green	26	A2
Dunsink Lane	24	C1
Dunsink Park	26	A2
Dunsink Road	26	A2
Dunsoghly Avenue	25	E1
Dunsoghly Close	25	E1
Dunsoghly Court	25	E1
Dunsoghly Drive	25	E1
Dunsoghly Green	25	E1
Dunsoghly Park	25	E1
Dunstaffnage Hall	69	D1
Dunville Avenue	50	A3
Durham Road	51	E2
Durrow Road	48	C3
Dwyer Park	73	E4

E

Eagle Park	19	E4
Eaglewood	70	C2
Earl Street North	80	B3
Earl Street South	79	C4
Earls Court	56	C1
Earls Place	80	B3
Earlscroft	77	D4
Earlsfort Avenue	35	F4
Earlsfort Close	35	F4
Earlsfort Court	35	F3
Earlsfort Drive	35	F4
Earlsfort Gardens	36	A4
Earlsfort Glade	35	F4
Earlsfort Grove	35	F4
Earlsfort Lane	36	A4
Earlsfort Lawn	36	A4
Earlsfort Park	35	F3
Earlsfort Rise	35	F4
Earlsfort Road	35	F4
Earlsfort Terrace	81	B6
Earlsfort Vale	35	F4
Earlsfort View	36	A4
Earlsfort Way	35	F4
Earlswood	25	E3
East Pier Howth Harbour	33	E1
East Road	41	E2
East Wall Road	41	F3
Eastmoreland Lane	81	D6
Eastwood	25	F2
Eaton Brae (Rathgar)	57	D2
Eaton Brae (Shankill)	75	F3
Eaton Place	60	B2
Eaton Road	49	D4
Eaton Square (Monkstown)	60	B3
Eaton Square (Terenure)	49	D4
Eaton Wood Avenue	75	E4
Eaton Wood Court	75	E4
Eaton Wood Grove	75	E4
Ebenezer Terrace	79	C6
Eblana Avenue	61	D3
Eccles Place	80	B1
Eccles Street	80	A1
Echlin Street	79	B4
Eden Avenue	66	C1
Eden Court	66	C1
Eden Crescent	66	C1
Eden Grove	66	C1
Eden Park	61	E4
Eden Park Avenue	58	B4
Eden Park Drive	58	B4
Eden Park Road	58	B4
Eden Quay	80	B3

Name	Page	Grid
Eden Road Lower	61	E4
Eden Road Upper	61	E4
Eden Terrace	61	E4
Eden Villas	61	E4
Edenbrook Court	56	B4
Edenbrook Drive	56	A4
Edenbrook Manor	56	B4
Edenbrook Park	56	A4
Edenmore Avenue	29	F1
Edenmore Crescent	30	A1
Edenmore Drive	29	F1
Edenmore Gardens	29	F1
Edenmore Green	29	F1
Edenmore Grove	29	F1
Edenmore Park	29	F1
Edenvale Road	50	A3
Edenwood	58	B4
Edgewood Lawn	14	B4
Edmondstown Road	66	A3
Edward Road	77	E2
Edward's Court	66	A2
Edwin Court	71	E1
Effra Road	49	E3
Eglinton Court	50	C3
Eglinton Park (Donnybrook)	50	C3
Eglinton Park (Dún Laoghaire)	61	D4
Eglinton Road (Bray)	77	D1
Eglinton Road (Donnybrook)	50	C3
Eglinton Terrace (Donnybrook)	50	C3
Eglinton Terrace (Dundrum)	57	F4
Elderberry	34	C4
Elderwood Road	36	C2
Elgin Heights	76	B3
Elgin Road	50	C2
Elgin Wood	76	B3
Elizabeth Street	40	C1
Elkwood Estate	55	F4
Ellenfield Road	28	A1
Ellensborough Avenue	63	F3
Ellensborough Close	63	F3
Ellensborough Copse	63	F3
Ellensborough Court	64	A3
Ellensborough Crescent	63	F3
Ellensborough Dale	63	F3
Ellensborough Downs	63	F3
Ellensborough Grange	63	F3
Ellensborough Green	63	F3
Ellensborough Grove	63	F3
Ellensborough Lane	63	F3
Ellensborough Lawns	63	F3
Ellensborough Lodge	63	F3
Ellensborough Meadows	63	F3
Ellensborough Park	63	F3
Ellensborough Rise	63	F3
Ellensborough View	63	F3
Ellensborough Walk	63	F3
Ellensborough Way	63	F3
Ellesmere Avenue	78	B1
Ellis Court	78	C3
Ellis Quay	78	C3
Elm Close	35	D4
Elm Court (Lucan)	35	E4
Elm Court (Tallaght)	62	C2
Elm Dene	35	D4
Elm Drive (Lucan)	35	E4
Elm Drive (Tallaght)	62	C2
Elm Green	35	D4
Elm Grove (Blackrock)	59	F3
Elm Grove (Lucan)	35	E4
Elm Grove (Tallaght)	62	C2
Elm Mount Avenue	28	B2
Elm Mount Close	28	B2
Elm Mount Court	28	C2
Elm Mount Crescent	28	C2
Elm Mount Drive	28	B2
Elm Mount Grove	28	B2
Elm Mount Heights	28	B2
Elm Mount Lawn	28	B2
Elm Mount Park	28	B2
Elm Mount Rise	28	B2
Elm Mount Road	28	C2
Elm Mount View	28	C2
Elm Park	51	D4
Elm Park Terrace	56	B1
Elm Road (Donnycarney)	28	C3
Elm Road (Fox & Geese)	46	C3
Elm Vale	35	E4
Elm View	35	E4
Elm Way	35	E4
Elm Wood	35	E4
Elmbrook Avenue	35	E3
Elmbrook Crescent	35	E3
Elmbrook Lawn	35	E3
Elmbrook Walk	35	E3
Elmcastle Close	54	B2
Elmcastle Court	54	B2
Elmcastle Drive	54	B2
Elmcastle Green	54	B2
Elmcastle Park	54	B2
Elmcastle Walk	54	B2
Elmdale Crescent	46	B1
Elmdale Drive	46	B1
Elmdale Park	46	B1
Elmfield	45	F2
Elmfield Avenue	21	D3
Elmfield Close	20	C3
Elmfield Court	21	D3
Elmfield Crescent	21	D3
Elmfield Drive	21	D3
Elmfield Green	21	D3
Elmfield Grove	21	D3
Elmfield Lawn	21	D3
Elmfield Park	21	D3
Elmfield Vale	21	D3
Elmfield Walk	20	C3
Elmfield Way	20	C3
Elmgrove	71	D4
Elmpark Avenue	50	A3
Elmwood Avenue Lower	50	A3
Elmwood Avenue Upper	50	A3
Elmwood Close	22	B1
Elmwood Drive	4	C2
Elmwood Park	4	C2
Elmwood Road	4	C2
Elner Court	10	C1
Elton Court (Ard na Greine)	20	B4
Elton Court (Dalkey)	72	A1
Elton Drive	20	B4
Elton Park (Coolock)	20	B4
Elton Park (Dalkey)	72	A1
Elton Walk	20	B4
Elvira Close	73	D1
Ely Close	64	B3
Ely Crescent	64	B3
Ely Drive	64	B3
Ely Green	64	B3
Ely Place	81	C5
Ely View	64	B3
Embassy Lawn	58	A1
Emerald Place	80	D2
Emerald Square	79	B6
Emerald Street	80	D2
Emmet Court	48	A1
Emmet Crescent	48	A1
Emmet Road	39	D4
Emmet Street	80	C1
Emor Street	81	A6
Emorville Avenue	79	D6
Empress Place	80	C1
Engine Alley	79	C4
Ennafort Avenue	29	F2
Ennafort Drive	29	F2
Ennafort Grove	29	F2
Ennafort Park	29	F2
Ennafort Road	29	F2
Ennel Avenue	29	E1
Ennel Court	75	E1
Ennel Drive	29	E1
Ennel Park	29	E1
Ennis Grove	81	D4
Enniskerry Road (Phibsborough)	40	B1
Enniskerry Road (Sandyford)	68	B4
Erne Place	81	D4
Erne Place Lower	81	D4
Erne Street Lower	81	D4
Erne Street Upper	81	D4
Erne Terrace Front	81	D4
Erne Terrace Rear	81	D4
Errigal Road	48	A2
Erris Road	39	F1
Esker Cottages	35	D4
Esker Drive	34	C3
Esker Lane (north of N4)	35	E2
Esker Lane (south of N4)	35	E3
Esker Lawns	35	D2
Esker Lodge	35	E3
Esker Lodge Avenue	35	E3
Esker Lodge Close	35	E3
Esker Lodge View	35	E3
Esker Manor	35	D3
Esker Meadow Close	35	E3
Esker Meadow Court	35	D3
Esker Meadow Green	35	E3
Esker Meadow Grove	35	E3
Esker Meadow Lawn	35	E3
Esker Meadow Rise	35	E3
Esker Meadow View	35	E3
Esker Park	35	D3
Esker Road	34	C4
Esker Villas	49	F3
Esker Wood Close	35	E3
Esker Wood Drive	35	E3
Esker Wood Walk	35	E3
Esmond Avenue	41	E1
Esposito Road	48	A3
Essex Quay	81	A4
Essex Street East	81	A4
Essex Street West	81	A4
Estate Avenue	51	E4
Estate Cottages	41	E4
Estuary Court	5	E2
Estuary Road (Malahide)	6	B2
Estuary Road (Swords)	5	E2
Eugene Street	79	B6
Eustace Street	81	B4
Evora Park	33	D1
Ewington Lane	79	B4
Exchange Place	80	C3
Exchange Street Lower	81	A4
Exchequer Street	81	B4

F

Name	Page	Grid
Fade Street	81	B4
Fairbrook Lawn	56	B3
Fairfield Avenue	41	E2
Fairfield Park	49	E4
Fairfield Road	27	D4
Fairlawn Park	26	B2
Fairlawn Road	26	B2
Fairview	41	E1
Fairview Avenue Upper	28	B4
Fairview Green	28	B4
Fairview Passage	41	E1
Fairview Strand	41	E1
Fairview Terrace	28	A4
Fairways	56	B3
Fairways Avenue	26	C2
Fairways Green	26	C2
Fairways Grove	26	C2
Fairways Park	26	C2
Fairyhill (Blackrock)	59	F4
Fairyhill (Bray)	76	C2
Faith Avenue	41	E1
Falcarragh Road	27	F2
Falls Road	75	D3
Farmhill Drive	58	A3
Farmhill Park	58	A3
Farmhill Road	58	A2
Farmleigh Avenue	69	E1
Farmleigh Close	69	E1
Farmleigh Park	69	E1
Farmleigh Woods Avenue	24	B4
Farmleigh Woods Close	24	B4
Farmleigh Woods Park	24	B4
Farmleigh Woods View	24	B4
Farney Park	51	D1
Farnham Crescent	26	A1
Farnham Drive	26	A2
Farrenboley Cottages	57	F1
Farrenboley Park	57	F2
Fassaugh Avenue	26	B4
Father Bidone Court	38	B4
Father Kitt Court	48	A3
Faughart Road	48	B3
Faussagh Road	40	A1
Feltrim Road	6	A4
Fenian Street	81	C4
Fergus Road	56	B1
Ferguson Road	27	E4
Fern Court Avenue	64	C3
Fern Court Close	64	C3
Fern Court Green	64	C2
Fern Court Park	64	C3
Fern Court View	64	C3
Fernbrook	73	D3
Ferndale	64	A1
Ferndale Avenue	26	C1
Ferndale Road (Finglas East)	26	C1
Ferndale Road (Shankill)	75	D4
Fernhill Avenue	55	D1
Fernhill Park	55	D1
Fernhill Road	55	D1
Fernleigh Avenue	68	B3
Fernleigh Close	23	D3
Fernleigh Court (Carpenterstown)	23	D3
Fernleigh Court (Leopardstown)	68	C3
Fernleigh Dale	23	D3
Fernleigh Dene	23	D4
Fernleigh Drive	23	D3
Fernleigh Green	23	D3
Fernleigh Lawn	23	D4
Fernleigh Park	23	D3
Fernleigh Rise	68	C3
Fernleigh Vale	23	D3
Fernleigh View	23	D4
Ferns Road	48	C3
Fernvale Drive	48	A3
Fernwood Avenue	53	E4
Fernwood Park	53	E4
Fernwood Way	53	E4
Ferrard Road	49	E4
Ferrycarrig Avenue	20	A3
Ferrycarrig Drive	19	F3
Ferrycarrig Green	20	A3
Ferrycarrig Park	20	A3
Ferrycarrig Road	20	A3
Ferryman's Crossing	80	D2
Fettercairn Road	53	D4
Fey Yerra	69	E2
Fforster Close	35	E3
Fforster Court	35	E3
Fforster Crescent	35	E3
Fforster Drive	35	E3
Fforster Green	35	E3
Fforster Grove	35	E3
Fforster Lawn	35	E3
Fforster Park	35	E3
Fforster Row	35	E3

Name	Page	Grid
Fforster Walk	35	E3
Fforster Way	35	E3
Field Avenue	48	A3
Findlater Place	80	B2
Findlater Street (Dún Laoghaire)	61	E4
Findlater Street (off Infirmary Road)	78	A2
Fingal Street	79	B6
Finglas Park	17	D4
Finglas Place	26	B1
Finglas Road	26	B2
Finglaswood Road	26	A1
Finn Street	78	B2
Finneber Square	26	B1
Finnstown Court	44	A1
Finnstown Green	44	A1
Finnstown Grove	44	A1
Finnstown Hall	34	C4
Finnstown Lawn	44	A1
Finnstown Park	44	A1
Finnstown Vale	44	A1
Finnstown View	44	A1
Finnstown Walk	34	C4
Finnstown Wood	44	A1
Finsbury Green	57	E3
Finsbury Park	57	E3
Firgrove	75	E1
Firhouse Road	55	E4
Firhouse Road West	63	F2
First Avenue (Inchicore)	38	B4
First Avenue (North Wall)	80	D2
Fishamble Street	81	A4
Fitzgerald Park	60	C4
Fitzgerald Street	49	E2
Fitzgibbon Lane	80	B1
Fitzgibbon Street	80	B1
Fitzroy Avenue	40	C1
Fitzwilliam Lane	81	C5
Fitzwilliam Place	50	A1
Fitzwilliam Quay	41	F4
Fitzwilliam Square East	81	C6
Fitzwilliam Square North	81	C5
Fitzwilliam Square South	81	C6
Fitzwilliam Square West	81	C5
Fitzwilliam Street	41	F4
Fitzwilliam Street Lower	81	C5
Fitzwilliam Street Upper	81	C5
Fleet Street	80	B3
Fleming Road	27	E3
Fleming's Place	81	D6
Flemingstown Park	57	E3
Fleurville	59	F4
Floraville Avenue	46	A4
Floraville Drive	46	A4
Floraville Lawn	46	A4
Florence Road	77	D1
Florence Street	49	F2
Florence Terrace	77	D1
Flower Grove	71	D2
Foley Street	80	C2
Fontenoy Street	78	D1
Fontenoy Terrace	77	E2
Fonthill Abbey	56	B4
Fonthill Court	56	B4
Fonthill Park	56	B4
Fonthill Road	36	A4
Fonthill Road (Rathfarnham)	56	B4
Fonthill Road South	45	F4
Forbes Lane	79	B5
Forbes Street	41	E3
Forest Avenue (Ballymount)	54	A1
Forest Avenue (Swords)	4	B4
Forest Boulevard	4	B4
Forest Close	54	A1
Forest Court	4	B4
Forest Crescent	4	B4
Forest Dale	4	B4
Forest Drive	54	A2
Forest Fields Road	4	C4
Forest Green (Ballymount)	54	A1
Forest Green (Swords)	4	B4
Forest Grove	4	B4
Forest Lawn	54	A1
Forest Park (Ballymount)	54	A1
Forest Park (Swords)	4	B4
Forest Road (Hilltown)	8	B2
Forest Road (Swords)	4	C4
Forest View	4	B4
Forest Walk	4	B4
Forest Way	4	B4
Forestwood Avenue	18	A3
Forrest Hills	8	C1
Fortfield Avenue	55	F2
Fortfield Court	56	A1
Fortfield Drive	56	A2
Fortfield Grove	56	A2
Fortfield Park	56	A2
Fortfield Road	56	A1
Fortfield Terrace	49	F4
Forth Road	41	E2
Fortlawn Avenue	23	D1
Fortlawn Drive	23	D1
Fortlawn Park	22	C1
Fortrose Park	55	F2
Fortunestown Crescent	52	C4
Fortunestown Lane	62	B1
Fortunestown Road	62	B2
Fortunestown Way	62	C1
Fortview Avenue	42	C1
Foster Place	81	B4
Foster Terrace	41	D1
Fosterbrook	59	D1
Fosters Avenue	58	C2
Fountain Road	39	E3
Fownes Street Upper	81	B4
Fox's Lane	30	C2
Foxborough Avenue	35	E4
Foxborough Close	35	F4
Foxborough Court	44	C1
Foxborough Downs	35	E4
Foxborough Drive	35	E4
Foxborough Gardens	44	C1
Foxborough Glen	44	C1
Foxborough Green	44	C1
Foxborough Hill	35	E4
Foxborough Lane	44	C1
Foxborough Lawn	44	C1
Foxborough Meadows	35	E4
Foxborough Park	35	E4
Foxborough Rise	44	C1
Foxborough Road	35	E4
Foxborough Walk	35	F4
Foxborough Way	44	C1
Foxdene Avenue	45	D1
Foxdene Drive	45	D1
Foxdene Gardens	45	D1
Foxdene Green	45	D1
Foxdene Grove	45	D1
Foxdene Park	36	A4
Foxes Grove	75	E4
Foxfield	34	C4
Foxfield Avenue	30	B2
Foxfield Crescent	30	C1
Foxfield Drive	30	C1
Foxfield Green	30	B1
Foxfield Grove	30	C1
Foxfield Heights	30	B2
Foxfield Lawn	30	C2
Foxfield Park	30	C2
Foxfield Road	30	B2
Foxfield Saint John	30	C1
Foxhill	64	A4
Foxhill Avenue	20	C4
Foxhill Close	20	C4
Foxhill Court	20	C4
Foxhill Crescent	20	C4
Foxhill Drive	20	C4
Foxhill Green	20	C3
Foxhill Grove	20	C3
Foxhill Lawn	20	C4
Foxhill Park	20	C4
Foxhill Way	20	C4
Foxpark	34	C4
Foxrock Avenue	70	A1
Foxrock Close	70	A1
Foxrock Court	70	A2
Foxrock Crescent	70	A2
Foxrock Green	70	A2
Foxrock Grove	70	A1
Foxrock Manor	69	E2
Foxrock Park	70	A2
Foxrock Wood	70	A2
Foxwood (Lucan)	34	C4
Foxwood (Swords)	5	E4
Foyle Road	28	A4
Francis Street	79	D4
Frankfort	57	F3
Frankfort Avenue	49	F4
Frankfort Court	57	F3
Frankfort Park	57	F3
Frascati Park	59	F2
Frederick Lane North	80	A2
Frederick Street North	40	B2
Frederick Street South	81	B4
Frenchman's Lane	80	C3
Frescati Road	59	F2
Friarsland Avenue	58	A2
Friarsland Road	58	A2
Friary Avenue	78	C3
Friel Avenue	46	A3
Furry Park Road	29	E3
Furze Road (Phoenix Park)	38	A1
Furze Road (Sandyford)	68	C2

G

Name	Page	Grid
Gaelic Street	80	D1
Gainsborough Avenue	6	B3
Gainsborough Close	6	A2
Gainsborough Court	6	A3
Gainsborough Crescent	6	A2
Gainsborough Downs	6	A3
Gainsborough Green	6	A3
Gainsborough Lawn	6	A3
Gallanstown Drive	46	B1
Gallanstown Green	46	B1
Gallaun Road	17	F3
Gallery Quay	41	E4
Galmoy Road	39	F1
Galtrim Grange	7	D4
Galtrim Park	77	D1
Galtrim Road	77	E1
Galtymore Close	48	A2
Galtymore Drive	48	B1
Galtymore Park	48	A2
Galtymore Road	48	B1
Gandon Close	49	E2
Garden Lane	79	D4
Gardiner Place	80	B2
Gardiner Row	80	B2
Gardiner Steet Upper	80	B1
Gardiner Street Lower	80	B2
Gardiner Street Middle	80	B2
Gardiners Lane	80	B1
Garrynisk Road	53	F2
Garrynure	29	F2
Garryowen Road	38	A4
Gartan Avenue	27	E4
Gartan Court	5	E2
Gartan Drive	5	E2
Garth Mews	61	D3
Garty Wood Apartments	65	E1
Garville Avenue	49	E4
Garville Avenue Upper	49	E4
Garville Lane	49	E4
Garville Mews	49	E4
Garville Road	49	E4
Gas Yard Lane	7	D2
Gateway Crescent	18	A4
Gateway Mews	18	A4
Gateway Place	17	F4
Gatlon Hall	49	D4
Gaybrook Lawns	6	B3
Gazelle Avenue	14	A1
Gazelle Lane	14	A1
Gazelle Terrace	14	A1
Gazelle Walk	14	A1
Geoffrey Keating Road	79	C6
George's Avenue	59	F2
George's Hill	78	D3
George's Lane	78	C3
George's Place (Blackrock)	59	F2
George's Place (Central Dublin)	80	B1
George's Place (Dún Laoghaire)	61	D3
George's Quay	80	C3
George's Street Lower	61	D3
George's Street Upper	61	D3
Georgian Hamlet	11	D3
Gerald Street	41	F4
Geraldine Street	80	A1
Geraldine Terrace	57	F1
Gilbert Road	79	C6
Gilford Avenue	51	E2
Gilford Court	51	E2
Gilford Drive	51	E2
Gilford Park	51	E2
Gilford Road	51	E2
Gilford Terrace	51	E2
Giltspur Brook	77	D3
Giltspur Wood	76	C2
Glandore Park	60	C4
Glandore Road	28	A3
Glasanaon Court	26	B1
Glasanaon Road	26	B1
Glasaree Road	26	B1
Glasilawn Avenue	27	D2
Glasilawn Road	26	C2
Glasmeen Road	26	C2
Glasmore Park	4	C3
Glasnamana Place	26	C2
Glasnamana Road	26	C2
Glasnevin Avenue	27	D1
Glasnevin Downs	26	C2
Glasnevin Drive	27	D1
Glasnevin Hill	27	D3
Glasnevin Park	27	D1
Glasson Court	57	F2
Glasthule Road	61	E4
Gleann na Rí	74	C2
Gleann na Smol (Killinarden)	63	F2
Gleann na Smol (Monkstown)	60	B3
Gledswood Avenue	57	F2
Gledswood Close	58	A2
Gledswood Park	57	F2
Glen Arm Square	27	E4
Glen Avenue	70	B3
Glen Close	70	B3
Glen Dale	70	B3
Glen Drive	70	B3
Glen Ellen Close	4	C2
Glen Ellen Court	4	C2
Glen Ellen Crescent	4	C2
Glen Ellen Drive	4	C2
Glen Ellen Green	4	C2
Glen Ellen Park	4	C2
Glen Ellen Pines	4	C2
Glen Garth	70	B3
Glen Grove	70	B3
Glen Lawn Drive	70	B3
Glen Lucan	76	C2

Name	Page	Grid
Glen na Smole	77	D3
Glen Park	77	D4
Glen Road	37	F2
Glen Walk	70	B3
Glenaan Road	27	F1
Glenabbey Road	58	C3
Glenageary Avenue	71	D1
Glenageary Court	71	D2
Glenageary Hall	71	E2
Glenageary Lodge	71	D2
Glenageary Park	71	D1
Glenageary Road Lower	61	D4
Glenageary Road Upper	71	D1
Glenageary Woods	71	D1
Glenalbyn Road	59	D4
Glenallin Green	37	E3
Glenalua Heights	71	F3
Glenalua Road	71	E3
Glenalua Terrace	71	F3
Glenanne	48	C4
Glenard Avenue	77	E1
Glenard Hall	58	A2
Glenarm Avenue	27	E4
Glenarriff Road	25	E3
Glenart Avenue	59	E3
Glenaulin	37	F2
Glenaulin Drive	37	F3
Glenaulin Park	37	F2
Glenaulin Road	37	E3
Glenavon Park	75	D1
Glenavy Park	56	A1
Glenayle Road	29	F1
Glenayr Road	56	C1
Glenbeigh Park	78	A1
Glenbeigh Road	78	A1
Glenbourne Avenue	69	D4
Glenbourne Close	69	D4
Glenbourne Drive	69	D4
Glenbourne Grove	69	D4
Glenbourne Road	69	D4
Glenbourne View	69	D4
Glenbourne Walk	69	D4
Glenbourne Way	69	D4
Glenbower Park	57	E3
Glenbrook Park	56	B3
Glenbrook Road	25	E3
Glencairn Avenue	68	C4
Glencairn Chase	68	C3
Glencairn Close	68	C4
Glencairn Copse	69	D4
Glencairn Court	69	D4
Glencairn Crescent	69	D4
Glencairn Dale	68	D4
Glencairn Drive	68	D4
Glencairn Garth	68	C3
Glencairn Glade	69	D4
Glencairn Green	68	C3
Glencairn Grove	69	D4
Glencairn Heights	69	D4
Glencairn Lawn	69	D4
Glencairn Oaks	69	D4
Glencairn Park	68	C3
Glencairn Place	69	D4
Glencairn Rise	69	D4
Glencairn Road	68	C3
Glencairn Thicket	69	D4
Glencar Lawn	75	D1
Glencarrig	32	B1
Glencarrig Court	64	B2
Glencarrig Drive	64	B2
Glencarrig Green	64	B2
Glencloy Road	27	F2
Glencorp Road	28	A2
Glencourt	76	C2
Glendale Drive	77	D3
Glendale Park	55	E1
Glendhu Park	25	E3
Glendhu Road	25	E3
Glendoher Avenue	56	B4
Glendoher Close	66	A1
Glendoher Drive	66	B1
Glendoher Park	66	B1
Glendoher Road	56	B4
Glendoo Close	54	C1
Glendown Avenue	55	E2
Glendown Close	55	E2
Glendown Court	55	E2
Glendown Drive	55	E2
Glendown Green	55	E2
Glendown Grove	55	E2
Glendown Lawn	55	E2
Glendown Park	55	E2
Glendown Road	55	E2
Glendun Road	27	F1
Glenealy Downs	13	D3
Glenealy Road	49	D2
Glenfarne Road	29	F1
Glenfield Avenue	36	B3
Glenfield Close	36	B3
Glenfield Drive	36	B3
Glenfield Grove	36	B3
Glenfield Park	36	A3
Glenfield Road	58	C2
Glengara Park	61	E4
Glengariff Parade	40	B1
Glenhill Avenue	26	B2
Glenhill Court	26	B2
Glenhill Drive	26	B2
Glenhill Grove	26	B2
Glenhill Road	26	B2
Glenhill Villas	26	B2
Glenlyon Crescent	65	D2
Glenlyon Grove	65	D2
Glenlyon Park	65	D2
Glenmalure Park	79	A5
Glenmalure Square	50	B4
Glenmaroon Park	37	E3
Glenmaroon Road	37	E3
Glenmore Court	66	B1
Glenmore Park	66	B2
Glenmore Road	78	A1
Glenomena Grove	58	C1
Glenomena Park	58	C1
Glenpark Drive	36	C2
Glenpark Road	36	C2
Glenshane Close	62	C1
Glenshane Crescent	62	C1
Glenshane Drive	62	D1
Glenshane Gardens	62	C1
Glenshane Green	62	C1
Glenshane Grove	62	C1
Glenshane Lawns	62	C1
Glenshane Park	62	C1
Glenshesk Road	28	A2
Glenthorn	76	B3
Glenties Drive	25	F2
Glenties Park	25	F2
Glentworth Park	20	B4
Glenvar Park	59	E2
Glenvara Park	65	D1
Glenview	71	D3
Glenview Drive	54	C4
Glenview Lawn	54	C4
Glenview Park	54	B4
Glenville Avenue	23	E2
Glenville Drive	23	E2
Glenville Garth	23	E2
Glenville Green	23	E2
Glenville Grove	23	E2
Glenville Lawn	23	E2
Glenville Road	23	E2
Glenville Way	23	E2
Glenwood	76	C1
Glenwood Road	29	F1
Glin Avenue	19	F3
Glin Crescent	19	F3
Glin Drive	19	F3
Glin Grove	19	F3
Glin Park	19	F3
Glin Road	19	F3
Gloucester Place North	80	C2
Gloucester Place Upper	80	C2
Gloucester Street South	80	C3
Glovers Alley	81	B5
Goatstown Avenue	58	A3
Goatstown Road	58	A3
Golden Lane	81	A4
Goldenbridge Avenue	48	B1
Goldsmith Street	40	B1
Golf Links Road	10	B4
Gordon Avenue	70	A3
Gordon Street	41	E4
Gorish Square	14	C4
Gort na Mona Drive	70	A3
Gortbeg Avenue	26	B2
Gortbeg Drive	26	B2
Gortbeg Park	26	B2
Gortbeg Road	26	B2
Gortmore Avenue	26	B2
Gortmore Drive	26	A2
Gortmore Park	26	B2
Gortmore Road	26	B2
Gosworth Park	71	F1
Gowrie Park	71	D1
Grace O'Malley Drive	33	D2
Grace O'Malley Road	33	D2
Grace Park Avenue	27	F4
Grace Park Court	28	A2
Grace Park Gardens	27	F4
Grace Park Heights	28	A2
Grace Park Manor	28	A3
Grace Park Meadows	28	B2
Grace Park Road	28	A3
Grace Park Terrace	28	A3
Gracefield Avenue	29	E2
Gracefield Road	29	E2
Grafton Street	81	B4
Graigue Court	17	E3
Granby Lane	80	A2
Granby Place	80	A2
Granby Row	80	A2
Grand Canal Place	79	B4
Grand Canal Plaza	41	E4
Grand Canal Quay	41	E4
Grand Canal Square	41	E3
Grand Canal Street Lower	81	D4
Grand Canal Street Upper	41	E4
Grand Canal View	48	B1
Grand Parade	50	A2
Grange Abbey Crescent	21	D3
Grange Abbey Drive	21	D3
Grange Abbey Grove	21	E3
Grange Avenue	21	E3
Grange Brook Avenue	66	B2
Grange Brook Close	66	B2
Grange Close	21	E4
Grange Crescent	70	B1
Grange Downs	57	D4
Grange Drive	21	F4
Grange Grove	60	B4
Grange Manor	44	A1
Grange Manor Avenue	56	C4
Grange Manor Close	56	C4
Grange Manor Drive	56	C4
Grange Manor Grove	56	C4
Grange Manor Road	56	C4
Grange Parade	21	E4
Grange Park	56	B4
Grange Park (Baldoyle)	21	F3
Grange Park (Cornelscourt)	70	A2
Grange Park Avenue	30	B1
Grange Park Close	30	B1
Grange Park Crescent	30	B1
Grange Park Drive	30	B1
Grange Park Green	30	B1
Grange Park Grove	30	A1
Grange Park Rise	30	B1
Grange Park Road	30	B1
Grange Park View	30	B1
Grange Park Walk	30	B1
Grange Rise	21	E3
Grange Road	66	C1
Grange Road (Baldoyle)	21	E3
Grange Road (Rathfarnham)	56	C4
Grange Terrace	70	A1
Grange View Court	44	C3
Grange View Drive	44	C3
Grange View Green	44	C3
Grange View Park	44	C3
Grange View Place	44	C2
Grange View Road	44	C3
Grange View Walk	44	C3
Grange View Way	44	C3
Grange View Wood	44	C2
Grange Way	21	E4
Grange Wood	67	D1
Grangecastle Road	44	C3
Grangefield	67	E3
Grangegorman Lower	78	C2
Grangegorman Upper	78	C1
Grangemore Avenue	21	D3
Grangemore Court	21	D3
Grangemore Crescent	20	C3
Grangemore Drive	21	D3
Grangemore Grove	21	D3
Grangemore Lawn	21	D3
Grangemore Park	21	D3
Grangemore Rise	21	D3
Grangemore Road	21	D3
Grangewood	70	B1
Granitefield	71	D3
Granitefield Mews	70	C3
Grant's Row	81	D5
Grantham Place	81	A6
Grantham Street	81	A6
Granville Close	71	D4
Granville Court	69	F1
Granville Crescent	70	D3
Granville Park	69	F1
Granville Road (Cabinteely)	70	C3
Granville Road (Dean's Grange)	69	F1
Grattan Court East	81	D5
Grattan Crescent	38	C4
Grattan Hall	21	D3
Grattan Lodge	21	D3
Grattan Parade	40	C1
Grattan Street	81	D5
Grattan Wood	21	D3
Gray Square	79	C5
Gray Street	79	C5
Great Western Square	40	A1
Great Western Villas	78	C1
Greek Street	78	D3
Green Park	57	E2
Green Park Road	73	E4
Green Road	59	E2
Green Street	78	D3
Green Street East	41	E3
Greenacre Court	55	E4
Greencastle Avenue	20	A4
Greencastle Crescent	20	A3
Greencastle Drive	19	F3
Greencastle Parade	20	A4
Greencastle Park	19	F3
Greencastle Road	19	F3
Greencastle Road	20	A4
Greendale Avenue	30	C1
Greendale Road	30	C1
Greenfield Avenue	51	D4
Greenfield Park (Donnybrook)	51	D4
Greenfield Park (Firhouse)	65	D2
Greenfield Road	32	B1

Greenfort Avenue	36	B3
Greenfort Close	36	B3
Greenfort Crescent	36	B3
Greenfort Drive	36	B3
Greenfort Gardens	36	B3
Greenfort Lawns	36	B2
Greenfort Park	36	B3
Greenhills Road	47	D4
Greenhills Road	54	B2
Greenlands	68	B2
Greenlea Avenue	56	A1
Greenlea Drive	56	A1
Greenlea Grove	56	B1
Greenlea Park	56	A1
Greenlea Road	56	A1
Greenmount Avenue	49	E2
Greenmount Lane	49	E2
Greenmount Lawns	56	C1
Greenmount Road	56	C1
Greenmount Square	49	E2
Greenpark Road	34	B3
Greenridge Court	14	B4
Greentrees Park	55	E1
Greentrees Road	55	E1
Greenville Avenue	79	C6
Greenville Lane	80	B1
Greenville Road	60	A3
Greenville Street	80	B2
Greenville Terrace	79	C6
Greenwood Avenue	20	C3
Greenwood Close	20	C3
Greenwood Court	20	C3
Greenwood Drive	20	B3
Greenwood Lawn	20	C3
Greenwood Park	20	C3
Greenwood Walk	20	C3
Greenwood Way	20	C3
Greygates	58	D2
Greys Lane	33	E2
Greythorn Park	71	D1
Griarian Fidh	68	B4
Griffeen Avenue	35	D4
Griffeen Glen Avenue	44	B1
Griffeen Glen Boulevard	44	B1
Griffeen Glen Chase	35	D4
Griffeen Glen Close	35	D3
Griffeen Glen Court	35	E4
Griffeen Glen Crescent	35	D4
Griffeen Glen Dale	44	B1
Griffeen Glen Dene	44	B1
Griffeen Glen Drive	35	E4
Griffeen Glen Green	35	D4
Griffeen Glen Grove	35	E4
Griffeen Glen Lawn	35	D4
Griffeen Glen Park	35	D4
Griffeen Glen Road	44	B1
Griffeen Glen Vale	35	D4
Griffeen Glen Way	35	E4
Griffeen Glen Wood	44	B1
Griffeen Road	35	E4
Griffeen Way	35	E3
Griffith Avenue	27	D2
Griffith Close	26	C2
Griffith Court	28	A4
Griffith Downs	27	F3
Griffith Drive	26	C2
Griffith Hall	28	A3
Griffith Heights	26	C2
Griffith Lawns	27	E3
Griffith Parade	26	C2
Griffith Road	26	C2
Griffith Walk	28	A3
Grosvenor Avenue	77	E2
Grosvenor Court (Clontarf)	29	E4
Grosvenor Court (Templeogue)	55	E2
Grosvenor Lodge	49	E3
Grosvenor Park	49	E3
Grosvenor Place	49	E3
Grosvenor Road	49	F3
Grosvenor Square	49	E3
Grosvenor Terrace	72	C3
Grosvenor Villas	49	E3
Grotto Avenue	59	D1
Grotto Place	59	D1
Grove Avenue (Finglas)	17	D4
Grove Avenue (Malahide)	7	E3
Grove Avenue (Mount Merrion)	59	E3
Grove Lane	20	B3
Grove Lawn	59	E3
Grove Lawns	7	E3
Grove Park	49	F2
Grove Park Avenue	26	C1
Grove Park Crescent	17	E4
Grove Park Drive	17	E4
Grove Park Road	26	C1
Grove Road (Blanchardstown)	23	E2
Grove Road (Finglas)	26	C1
Grove Road (Malahide)	7	E2
Grove Road (Rathmines)	49	E2
Grove Wood	17	D4
Guild Street	80	D3
Guiltspur Lane	76	B4
Gulistan Cottages	49	F2
Gulistan Terrace	49	F3
Gurteen Avenue	37	E4
Gurteen Park	37	E4
Gurteen Road	37	E3

H

Hackets Land	75	E2
Haddington Park	71	E1
Haddington Place	50	B1
Haddington Road	50	B1
Haddington Terrace	61	E3
Haddon Park	42	A1
Haddon Road	42	A1
Hadleigh Court	24	B3
Hadleigh Green	24	B3
Hadleigh Park	24	B3
Hagan's Court	81	C5
Haigh Terrace	61	D3
Hainault Drive	70	A3
Hainault Grove	70	A3
Hainault Lawn	70	A3
Hainault Park	69	F3
Hainault Road	69	F3
Halliday Road	78	B2
Halliday Square	78	B2
Halston Street	78	D3
Hamilton Street	79	C6
Hammond Lane	78	D3
Hammond Street	79	D6
Hampstead Avenue	27	E2
Hampstead Park	27	E2
Hampton Court	29	E4
Hampton Crescent	59	D2
Hampton Green	39	E1
Hampton Park	59	D2
Hampton Wood	17	D2
Hanbury Lane	79	C4
Hannaville Park	56	B1
Hanover Dock	41	E3
Hanover Lane	79	D5
Hanover Quay	41	E3
Hanover Street East	81	D4
Hanover Street West	79	D5
Hansfield	13	D3
Hansted Close	44	A1
Hansted Crescent	44	A1
Hansted Drive	44	A1
Hansted Park	44	A1
Hansted Road	44	A1
Hansted Way	44	A1
Harbour Cottages	61	D3
Harbour Court	81	B3
Harbour Road (Dalkey)	72	B2
Harbour Road (Dún Laoghaire)	61	E3
Harbour Road (Howth)	33	D1
Harbour View	33	D1
Harcourt Lane	81	B6
Harcourt Road	81	B6
Harcourt Street	81	B5
Harcourt Terrace	81	B6
Hardebeck Avenue	47	F4
Hardiman Road	27	E3
Hardwicke Lane	80	B1
Hardwicke Street	80	B1
Harelawn Avenue	36	B4
Harelawn Crescent	36	B3
Harelawn Drive	36	B3
Harelawn Green	36	B4
Harelawn Grove	36	B3
Harelawn Park	36	B3
Harlech Crescent	58	B2
Harlech Downs	58	A2
Harman Street	79	C6
Harmonstown Road	29	F2
Harmony Avenue	50	C3
Harmony Row	81	D4
Harmsworth	49	E2
Harold Bridge Court	49	E2
Harold Crescent	61	E4
Harold Road	78	B2
Harold's Cross Road	49	E3
Harold's Grange Road	67	E3
Haroldville Avenue	79	B6
Harrington Street	81	A6
Harrison Row	49	E4
Harriston Lane	16	C1
Hartstown Road	22	B1
Harty Avenue	47	F3
Harty Place	79	D6
Harvard	58	A2
Hastings Street	41	E4
Hatch Place	81	B6
Hatch Street Lower	81	B6
Hatch Street Upper	81	B6
Havelock Square	50	C1
Havelock Terrace	50	C1
Haverty Road	28	B4
Hawkins Street	80	B3
Hawthorn Avenue	41	E2
Hawthorn Drive	67	E1
Hawthorn Lawn	24	A3
Hawthorn Lodge	24	A3
Hawthorn Park	4	C4
Hawthorn Road (Bray)	73	D4
Hawthorn Road (Fox & Geese)	46	C3
Hawthorns Road	68	B2
Hayden's Lane	44	A2
Haydens Park Avenue	44	B1
Haydens Park Close	44	B1
Haydens Park Dale	44	B1
Haydens Park Drive	44	B1
Haydens Park Glade	44	B1
Haydens Park Green	44	B1
Haydens Park Lawn	44	B1
Haydens Park View	44	B1
Haydens Park Walk	44	B1
Haydens Park Way	44	B1
Haymarket	78	C3
Hayworth Close	22	A1
Hayworth Court	12	C4
Hayworth Drive	22	A1
Hayworth Mews	22	A1
Hayworth Place	12	C4
Hazel Avenue	58	C4
Hazel Grove (Jobstown)	63	D2
Hazel Grove (Portmarnock)	10	B4
Hazel Lawn	23	F2
Hazel Road	28	C3
Hazelbrook	56	B1
Hazelbrook Drive	48	C4
Hazelbrook Park	54	B2
Hazelbrook Road	48	C4
Hazelbury Green	12	C3
Hazelbury Park	12	C3
Hazelcroft Gardens	26	B2
Hazelcroft Park	26	B2
Hazelcroft Road	26	B2
Hazeldene	50	C3
Hazelgrove Court	63	D2
Hazelwood	18	A3
Hazelwood (Bray)	73	D4
Hazelwood (Shankill)	75	D3
Hazelwood Avenue	13	D4
Hazelwood Close	52	C1
Hazelwood Court (Hartstown)	13	D4
Hazelwood Court (Kilmore)	28	C1
Hazelwood Crescent (Clondalkin)	52	C1
Hazelwood Crescent (Hartstown)	13	D4
Hazelwood Drive	28	C1
Hazelwood Green	13	D4
Hazelwood Lane	52	C1
Hazelwood Park	29	D1
Hazelwood View	52	C1
Headford Grove	57	E3
Headlands	77	E2
Healthfield Road	49	E4
Heaney Avenue	46	C2
Heather Close	67	D2
Heather Drive	67	D2
Heather Grove (Ballinteer)	67	D2
Heather Grove (Palmerston)	36	C3
Heather Lawn	67	D2
Heather Park	67	D2
Heather Road	68	C2
Heather View Avenue	63	F2
Heather View Close	63	F2
Heather View Drive	63	F2
Heather View Lawn	63	F2
Heather View Park	63	F2
Heather View Road	63	F2
Heather Walk	10	C2
Heathfield	60	B3
Heidelberg	58	B2
Hendrick Street	78	C3
Henley Park	57	E3
Henley Villas	57	E3
Henlons Lane	7	D2
Henrietta Lane	80	A2
Henrietta Place	78	D2
Henrietta Street	80	A2
Henry Place	80	B3
Henry Street	80	B3
Hepenstal Terrace	51	E1
Herbert Avenue	51	E4
Herbert Lane	81	D5
Herbert Park (Ballsbridge)	50	C2
Herbert Park (Bray)	76	B3
Herbert Park Lane	50	C2
Herbert Place	81	D5
Herbert Road (Blanchardstown)	23	F1
Herbert Road (Bray)	76	B3
Herbert Road (Sandymount)	51	D1
Herbert Street	81	D5
Herberton Drive	48	C2
Herberton Park	79	A6
Herberton Road	79	A6
Hermitage Avenue	66	C1
Hermitage Close	56	C4
Hermitage Court	56	C4
Hermitage Crescent	35	F2
Hermitage Downs	66	C1
Hermitage Drive	56	C4
Hermitage Gardens	35	F2
Hermitage Green	35	F2

Hermitage Grove	66	C1
Hermitage Lawn	56	C4
Hermitage Manor	35	F2
Hermitage Park	66	C1
Hermitage Place	35	F2
Hermitage Road	35	F2
Hermitage Valley	35	F2
Hermitage View	66	C1
Hermitage Way	35	E3
Heytesbury Lane	50	B2
Heytesbury Street	81	A6
High Park	29	A2
High Street (Central Dublin)	79	D4
High Street (Tallaght)	54	A4
Highfield Avenue	66	D1
Highfield Close	4	C4
Highfield Court Apartments	49	E4
Highfield Crescent	4	C4
Highfield Downs	4	C4
Highfield Drive	66	D1
Highfield Green	4	C3
Highfield Grove	49	F4
Highfield Lawn	4	C4
Highfield Park	57	F2
Highfield Road	49	F4
Highland Avenue	70	A3
Highland Grove	70	A4
Highland Lawn	70	B4
Highland View	70	A3
Highridge Green	58	C4
Highthorn Park	61	D4
Hill Cottages	71	F3
Hill Court	10	B2
Hill Drive	7	D3
Hill Street	80	B1
Hill Top Lawn	75	E4
Hillbrook Woods	23	D1
Hillcourt Park	71	D2
Hillcourt Road	71	E2
Hillcrest	55	E3
Hillcrest Avenue	34	C3
Hillcrest Close	34	B3
Hillcrest Court	34	C3
Hillcrest Drive	34	C3
Hillcrest Green	34	B3
Hillcrest Grove	34	C3
Hillcrest Heights	34	C3
Hillcrest Lawns	34	C3
Hillcrest Park (Finglas)	26	C1
Hillcrest Park (Lucan)	34	C3
Hillcrest Road (Lucan)	34	C3
Hillcrest Road (Sandyford)	68	B3
Hillcrest View	34	B3
Hillcrest Walk	34	B3
Hillcrest Way	34	B3
Hillsbrook Avenue	48	A4
Hillsbrook Drive	55	E1
Hillsbrook Grove	48	A4
Hillside	72	A3
Hillside Drive	57	D2
Hillside Park	56	A4
Hillside View	31	D1
Hilltown Close	4	C4
Hilltown Court	4	C4
Hilltown Green	4	C4
Hilltown Grove	4	B4
Hilltown Lawn	4	B4
Hilltown Park	4	C4
Hilltown Road	4	C4
Hilltown Way	4	C3
Hillview Drive	70	C2
Hillview Grove	67	D1
Hillview Lawn	70	C2
Hilton Gardens	67	F2
Holles Row	81	D4
Holles Street	41	D4
Holly Court	75	D1
Holly Park	75	E4
Holly Park Avenue	69	F1
Holly Road (Donnycarney)	28	C3
Holly Road (Fox & Geese)	46	C3
Hollybank Avenue Lower	50	B3
Hollybank Avenue Upper	50	B3
Hollybank Road	27	E4
Hollybrook	69	F3
Hollybrook Court	42	A1
Hollybrook Grove	28	C4
Hollybrook Park	28	C4
Hollybrook Road	28	C4
Hollyville Lawns	37	D2
Hollywood Drive	58	B3
Hollywood Park	58	B3
Holmston Avenue	61	D4
Holmwood	70	B4
Holybrooke Park	77	D4
Holyrood Park	51	D2
Holywell (Goatstown)	58	B4
Holywell (Poppintree)	17	E3
Holywell Avenue	9	E1
Holywell Court	9	E1
Holywell Crescent	21	D4
Holywell Drive	9	E1
Holywell Gardens	9	E1
Holywell Grove	9	E1
Holywell Heath	9	E1
Holywell Place	9	E1
Holywell Road (Donaghmede)	21	D4
Holywell Road (Swords)	9	E1
Holywell Square	9	E1
Holywell View	9	E1
Holywell Walk	9	E1
Home Villas	50	C2
Homefarm Park	27	E3
Homefarm Road	27	E3
Homelawn Avenue	64	B1
Homelawn Drive	64	B1
Homelawn Gardens	64	B1
Homelawn Road	64	B1
Homeleigh	23	D4
Honey Park	71	D1
Hope Avenue	41	E1
Hope Street	41	E4
Horton Court	56	B1
Hospital Lane	39	D3
Hotel Lane	80	B3
Howard Street	41	E4
Howth Junction Cottages	30	C1
Howth Road (Howth)	33	D1
Howth Road (Marino)	28	C4
Howth Road (Raheny)	30	C2
Howth Road, 150	29	D3
Howth View Park	21	D4
Huband Road	47	F2
Hudson Park	61	F4
Hudson Road	61	F4
Hughes Road East	48	A3
Hughes Road North	47	F3
Hughes Road South	48	A3
Hume Avenue	46	C2
Hume Street	81	C5
Hunters Avenue	65	D2
Hunters Court	65	D3
Hunters Green	65	D3
Hunters Grove	65	D3
Hunters Hall Apartments	65	D3
Hunters Hill	65	D3
Hunters Lane	65	D3
Hunters Parade	65	D3
Hunters Place	65	D3
Hunters Run The Close	13	D3
Hunters Run The Drive	13	D3
Hunters Run The Glade	13	D3
Hunters Run The Grove	13	D3
Hunters Run The Park	13	D3
Hunters Run The Rise	13	D3
Hunters Run The View	13	D3
Hunters Run The Way	13	D3
Hunters Walk	65	D3
Hunters Way	65	D3
Huntstown Avenue	13	E4
Huntstown Close	13	E3
Huntstown Court	13	E3
Huntstown Drive	13	E3
Huntstown Glen	13	D3
Huntstown Green	13	E3
Huntstown Grove	13	E3
Huntstown Park	13	E3
Huntstown Rise	13	E3
Huntstown Road	13	E4
Huntstown Way	13	E3
Huntstown Wood	13	E3
Hutchinsons Strand	5	F2
Hyacinth Street	80	D1
Hybreasal	48	B1
Hyde Park (Dalkey)	72	A2
Hyde Park (Templeogue)	56	A2
Hyde Park Avenue	59	E2
Hyde Park Garden	59	E2
Hyde Road	72	B2

I

Idrone Avenue	65	E1
Idrone Drive	55	E4
Idrone Park	55	E4
Idrone Terrace	59	F2
Imaal Road	39	F1
Inagh Road	37	E4
Inbhir Ide Close	6	C2
Inbhir Ide Drive	6	C2
Inchicore Parade	38	C4
Inchicore Road	39	D4
Inchicore Square	38	C4
Inchicore Terrace South	38	C4
Infirmary Road	78	A3
Inglewood Close	22	C1
Inglewood Crescent	22	C1
Inglewood Drive	22	C1
Inglewood Road	22	C1
Ingram Road	79	C6
Inis Fail	63	F2
Inis Thiar	64	A2
Inn's Quay	78	D3
Innisfallen Parade	40	B1
Innismore	48	A3
Inver Road	39	E1
Invermore Grove	20	C4
Inverness Road	28	A4
Iona Crescent	27	E4
Iona Drive	27	E4
Iona Park	27	E4
Iona Road	27	D4
Iona Villas	27	E4
Iris Grove	58	C2
Irishtown Road	41	F4
Irvine Terrace	41	E2
Irwin Court	79	A4
Island Street	78	C3
Island View (Kilbarrack)	31	D1
Island View (Malahide)	7	E2
Islandbridge Court	39	D3
Islington Avenue	61	E4
Isolda Road	42	A4
Ivar Street	78	B2
Iveagh Gardens	48	B2
Iveragh Road	27	F2
Ivy Court	19	D4

J

James Connolly Park	45	F2
James Connolly Square	77	D1
James Everett Park	73	D4
James Larkin Road	30	C2
James McCormack Gardens	11	E4
James Street North	41	E2
James's Court	79	B4
James's Place	81	D5
James's Street	79	B4
James's Street East	81	D5
James's Terrace	7	D2
James's Walk	79	A5
Jamestown Avenue	47	F1
Jamestown Court	47	F1
Jamestown Road (Finglas)	17	D3
Jamestown Road (Inchicore)	47	E1
Jervis Lane Lower	80	A3
Jervis Lane Upper	80	A3
Jervis Street	40	B3
Jobstown Road	62	C2
John Dillon Street	79	D4
John F Kennedy Avenue	47	D2
John F Kennedy Drive	47	E2
John F Kennedy Road	46	C2
John McCormack Avenue	47	F3
John Street North	78	C3
John Street South	79	C5
John Street West	79	C4
John's Lane West	79	C4
Johnsbridge Avenue	35	D4
Johnsbridge Close	35	D4
Johnsbridge Green	35	D4
Johnsbridge Grove	35	D4
Johnsbridge Meadows	35	D4
Johnsbridge Park	35	D4
Johnsbridge Walk	35	D4
Johnstown Avenue	70	C2
Johnstown Court	70	C2
Johnstown Grove	70	C3
Johnstown Park (Cornelscourt)	70	C3
Johnstown Park (Glasnevin)	26	C2
Johnstown Road	70	C4
Jones Road	40	C1
Joy Street	41	E4
Joyce Avenue	70	A3
Joyce Road	27	E3
Joyce Way	46	B2
Jugback Green	4	C1
Jugback Lane	4	C2
Jugback Place	4	C1

K

Karrickmines Little	70	A4
Kavanagh Avenue	46	C2
Keadeen Avenue	54	C1
Kearn's Place	39	E4
Keeper Road	48	C2
Kells Road	48	C3
Kelly's Avenue	61	D3
Kelly's Row	80	B1
Kellystown Road	67	D3
Kelston Avenue	69	E1
Kelston Drive	69	E1
Kelston Park	69	E2
Kelston View	69	E1
Kelvin Close	10	C2
Kempton Avenue	25	E3
Kempton Green	25	E3
Kempton Grove	25	E3
Kempton Heath	25	E3
Kempton Lawn	25	E3
Kempton Park	25	E3
Kempton Rise	25	E3

Name	Page	Grid
Kempton View	25	E3
Kempton Way	25	E3
Kengar Mews	49	E3
Kenilworth Lane	49	E3
Kenilworth Manor	49	E4
Kenilworth Park	49	D3
Kenilworth Road	49	E3
Kenilworth Square East	49	E3
Kenilworth Square North	49	E3
Kenilworth Square West	49	E3
Kenmare Parade	40	B1
Kennedy Park	77	D3
Kennelsfort Green	37	D3
Kennelsfort Road Lower	37	D2
Kennelsfort Road Upper	37	D3
Kennington Close	55	D3
Kennington Crescent	55	D2
Kennington Lawn	55	D3
Kennington Road	55	D2
Kentfield	75	E3
Kerlogue Road	42	A4
Kerrymount Avenue	69	F4
Kerrymount Close	70	A3
Kerrymount Green	70	A3
Kerrymount Mall	70	A3
Kerrymount Rise	70	A3
Kettles Lane	9	D2
Kevin Street Lower	81	A5
Kevin Street Upper	81	A5
Kew Park	34	B2
Kew Park Avenue	34	A2
Kew Park Crescent	34	A2
Kickham Road	39	D4
Kilakee Close	54	C1
Kilbarrack Avenue	30	C1
Kilbarrack Gardens	30	C1
Kilbarrack Grove	30	C1
Kilbarrack Parade	21	E4
Kilbarrack Road	30	C1
Kilbarrack Way	21	E4
Kilbarron Avenue	19	D4
Kilbarron Drive	19	D4
Kilbarron Park	19	E4
Kilbarron Road	19	E4
Kilbegnet Close	72	B2
Kilbogget Grove	74	C1
Kilbride Lane	76	B3
Kilbride Road	29	D3
Kilcarrig Avenue	53	D4
Kilcarrig Close	53	D4
Kilcarrig Crescent	53	D3
Kilcarrig Green	53	D4
Kilclare Avenue	63	D1
Kilclare Drive	63	D1
Kilclare Gardens	63	D1
Kilcolman Court	71	E1
Kilcronan Avenue	44	C2
Kilcronan Close	44	C2
Kilcronan Court	44	C2
Kilcronan Crescent	44	C2
Kilcronan Green	44	C2
Kilcronan Grove	44	C2
Kilcronan Lawn	44	C2
Kilcronan View	44	C2
Kilcroney Lane	76	A4
Kilcross Avenue	68	A3
Kilcross Court	68	A3
Kilcross Crescent	68	A3
Kilcross Drive	68	A3
Kilcross Grove	68	A2
Kilcross Lawn	68	A2
Kilcross Park	68	A3
Kilcross Road	68	A3
Kildare Park	48	B2
Kildare Road	48	B3
Kildare Street	81	C5
Kildonan Avenue	25	F1
Kildonan Drive	25	F1
Kildonan Road	16	B4
Kilfenora Drive	20	C4
Kilfenora Road	48	C3
Kilgobbin Road	68	B3
Kilgobbin Wood	68	C4
Kilians Road	76	C3
Kilins Square	10	A4
Kilkieran Court	26	B4
Kilkieran Road	26	A4
Kill Avenue	70	B1
Kill Lane	70	A2
Killakee Avenue	64	C1
Killakee Court	64	C2
Killakee Drive	54	C1
Killakee Gardens	64	C2
Killakee Green	64	C2
Killakee Grove	64	C1
Killakee Lawns	64	C2
Killakee Park	64	C2
Killakee Rise	64	C1
Killakee Road	65	E4
Killakee Walk	64	C1
Killakee Way	64	C2
Killala Road	26	B4
Killane Road	41	E2
Killarney Heights	76	B2
Killarney Lane	76	C2
Killarney Parade	40	B1
Killarney Park	76	C2
Killarney Road	76	C2
Killarney Street	80	C2
Killarney Villas	77	D2
Killary Grove	21	D4
Killeen Avenue	6	B2
Killeen Court	6	B2
Killeen Crescent	6	B2
Killeen Road (Fox & Geese)	47	D3
Killeen Road (Rathmines)	50	A3
Killester Avenue	29	D3
Killester Court	29	D2
Killester Park	29	D3
Killinarden Estate	63	E1
Killinarden Heights	63	D2
Killinarden Road	63	E3
Killiney Avenue	71	E4
Killiney Court	75	E2
Killiney Gate	75	E1
Killiney Heath	71	E4
Killiney Hill Road	75	E1
Killiney Road	71	F2
Killiney Towers	71	F2
Kilmacud Avenue	58	C4
Kilmacud Park	58	C4
Kilmacud Road (Dundrum)	57	F4
Kilmacud Road (Stillorgan)	68	C1
Kilmacud Road Lower	59	B4
Kilmacud Road Upper	58	B4
Kilmahuddrick Avenue	44	C2
Kilmahuddrick Close	44	C3
Kilmahuddrick Court	44	C2
Kilmahuddrick Crescent	44	C2
Kilmahuddrick Drive	44	C2
Kilmahuddrick Green	44	C3
Kilmahuddrick Grove	44	C3
Kilmahuddrick Lawn	44	C2
Kilmahuddrick Road	44	C2
Kilmainham Bank	39	D4
Kilmainham Lane	39	E4
Kilmantain Place	77	D1
Kilmartin Avenue	53	D4
Kilmartin Crescent	53	D4
Kilmartin Drive	52	C4
Kilmartin Gardens	53	D4
Kilmartin Green	52	C4
Kilmashogue Close	54	C1
Kilmashogue Drive	54	C1
Kilmashogue Grove	54	C1
Kilmashogue Lane	66	C3
Kilmore Avenue (Coolock)	19	E4
Kilmore Avenue (Killiney)	71	F4
Kilmore Close	28	D1
Kilmore Court	19	E4
Kilmore Crescent	19	F4
Kilmore Drive	28	D1
Kilmore Road	19	E4
Kilmore Road	28	C1
Kilmorony Close	21	D4
Kilnamanagh Road	47	F3
Kilrock Road	33	E2
Kilshane Cross	15	E2
Kilshane Road	25	F2
Kiltalown Avenue	62	C2
Kiltalown Close	62	C2
Kiltalown Court	62	C2
Kiltalown Crescent	62	C2
Kiltalown Drive	62	C2
Kiltalown Green	62	C2
Kiltalown Heights	62	C2
Kiltalown Park	62	C2
Kiltalown Road	62	C2
Kiltalown View	62	C2
Kiltalown Walk	62	C2
Kiltalown Way	62	C2
Kilteragh Drive	70	A3
Kilteragh Pines	69	F3
Kilteragh Road	70	A3
Kiltipper Avenue	64	A2
Kiltipper Close	64	A2
Kiltipper Drive	64	A2
Kiltipper Gate	63	F3
Kiltipper Gate Apartments	63	F3
Kiltipper Rise	63	F3
Kiltipper Road	64	A3
Kiltipper View	63	F3
Kiltipper Way	63	F2
Kilvere	55	F3
Kilvere Park	55	E3
Kilworth Road	47	F2
Kilworth Road	48	A2
Kimmage Court	48	C4
Kimmage Grove	49	D4
Kimmage Road Lower	48	C4
Kimmage Road West	48	B4
Kinahan Street	78	A2
Kincora Avenue	29	D4
Kincora Avenue	42	B1
Kincora Court	43	D1
Kincora Drive	29	D4
Kincora Grove	29	D4
Kincora Lodge	74	A1
Kincora Park	42	B1
Kincora Road	42	B1
King Edward Court	77	D1
King Edward Lawn	76	C1
King Edward Park	76	C1
King Edward Road	76	C1
King Street North	78	C3
King Street South	81	B5
King's Avenue	41	D1
King's Inns Street	80	A2
Kingram Place	81	C6
Kings Hall	5	F4
Kingsland Parade	49	E3
Kingsland Park Avenue	49	F1
Kingsmill Road	77	E1
Kingston Avenue	67	E3
Kingston Close	67	E3
Kingston Crescent	67	E3
Kingston Drive	67	F2
Kingston Green	67	E3
Kingston Grove	67	E3
Kingston Heights	67	F2
Kingston Lawn	67	F3
Kingston Park	67	E3
Kingston Rise	67	E3
Kingston View	67	E3
Kingston Walk	67	E3
Kingswood Avenue	53	F2
Kingswood Castle	54	A1
Kingswood Drive	53	F2
Kingswood Heights	53	F2
Kingswood View	53	F2
Kinsaley Lane	6	C2
Kinvara Avenue	25	F4
Kinvara Drive	25	F3
Kinvara Grove	25	E4
Kinvara Park	25	F4
Kinvara Road	25	F4
Kippure Avenue	54	C2
Kippure Park	26	A2
Kirkpatrick Avenue	23	E3
Kirkpatrick Drive	23	E3
Kirkwood	51	E2
Kirwan Street	78	C2
Kitestown Road	33	E3
Knapton Lawn	60	C3
Knapton Road	60	C3
Knight's Bridge	29	D4
Knightswood	18	C3
Knockaire	65	E1
Knockcullen Drive	55	F4
Knockcullen Lawn	55	F4
Knockcullen Park	55	F4
Knockcullen Rise	55	F4
Knockfield Manor	65	D1
Knocklyon Avenue	55	E4
Knocklyon Close	55	D4
Knocklyon Cottages	65	F1
Knocklyon Court	55	E4
Knocklyon Drive	55	F3
Knocklyon Green	55	F3
Knocklyon Grove	65	E1
Knocklyon Heights	65	D1
Knocklyon Park	55	E4
Knocklyon Road	65	E1
Knockmaroon Hill	37	F2
Knockmaroon Road	37	F2
Knockmeenagh Lane	46	A4
Knockmeenagh Road	46	A4
Knockmitten Lane North	46	C3
Knockmitten Road	46	C3
Knockmore Avenue	63	D2
Knockmore Crescent	63	D2
Knockmore Drive	63	D2
Knockmore Gardens	63	D2
Knockmore Green	63	D2
Knockmore Grove	63	D2
Knockmore Park	63	D2
Knocknacree Grove	72	B3
Knocknacree Park	72	B3
Knocknacree Road	72	B3
Knocknagow	60	B3
Knocknarea Avenue	48	B2
Knocknarea Road	48	A2
Knocknashee	58	A4
Knocksinna	69	F2
Knocksinna Crescent	69	F1
Knocksinna Grove	69	F1
Knocksinna Park	69	F2
Knowth Court	17	E3
Kyber Road	38	C2
Kylemore Avenue	47	D1
Kylemore Drive	47	D1
Kylemore Park North	47	D1
Kylemore Park South	47	D1
Kylemore Park West	47	D1
Kylemore Road	47	D1

L

Name	Page	Grid
La Touche Court	67	D2
La Touche Drive	47	E2

Name	Page	Grid
La Touche Road	47	F2
La Vallee	76	B2
La Vista Avenue	32	B2
Labre Park	47	D2
Laburnum Road	57	F1
Laburnum Walk	36	C2
Lad Lane	81	C6
Lady's Well	13	F2
Lady's Well Road	13	E2
Lagan Road	26	B3
Lakelands Avenue	68	B1
Lakelands Close	68	C1
Lakelands Crescent	68	C1
Lakelands Drive	68	C1
Lakelands Grove	68	B1
Lakelands Lawn	58	C4
Lakelands Park	56	B1
Lakelands Road	68	C1
Lakeview Drive	5	D4
Lally Road	38	B4
Lamb Alley	79	D4
Lamb's Brook	68	B3
Lambay Close	75	E2
Lambay Court	7	F3
Lambay Drive	75	E2
Lambay Road	27	E3
Lambourn Avenue	22	C2
Lambourn Court	22	C2
Lambourn Drive	22	C2
Lambourn Park	22	C2
Lambourn Road	22	C2
Lambourne Village	29	D4
Lambourne Wood	70	B4
Landen Road	38	B4
Landscape Avenue	57	D2
Landscape Crescent	57	D2
Landscape Gardens	57	E2
Landscape Park	57	D2
Landscape Road	57	D2
Lanesborough Avenue	17	D3
Lanesborough Castle	17	D3
Lanesborough Crescent	16	C3
Lanesborough Drive	17	D3
Lanesborough Gardens	17	D3
Lanesborough Grove	17	D3
Lanesborough Mews	17	D3
Lanesborough Park	16	C3
Lanesborough Road	17	D3
Lanesborough Square	17	D2
Lanesborough Terrace	16	D2
Lanesborough View	17	D3
Lanesville	60	B4
Lanewood Mews	50	B1
Lanndale Lawns	53	E4
Lansdowne Park (Ballsbridge)	50	C1
Lansdowne Park (Templeogue)	55	F4
Lansdowne Road	50	C1
Lansdowne Square	51	D1
Lansdowne Valley Park	47	F1
Lansdowne Village	51	D1
Laracor Gardens	21	D4
Laragh	71	E4
Laragh Close	20	C4
Laragh Grove	20	C4
Laraghcon	34	C1
Larch Grove	50	B3
Larch View	66	A1
Larchfield	57	F3
Larchfield Park	58	A3
Larchfield Road	58	A2
Larchford Terrace	12	C4
Larchford The Court	12	C4
Larchford The Green	12	C4
Larchford The Square	12	C4
Larkfield Avenue (Harold's Cross)	49	D3
Larkfield Avenue (Lucan)	35	F3
Larkfield Close	35	F3
Larkfield Gardens	49	D4
Larkfield Green	35	F2
Larkfield Grove (Harold's Cross)	49	D4
Larkfield Grove (Lucan)	35	F3
Larkfield Park	49	D3
Larkfield Place	35	F3
Larkfield Rise	35	F3
Larkfield Square	35	F2
Larkfield View	35	F3
Larkfield Way	35	F2
Larkhill Road	27	F1
Larkhill Road	28	A1
Lauderdale Estate	77	D2
Laurel Avenue (Ballybrack)	75	E1
Laurel Avenue (Dundrum)	57	E4
Laurel Drive	57	E4
Laurel Hill	71	D1
Laurel Lodge Road	23	F3
Laurel Park	45	F3
Laurel Road	57	E4
Laurelton (Swords)	4	B2
Laurelton (Terenure)	56	C1
Laurence Court	38	B4
Laurleen	69	E1
Laverna Avenue	23	F3
Laverna Dale	23	E3
Laverna Grove	56	A1
Laverna Road	56	A1
Laverna Way	23	F3
Laverty Court	81	C5
Lavery Avenue	46	C1
Lawnswood Park	69	D1
Lawrence Grove	28	C4
Le Fanu Road	37	F4
Lea Crescent	51	E2
Lea Road	51	E2
Leahy's Terrace	51	D1
Lealand Avenue	45	D3
Lealand Close	45	D3
Lealand Drive	45	D3
Lealand Grove	45	D2
Lealand Road	45	D3
Lealand Walk	45	D2
Lee Road	26	B3
Leeson Close	81	C6
Leeson Lane	81	C5
Leeson Park	50	A2
Leeson Park Avenue	50	B2
Leeson Place	81	C6
Leeson Street Lower	81	C6
Leeson Street Upper	50	A2
Leeson Walk	81	C6
Leicester Avenue	49	E4
Leighlin Road	48	C3
Lein Gardens	29	F2
Lein Park	29	F2
Lein Road	29	F2
Leinster Avenue	41	E1
Leinster Lane	81	C4
Leinster Road	49	E3
Leinster Road West	49	E3
Leinster Square	49	F3
Leinster Street North	40	A1
Leinster Street South	81	C4
Leix Road	39	F1
Leixlip Road	34	A2
Lemon Street	81	B4
Lennox Place	49	F2
Lennox Street	49	F2
Lennox Terrace	49	F2
Lentisk Lawn	20	C4
Leo Street	40	B2
Leonards Court	79	D6
Leopardstown Avenue	69	E1
Leopardstown Drive	69	D2
Leopardstown Gardens	69	E1
Leopardstown Grove	69	E1
Leopardstown Oaks	69	D1
Leopardstown Park	69	D2
Leopardstown Rise	68	C3
Leopardstown Road	69	E2
Leslie Avenue	72	B2
Leukos Road	42	A4
Liberty Lane	81	A5
Library Road (Dún Laoghaire)	61	D3
Library Road (Shankill)	75	E4
Library Terrace	61	D3
Liffey Avenue	36	A3
Liffey Close	35	F3
Liffey Court	35	F3
Liffey Crescent	35	F3
Liffey Dale	35	F3
Liffey Downs	35	F3
Liffey Glen	35	F3
Liffey Green	35	F3
Liffey Grove	35	F3
Liffey Hall	35	F3
Liffey Lawn	36	A3
Liffey Park	35	F3
Liffey Place	35	F3
Liffey Rise	35	F3
Liffey Road	35	F3
Liffey Row	35	F3
Liffey Street Lower	80	B3
Liffey Street South	38	B4
Liffey Street Upper	80	B3
Liffey Street West	78	C3
Liffey Vale	35	F3
Liffey Walk	36	A3
Liffey Way	36	A3
Liffey Wood	36	A3
Lilmar Avenue	18	C3
Lilys Way	12	B4
Lime Street	41	D3
Limekiln Avenue	54	D1
Limekiln Close	55	E1
Limekiln Drive	55	E2
Limekiln Green	54	C2
Limekiln Grove	55	D1
Limekiln Lane	55	D1
Limekiln Park	55	D1
Limekiln Road	54	C2
Limelawn Court	23	D2
Limelawn Glade	23	D2
Limelawn Green	23	D2
Limelawn Rise	23	D2
Limelawn Wood	23	D2
Limes Road	68	B2
Limetree Avenue	10	B1
Limewood Avenue	20	B4
Limewood Close	20	B4
Limewood Mews	18	A3
Limewood Park	20	B4
Limewood Road	20	B4
Lincoln Place	81	C4
Linden Court	59	E3
Linden Fields	59	E3
Linden Grove	59	E3
Linden Lea Park	59	D4
Linden Place	59	E3
Linden Square	59	E3
Lindenvale	59	F3
Lindisfarne Avenue	45	D2
Lindisfarne Drive	45	D2
Lindisfarne Green	45	D2
Lindisfarne Grove	45	D3
Lindisfarne Lawns	45	D2
Lindisfarne Park	45	D2
Lindisfarne Vale	45	D2
Lindisfarne Walk	45	D2
Lindsay Road	27	D4
Linenhall Parade	78	D2
Linenhall Terrace	78	D2
Link Road	61	E4
Linnetfields Avenue	12	C3
Linnetfields Close	12	C3
Linnetfields Court	12	B4
Linnetfields Drive	12	C3
Linnetfields Green	12	B4
Linnetfields Park	12	B4
Linnetfields Rise	12	C3
Linnetfields Square	12	C3
Linnetfields View	12	C3
Linnetfields Walk	12	B4
Lios na Sidhe	63	F2
Lioscian	4	B2
Lisburn Street	78	D2
Liscannor Road	26	B4
Liscarne Court	36	B4
Liscarne Dale	36	B4
Liscarne Gardens	36	B4
Lisle Road	48	A3
Lismore Road	48	C3
Lissadel Avenue	48	B2
Lissadel Court	48	B2
Lissadel Crescent	6	A2
Lissadel Drive	48	B2
Lissadel Grove	6	A2
Lissadel Park	6	A2
Lissadel Road	48	B2
Lissadel Wood	6	A2
Lissen Hall Avenue	5	E2
Lissen Hall Court	5	E2
Lissen Hall Drive	5	E2
Lissen Hall Park	5	E2
Little Britain Street	78	D3
Little Green	78	D3
Littlepace Court	12	C3
Littlepace Crescent	12	C3
Littlepace Drive	12	C3
Littlepace Gallops	12	C3
Littlepace Meadows	12	C3
Littlepace Park	12	C3
Littlepace View	12	C3
Littlepace Walk	12	C3
Littlepace Way	12	C3
Littlepace Woods	12	C3
Llewellyn Close	67	D1
Llewellyn Court	67	D1
Llewellyn Grove	67	D1
Llewellyn Lawn	67	D1
Llewellyn Way	67	D1
Llewllyn Park	67	D1
Lock Road	44	A1
Loftus Lane	80	A3
Lohunda Crescent	22	C1
Lohunda Dale	23	D2
Lohunda Downs	23	D1
Lohunda Drive	22	C1
Lohunda Grove	23	D2
Lohunda Park	22	C1
Lohunda Road	22	C2
Lombard Street East	81	C4
Lombard Street West	79	D6
Lomond Avenue	28	A4
London Bridge Drive	51	D1
London Bridge Road	41	F4
Long Lane	81	A5
Long Mile Road	47	D3
Long's Place	79	B5
Longboat Quay	41	E3
Longdale Terrace	18	A4
Longdale Way	18	A4
Longford Place	60	C3
Longford Street Great	81	A4
Longford Terrace	60	C3
Longlands	5	D3
Longmeadow Grove	70	C3
Longwood Avenue	49	E2
Longwood Park	56	C4
Lorcan Avenue	18	C4
Lorcan Crescent	18	C4
Lorcan Drive	18	C4
Lorcan Green	19	D4
Lorcan Grove	18	C4

Lorcan O'Toole Park 48 B4
Lorcan Park 28 A1
Lorcan Road 18 C4
Lorcan Villas 19 D4
Lord Edward Street 81 A4
Lord's Road 39 D2
Loreto Abbey Apartments 56 C3
Loreto Avenue 56 C4
Loreto Crescent 56 C4
Loreto Grange 77 D2
Loreto Park 56 C3
Loreto Road 79 B5
Loreto Row 57 D4
Loreto Terrace 56 C3
Lough Conn Avenue 37 F3
Lough Conn Drive 37 F3
Lough Conn Road 37 F3
Lough Derg Road 30 A2
Loughlinstown Drive 75 D2
Loughlinstown Park 75 D2
Loughlinstown Wood 75 D2
Louis Lane 49 F3
Lourdes Road 79 B5
Louvain 58 B2
Louvain Glade 58 B2
Love Lane 41 E4
Lower Dargle Road 76 C1
Lower Lucan Road 22 C4
Lower Lucan Road 35 D2
Lower Lucan Road 37 D1
Lower Road 75 E4
Luby Road 39 D4
Lucan Bypass 34 C3
Lucan Heights 35 D2
Lucan Newlands Road 36 A4
Lucan Road 37 D2
Ludford Drive 67 E1
Ludford Park 67 E1
Ludford Road 67 E1
Lugnaquilla Avenue 54 C1
Luke Street 80 C3
Lullymore Terrace 49 D2
Luttrell Close 23 E3
Luttrell Court 23 E3
Luttrell Crescent 23 E3
Luttrell Drive 23 E3
Luttrell Green 23 E3
Luttrell Grove 23 E3
Luttrell Park 23 E3
Luttrell View 23 E3
Luttrellstown Avenue 23 E4
Luttrellstown Chase 23 D4
Luttrellstown Close 23 E4
Luttrellstown Court 23 D4
Luttrellstown Dale 23 D4
Luttrellstown Drive 23 D4
Luttrellstown Glade 23 D4
Luttrellstown Green 23 E4
Luttrellstown Grove 23 D4
Luttrellstown Heath 23 D4
Luttrellstown Heights 23 E4
Luttrellstown Lawns 23 D4
Luttrellstown Oaks 23 E4
Luttrellstown Park 23 E4
Luttrellstown Place 23 D4
Luttrellstown Rise 23 E3
Luttrellstown Thicket 23 D4
Luttrellstown View 23 E4
Luttrellstown Walk 23 E4
Luttrellstown Way 23 D3
Lynche's Lane 35 D3
Lynche's Lane 44 C1
Lynwood 57 F4

M

Mabbot Lane 80 C2
Mabel Street 40 C1
Mabestown 6 B4
Macetown Road 13 E1
Macken Street 81 D4
Mackintosh Park 70 B2
Macroom Avenue 19 F3
Macroom Road 20 A3
Madden Road 79 C6
Madden's Lane 75 E1
Madison Road 48 C1
Magennis Place 81 C4
Magenta Crescent 18 C4
Magenta Hall 18 C4
Magenta Place 61 E4
Magna Drive 62 B1
Maidens Row 38 A3
Main Road 34 C2
Main Street (Baldoyle) 11 D3
Main Street (Blackrock) 59 F2
Main Street (Blanchardstown) 23 F1
Main Street (Clondalkin) 45 F3
Main Street (Clonsilla) 12 B4
Main Street (Finglas) 26 B1
Main Street (Howth) 33 E2
Main Street (Lucan) 34 C2
Main Street (Raheny) 30 A2
Main Street (Rathfarnham) 56 B2
Main Street (Swords) 5 D3
Main Street (Tallaght) 54 A4
Maitland Street 73 E4
Malachi Road 78 B2
Malahide Marina Village 7 D2
Malahide Road (Ard na Greine) 20 B3
Malahide Road (Artane) 28 C2
Malahide Road (Malahide) 6 A2
Malahide Road (Swords) 5 D3
Mallin Avenue 79 B5
Malone Gardens 41 E4
Malpas Street 79 D5
Malpas Street 79 D5
Mander's Terrace 50 A2
Mannix Road 27 E4
Manor Avenue 56 A1
Manor Close 67 D1
Manor Drive 20 C3
Manor Green 67 D1
Manor Heath 67 D1
Manor Park 37 E3
Manor Place 12 B4
Manor Place 78 B2
Manor Rise 67 D1
Manor Road 37 D3
Manor Square 12 B4
Manor Street 40 A2
Manorfields Avenue 13 D4
Manorfields Close 13 D4
Manorfields Crescent 12 C4
Manorfields Dale 13 D4
Manorfields Drive 12 C4
Manorfields Green 13 D4
Manorfields Rise 13 D4
Manorfields Road 13 D4
Mapas Avenue 72 A3
Mapas Road 72 A3
Maple Avenue 23 E3
Maple Close 23 F3
Maple Drive (Carpenterstown) 23 F3
Maple Drive (Kimmage) 49 D4
Maple Green 23 E3
Maple Grove 73 D4
Maple Manor 70 C3
Maple Road 57 F1
Maples Road 68 B1
Maplewood Avenue 63 E1
Maplewood Close 63 E1

Maplewood Court 63 E1
Maplewood Drive 63 E1
Maplewood Green 63 E1
Maplewood Lawn 63 E1
Maplewood Park 63 E1
Maplewood Road 53 E4
Maplewood Way 63 E1
Maretimo Gardens East 60 A2
Maretimo Road 60 A2
Marewood Drive 17 E3
Margaret Place 41 E4
Marguerite Road 27 D4
Marian Crescent 56 A3
Marian Drive 56 A3
Marian Grove 56 B3
Marian Park (Baldoyle) 21 F4
Marian Park (Blackrock) 60 A4
Marian Park (Templeogue) 56 A3
Marian Road 56 A3
Marigold Avenue 20 B3
Marigold Court 20 B3
Marigold Crescent 20 A3
Marigold Grove 20 A3
Marigold Park 20 B3
Marigold Road 20 A3
Marine Avenue 61 F4
Marine Court 61 F4
Marine Drive 51 E1
Marine Parade 61 F4
Marine Road 61 D3
Marine Terrace 61 E3
Mariners Court 61 E3
Mariners Cove 33 E2
Mariners Port D2 D2
Marino Avenue 28 B4
Marino Avenue East 75 F1
Marino Avenue West 75 F1
Marino Green 28 B4
Marino Park (Blackrock) 59 E2
Marino Park (Marino) 28 B4
Marino Park Avenue 28 B4
Marion Villas 79 C5
Mark Street 81 C4
Mark's Lane 81 C4
Marlborough Court 71 E1
Marlborough Mews 78 A1
Marlborough Park 71 E1
Marlborough Place 80 B3
Marlborough Road
  (Donnybrook) 50 B3
Marlborough Road (Glenageary) 71 E1
Marlborough Road
  (McKee Barracks) 78 A2
Marlborough Street 80 B2
Marley Avenue (Malahide) 7 E2
Marley Avenue (Rathfarnham) 57 D4
Marley Close 57 D4
Marley Court 57 D4
Marley Court South 57 D4
Marley Drive 66 C1
Marley Grange 66 C1
Marley Grove 67 D1
Marley Lawn 66 C1
Marley Rise 66 C1
Marley View 67 E2
Marley Villas 66 D1
Marley Walk 66 C1
Marlfield Court 63 F3
Marlfield Crescent 63 F3
Marlfield Gardens 70 C3
Marlfield Grove 63 F3
Marlfield Lawn 63 F3
Marlfield Mall 63 F3
Marlfield Place 63 F3
Marlfield Row 63 F3
Marne Villas 78 C1
Marrowbone Lane 79 B5
Marsham Court 58 C4

Mart Lane 70 A3
Martello Avenue 61 E3
Martello Court 10 B2
Martello Mews 51 E3
Martello Terrace 73 F4
Martello View 51 E1
Martin Savage Park 25 D3
Martin Street 49 F2
Martin's Row 38 A3
Marville Avenue 41 E1
Mary Street 80 A3
Mary Street Little 80 A3
Mary's Abbey 80 A3
Mary's Lane 78 D3
Maryfield Crescent 28 D1
Maryfield Drive 28 C1
Maryville Road 29 F3
Mask Avenue 29 E1
Mask Crescent 29 E2
Mask Drive 29 E2
Mask Green 29 E2
Mask Road 29 E2
Mather Road North 58 C2
Mather Road South 58 C2
Maxwell Lane 49 F4
Maxwell Road 49 F4
Maxwell Street 79 B5
May Lane 78 D3
May Street 40 C1
Mayberry Road 54 A3
Mayfair 7 E2
Mayfield Park 46 A2
Mayfield Road (Dolphin's Barn) 48 C1
Mayfield Road (Terenure) 49 D4
Mayfield Road East 56 B1
Mayfield Terrace 67 F1
Mayne Road 21 E1
Mayor Street Lower 41 D3
Mayor Street Upper 41 E3
Mayville Terrace 72 B2
Maywood Avenue 30 B2
Maywood Close 30 B2
Maywood Crescent 30 B2
Maywood Drive 30 B2
Maywood Grove 30 B2
Maywood Lawn 30 B2
Maywood Park 30 B2
Maywood Road 30 B2
McAuley Avenue 29 E2
McAuley Drive 29 F2
McAuley Park 29 E2
McAuley Road 29 E2
McCabe Villas 59 D1
McDowell Avenue 79 A4
McKee Avenue 16 C4
McKee Park 78 A2
McKee Road 17 D4
McKelvey Avenue 16 C3
McKelvey Road 16 C3
McMahon Street 81 A6
Meade's Terrace 81 D4
Meadow Avenue 57 E4
Meadow Close (Churchtown) 57 D4
Meadow Close
  (Newtownpark Ave) 59 F4
Meadow Copse 13 D4
Meadow Court 75 D1
Meadow Downs 13 D4
Meadow Drive 13 D4
Meadow Green 13 D4
Meadow Grove 57 D4
Meadow Mount 57 E4
Meadow Park 57 D4
Meadow Vale 70 B2
Meadow View 57 D4
Meadow View Grove 34 B3
Meadow Way 13 D4
Meadowbank 56 C1

Name	Page	Grid
Meadowbrook Avenue	11	D4
Meadowbrook Lawn	11	D4
Meadowbrook Park	11	D4
Meadowfield	68	C4
Meadowlands Avenue	60	C4
Meadowlands Mews	60	C4
Meadowlands Park	60	C4
Meadowpark Avenue	57	D3
Meakstown Cottages	17	D2
Meany Avenue	72	C2
Meath Place (Bray)	77	E1
Meath Place (Central Dublin)	79	C4
Meath Road	77	E1
Meath Street	79	C4
Meath Terrace	79	C4
Meile an Rí Crescent	45	D1
Meile an Rí View	36	A4
Mellifont Avenue	61	E3
Mellowes Avenue	25	F1
Mellowes Court	26	A1
Mellowes Crescent	26	A1
Mellowes Park	16	B4
Mellowes Road	25	F1
Melrose Avenue (Clondalkin)	45	D2
Melrose Avenue (Marino)	28	A4
Melrose Crescent	45	D2
Melrose Green	45	D2
Melrose Grove	45	D2
Melrose Lawn	45	D2
Melrose Park (Clondalkin)	45	D3
Melrose Park (Swords)	9	F1
Melrose Road	45	D2
Melville Close	17	D3
Melville Court	17	D3
Melville Crescent	17	D3
Melville Drive	17	D3
Melville Green	17	D3
Melville Park	17	D3
Melville Terrace	17	D3
Melville View	17	D3
Melville Way	17	D3
Melvin Road	49	D4
Memorial Road (Central Dublin)	80	C3
Memorial Road (Inchicore)	39	D4
Mercer Street Lower	81	B5
Merchamp	42	C1
Merchant's Quay	79	C4
Merchant's Road	41	F2
Merchant's Square	41	F2
Merlyn Drive	51	E2
Merlyn Park	51	E3
Merlyn Road	51	E3
Merrion Grove	59	D2
Merrion Park	59	D2
Merrion Place	81	C5
Merrion Road	51	D2
Merrion Row	81	C5
Merrion Square East	81	D5
Merrion Square North	81	C4
Merrion Square South	81	C5
Merrion Square West	81	C4
Merrion Strand	51	E3
Merrion Street Lower	81	C4
Merrion Street Upper	81	C5
Merrion View Avenue	51	E3
Merrion Village	51	E3
Merrion Woods	59	D2
Merton Avenue	79	C6
Merton Crescent	50	B4
Merton Drive	50	B3
Merton Park	79	C6
Merton Road	50	A4
Merton Walk	50	A4
Merville Avenue	59	D4
Merville Road	59	D4
Mespil Road	81	C6
Metropolitan Apartments	39	D4
Michael Collins Park	45	F2
Middle Third	29	D3
Milesian Avenue	5	E4
Milesian Court	5	E4
Milesian Grove	5	E4
Milesian Lawn	5	E4
Milford	6	B2
Military Road (Killiney)	75	E1
Military Road (Kilmainham)	79	A4
Military Road (Rathmines)	49	F2
Mill Court	45	D3
Mill Court Way	45	D4
Mill Lane (Ashtown)	25	D3
Mill Lane (Bray)	73	E4
Mill Lane (Central Dublin)	79	C5
Mill Lane (Palmerstown)	37	E2
Mill Lane (Shankill)	75	E3
Mill Race	38	A3
Mill Road	23	F2
Mill Street	79	C5
Millbank	10	A4
Millbourne Avenue	27	E4
Millbrook Avenue	20	C4
Millbrook Drive	20	C4
Millbrook Grove	20	C4
Millbrook Road	20	C4
Millbrook Village	50	B4
Millers Wood	76	C2
Millfield	10	A4
Millgate Drive	55	E1
Millmount Avenue	27	E4
Millmount Grove	57	F1
Millmount Place	27	E4
Millmount Villas	27	E4
Millpark	45	E3
Millstead	24	A1
Millstream	10	A4
Milltown Bridge Road	57	F1
Milltown Drive	57	D2
Milltown Grove (Milltown)	57	F1
Milltown Grove (Rathfarnham)	57	D2
Milltown Road	50	B4
Milltown Village	50	B4
Millview Close	6	B2
Millview Court	6	B2
Millview Lawns	6	B2
Millview Road	6	B2
Millwood Court	20	C4
Millwood Park	30	A1
Millwood Villas	20	C4
Milners Hall	27	F1
Moatfield Avenue	29	E1
Moatfield Park	29	E1
Moatfield Road	29	E1
Moatview Avenue	19	F3
Moatview Court	19	F2
Moatview Drive	19	F2
Moatview Gardens	20	A3
Mobhi Court	27	E3
Mobhi Drive	27	D3
Mobhi Road	27	E3
Moeran Road	48	A4
Moland Place	80	C2
Molesworth Place	81	B4
Molesworth Street	81	B4
Molyneaux Yard	79	C4
Monalea Grove	65	D1
Monalea Park	65	D1
Monalea Wood	65	D1
Monaloe Avenue	70	B3
Monaloe Drive	70	B3
Monaloe Park	70	B3
Monaloe Park Road	70	B3
Monasterboice Road	48	B3
Monastery Drive	46	A3
Monastery Gate Avenue	46	B3
Monastery Gate Close	46	B3
Monastery Gate Copse	46	B4
Monastery Gate Green	46	B3
Monastery Gate Lawn	46	B3
Monastery Gate Villas	46	A3
Monastery Heath Avenue	46	B4
Monastery Heath Court	46	B4
Monastery Heath Green	46	B4
Monastery Heath Square	46	B4
Monastery Park	46	A3
Monastery Rise	46	A3
Monastery Walk	46	A3
Monck Place	78	D1
Monksfield Court	46	B3
Monksfield Downs	46	B3
Monksfield Grove	46	B3
Monksfield Heights	46	B3
Monksfield Lawn	46	B3
Monksfield Meadows	46	B3
Monksfield Walk	46	B3
Monkstown Avenue	60	B4
Monkstown Crescent	60	C3
Monkstown Farm	60	B4
Monkstown Grove	60	B4
Monkstown Road	60	B3
Monkstown Square	60	B4
Monkstown Valley	60	B3
Montague Lane	81	B5
Montague Place	81	B5
Montague Street	81	B5
Montpelier Drive	78	B3
Montpelier Gardens	78	A3
Montpelier Hill	78	B3
Montpelier Parade	60	B3
Montpelier Park	78	B3
Montpelier View	62	C2
Montrose Avenue	28	C1
Montrose Close	28	B1
Montrose Court	28	C1
Montrose Crescent	28	C1
Montrose Drive	28	C1
Montrose Grove	28	C1
Montrose Park	28	C1
Moore Lane	80	B2
Moore Street	80	B2
Mooretown Avenue	4	C2
Mooretown Grove	4	C2
Mooretown Park	4	C2
Mooretown Road	4	C2
Moorfield Avenue	45	F1
Moorfield Drive	45	E1
Moorfield Grove	45	E1
Moorfield Lawns	45	F1
Moorfield Walk	45	E1
Moracrete Cottages	48	C2
Moreen Avenue	68	B2
Moreen Close	68	B2
Moreen Park	68	B2
Moreen Road	68	B2
Morehampton Lane	50	B2
Morehampton Road	50	B2
Morehampton Square	50	B2
Morehampton Terrace	50	B2
Morgan Place	78	D3
Morning Star Avenue	78	C2
Morning Star Road	79	B5
Mornington Grove	29	D2
Mornington Road	50	A3
Morrogh Terrace	28	A3
Moss Street	41	D3
Mount Albany	60	A4
Mount Albion Road	57	E4
Mount Alton	65	E1
Mount Andrew Avenue	36	A2
Mount Andrew Close	36	A2
Mount Andrew Court	36	A2
Mount Andrew Crescent	36	A2
Mount Andrew Dale	36	A2
Mount Andrew Grove	36	A2
Mount Andrew Place	36	A2
Mount Andrew Rise	36	A2
Mount Anville Lawn	58	B3
Mount Anville Park	58	B3
Mount Anville Road	58	B3
Mount Anville Wood	58	C4
Mount Argus Avenue	49	D3
Mount Argus Close	49	D3
Mount Argus Court	49	D3
Mount Argus Crescent	49	D3
Mount Argus Drive	49	D3
Mount Argus Green	49	D3
Mount Argus Grove	49	D3
Mount Argus Lawn	49	D3
Mount Argus Park	49	D3
Mount Argus Road	49	D3
Mount Argus Terrace	49	D3
Mount Argus View	49	D3
Mount Argus Way	49	D3
Mount Bellew Avenue	35	E3
Mount Bellew Crescent	35	F3
Mount Bellew Green	35	E3
Mount Bellew Rise	35	E3
Mount Brown	79	A4
Mount Carmel Avenue	57	F3
Mount Carmel Park	55	D4
Mount Carmel Road	58	A3
Mount Drinan Avenue	9	F1
Mount Drinan Grove	9	F1
Mount Drinan Lawn	9	F1
Mount Drinan Park	9	F1
Mount Drinan Walk	9	F1
Mount Drummond Avenue	49	E2
Mount Drummond Square	49	E2
Mount Eagle Drive	68	C3
Mount Eagle Green	68	C3
Mount Eagle Grove	68	C3
Mount Eagle Lawn	68	C3
Mount Eagle Park	68	C3
Mount Eagle Rise	68	C3
Mount Eagle View	68	C3
Mount Eagle Way	68	C3
Mount Eden Road	50	C3
Mount Merrion Avenue	59	D2
Mount Olive Grove	30	B1
Mount Olive Park	30	B1
Mount Olive Road	21	D4
Mount Prospect Avenue	30	A4
Mount Prospect Drive	29	F4
Mount Prospect Grove	29	F4
Mount Prospect Lawns	29	F4
Mount Prospect Park	29	F4
Mount Saint Annes	50	B4
Mount Salus Road	72	C3
Mount Sandel	70	A4
Mount Sandford	50	B3
Mount Shannon Road	48	C1
Mount Souci Wood	77	D2
Mount Street Lower	81	D5
Mount Street Upper	81	D5
Mount Symon Avenue	22	B2
Mount Symon Close	22	B1
Mount Symon Crescent	22	B1
Mount Symon Green	22	B1
Mount Symon Lawn	22	B1
Mount Symon Park	22	B1
Mount Tallant Avenue	49	D4
Mount Temple Road	78	B2
Mount Venus Road	65	F4
Mount Wood	60	C4
Mountain Park	64	A1
Mountain View Avenue	49	E3
Mountain View Drive (Bray)	77	D3
Mountain View Drive (Nutgrove Ave)	57	D4
Mountain View Park	57	D3
Mountain View Road	50	A3
Mountdown Avenue	55	D1
Mountdown Park	55	D2
Mountdown Road	55	D1
Mountfield	7	E3

Mountfield Lawns 7 E3
Mountfield Lodge 7 E3
Mountfield The Park 7 E3
Mountgorry Wood 5 E4
Mountjoy Square East 80 B1
Mountjoy Square North 80 B1
Mountjoy Square South 80 B1
Mountjoy Square West 80 B1
Mountjoy Street 80 A1
Mountjoy Street Middle 78 D2
Mountpleasant Avenue Lower 49 F2
Mountpleasant Avenue Upper 49 F2
Mountpleasant Square 50 A2
Mountpleasant Terrace 50 A2
Mountseskin Road 62 C3
Mounttown Park 60 C4
Mounttown Road Lower 60 C4
Mounttown Road Upper 60 C3
Mountview Road 22 C1
Mourne Road 47 F2
Mourne Road 48 B1
Moy Elta Road 41 E2
Moy Glas Avenue 35 E4
Moy Glas Chase 35 E4
Moy Glas Close 35 E4
Moy Glas Court 35 E4
Moy Glas Crescent 35 E4
Moy Glas Dale 35 E4
Moy Glas Dene 35 E4
Moy Glas Drive 35 E4
Moy Glas Glen 35 E4
Moy Glas Green 35 E4
Moy Glas Grove 35 E4
Moy Glas Lawn 35 E4
Moy Glas Park 35 E4
Moy Glas Vale 35 E4
Moy Glas View 35 E4
Moy Glas Way 35 E4
Moy Glas Wood 35 E4
Moyclare Avenue 11 D4
Moyclare Close 11 D4
Moyclare Drive 11 D4
Moyclare Park 11 D4
Moyclare Road 11 D4
Moycullen Road 37 E4
Moyle Road 26 B3
Moyne Road 50 A3
Moyola Court 57 E2
Moyville 66 A2
Moyville Lawn 66 A1
Muckross Avenue 55 E1
Muckross Crescent 55 E1
Muckross Drive 55 E1
Muckross Green 48 B4
Muckross Grove 55 E1
Muckross Park 55 E1
Muirfield Drive 47 F2
Mulberry Drive 23 F4
Mulberry Park 23 F4
Muldowney Court 7 F2
Mulgrave Street 61 D3
Mulgrave Terrace 61 D4
Mullinastill Road 75 D3
Mullingar Terrace 38 A3
Mulroy Road 26 B4
Mulvey Park 57 F2
Munster Street 40 B1
Murphystown Road 68 C3
Murtagh Road 78 B2
Muskerry Road 38 A4
Myra Close 39 D4
Myrtle Grove 69 D1
Myrtle Park 61 D4
Myrtle Street 78 D1

N

Naas Road 46 C3
Nangor Road 45 E3
Nanikin Avenue 29 F3
Nash Street 47 F1
Nashfield Road 33 E2
Nassau Street 81 B4
Naul Road 8 B2
Navan Road (Blanchardstown) 14 A3
Navan Road (Cabra) 39 E1
Navan Road (Castleknock) 24 C3
Navan Road (Clonee) 12 C2
Neagh Road 49 D4
Neilstown Avenue 45 F1
Neilstown Crescent 45 F1
Neilstown Drive 36 B4
Neilstown Gardens 45 F1
Neilstown Park 45 F1
Neilstown Road 36 B4
Nelson Street 80 A1
Nephin Road 39 D1
Nerano Road 72 C3
Nerney's Court 80 B1
Neville Road 49 F4
Nevinstown Lane 9 D1
New Bawn Drive 64 B1
New Bawn Park 64 B1
New Bride Street 81 A5
New Cabra Road 39 F1
New Grange Road 69 F1
New Hall Court 62 C2
New Ireland Road 48 C1
New Link Road 63 F1
New Nangor Road 45 D3
New Park Road 70 A1
New Road (Clondalkin) 45 F4
New Road (Inchicore) 47 F1
New Row South 79 D5
New Row Square 79 D5
New Street 7 D2
New Street Gardens 81 A5
New Street South 79 D5
New Vale Cottages 75 D4
New Vale Crescent 75 E4
New Waltham Terrace 59 E2
New Wapping Street 41 E3
Newbridge Avenue 51 D1
Newbridge Drive 51 D1
Newbrook Avenue 21 D4
Newbrook Road 21 D4
Newbury Avenue 19 E3
Newbury Drive 19 E3
Newbury Grove 19 E3
Newbury Lawns 19 F3
Newbury Park 19 E3
Newbury Terrace 19 E3
Newcastle Road 34 C4
Newcomen Avenue 80 D1
Newcourt 5 E2
Newcourt Avenue 77 E2
Newcourt Road 77 E3
Newgrange Park 77 E2
Newgrange Road 40 A1
Newgrove Avenue 51 E1
Newgrove Estate 21 D3
Newlands Drive 46 A4
Newlands Manor Court 52 C1
Newlands Manor Drive 52 C1
Newlands Manor Green 52 C1
Newlands Manor Park 52 C1
Newlands Park 46 A4
Newlands Road 46 A4
Newmarket 79 C5
Newpark 69 E1
Newport Street 79 B5
Newtown Avenue 60 A2
Newtown Cottages 20 A4

Newtown Court 20 B3
Newtown Drive 20 B4
Newtown House 60 A2
Newtown Park (Blackrock) 59 F4
Newtown Park (Tallaght) 54 B4
Newtown Villas (Blackrock) 60 A2
Newtown Villas (Churchtown) 57 D2
Newtownpark Avenue 69 F1
Newtownsmith 61 E3
Niall Street 78 B2
Nicholas Avenue 78 D3
Nicholas Street 79 D4
Ninth Lock Road 45 F2
Nore Road 26 B3
Norfolk Road 40 A1
Norseman Place 78 C2
North Avenue 58 C2
North Circular Road 39 E2
North Circular Road 40 C1
North Great George's Street 80 B2
North Lotts 80 B3
North Road (Finglas West) 16 C3
North Road (Phoenix Park) 25 E4
North Strand Road 41 D2
North Street (Clonsilla) 12 B4
North Street (Swords) 5 D3
North Wall Quay 41 D3
Northbrook Avenue 50 A2
Northbrook Avenue Lower 41 E1
Northbrook Lane 50 A2
Northbrook Road 50 A2
Northbrook Terrace 41 E2
Northcliffe 38 A3
Northcote Avenue 61 D3
Northland Drive 26 C2
Northumberland Avenue 61 D3
Northumberland Place 41 E4
Northumberland Road 50 C1
Northway Estate 16 B3
Norton's Avenue 78 D1
Norwood 75 E2
Norwood Park 50 B3
Nottingham Street 41 D1
Novara Avenue 77 D1
Novara Park 77 D1
Nugent Road 57 D3
Nutgrove Avenue 56 C3
Nutgrove Crescent 57 D4
Nutgrove Park 58 A1
Nutgrove Way 57 D3
Nutley Avenue 51 D3
Nutley Lane 51 D4
Nutley Park 51 D4
Nutley Road 51 D3

O

O'Briens Place 27 E3
O'Byrne Road 77 D3
O'Carolan Road 79 C5
O'Casey Avenue 46 B1
O'Connell Avenue 80 A1
O'Connell Gardens 51 D1
O'Connell Street 80 B2
O'Curry Avenue 79 c5
O'Curry Road 79 C6
O'Daly Road 27 E3
O'Devaney Gardens 78 A2
O'Dohoghue Street 47 F1
O'Donnell Gardens 61 E4
O'Donovan Road 79 C6
O'Dwyer Road 48 A4
O'Hogan Road 38 B4
O'Leary Road 48 B1
O'Moore Road 38 B4
O'Neachtain Road 27 E3

O'Reilly Avenue 79 A4
O'Rourke Park 70 C1
O'Sullivan Avenue 41 D1
Oak Apple Green 56 C1
Oak Avenue 18 C3
Oak Court 18 C3
Oak Crescent 18 C3
Oak Downs 45 E4
Oak Drive 18 C3
Oak Glen View 77 D4
Oak Green 18 C3
Oak Grove 18 C3
Oak Lawn 24 A3
Oak Lodge 24 B4
Oak Park 24 C4
Oak Rise (Clondalkin) 52 C1
Oak Rise (Santry) 18 C3
Oak Road (Clondalkin) 46 B3
Oak Road (Donnycarney) 28 C3
Oak Way (Clondalkin) 45 E4
Oak Way (Clondalkin) 52 C1
Oakcourt Avenue 37 E3
Oakcourt Close 37 E3
Oakcourt Drive 37 D3
Oakcourt Grove 37 D3
Oakcourt Lawn 37 E3
Oakcourt Park 37 D3
Oakdale Close 64 C3
Oakdale Crescent 64 C3
Oakdale Drive 70 C2
Oakdale Drive (Firhouse) 64 C2
Oakdale Grove 64 C3
Oakdale Park (Firhouse) 64 C3
Oakdale Park (Killiney) 75 D1
Oakdale Road 64 C3
Oakdene 71 E3
Oakdown Road 57 D3
Oakfield 45 F3
Oakfield Place 79 D6
Oaklands Avenue 5 D3
Oaklands Crescent 49 F4
Oaklands Drive (Rathgar) 49 F4
Oaklands Drive (Sandymount) 51 D1
Oaklands Park (Sandymount) 51 D2
Oaklands Park (Swords) 5 D3
Oaklands Terrace 49 E4
Oakley Grove 59 F3
Oakley Park (Blackrock) 59 F3
Oakley Park (Clontarf) 29 E4
Oakley Road 50 A3
Oakpark Avenue 18 C4
Oakpark Close 18 C4
Oakpark Drive 18 C4
Oakpark Grove 18 C4
Oakton Drive 71 E4
Oakton Green 75 D1
Oakton Park 75 D1
Oaktree Avenue 23 F3
Oaktree Drive 23 F3
Oaktree Green 23 F3
Oaktree Grove 23 F3
Oaktree Lawn 23 F3
Oaktree Road 69 D1
Oakview 18 C3
Oakview Avenue 22 C1
Oakview Close 22 C1
Oakview Court 22 C1
Oakview Drive 13 D4
Oakview Lawn 22 B1
Oakview Park 13 E4
Oakview Rise 22 C1
Oakview Walk 22 C1
Oakview Way 22 C1
Oakwood 61 D4
Oakwood Avenue (Finglas East) 17 D4
Oakwood Avenue (Swords) 4 C3
Oakwood Close 17 D4
Oakwood Grove 45 E2

Name	Grid		Name	Grid		Name	Grid		Name	Grid
Oakwood Park	17	D4	Oldcourt Grove	76	C3	Ormond Crescent	4	B2	Palmers Close	36	C3
Oakwood Road	17	D4	Oldcourt Manor	64	B2	Ormond Drive	4	B3	Palmers Copse	36	C3
Oatfield Avenue	36	B4	Oldcourt Park	76	C3	Ormond Grove	4	B2	Palmers Court	36	C3
Oatfield Close	36	C4	Oldcourt Road	64	B3	Ormond Lawn	4	B2	Palmers Crescent	37	D3
Oatfield Grove	36	C4	Oldcourt View	64	B2	Ormond Place	78	D3	Palmers Drive	36	C3
Oatfield Lawn	36	B4	Oldtower Crescent	36	B3	Ormond Quay Lower	80	A3	Palmers Glade	36	C3
Oatfield Park	36	B4	Oldtown Avenue	18	A4	Ormond Quay Upper	80	A3	Palmers Grove	37	D3
Obelisk Court	59	F4	Oldtown Park	18	A4	Ormond Road	27	F4	Palmers Lawn	36	C3
Obelisk Rise	59	F4	Oldtown Road	18	A4	Ormond Road South	50	A3	Palmers Road	36	C3
Offaly Road	39	F1	Olivemount Grove	57	F2	Ormond Square	78	D3	Palmers Walk	37	D3
Offington Avenue	32	B1	Olivemount Road	57	F2	Ormond Street	79	C5	Palmerston Gardens	50	A4
Offington Court	32	B2	Oliver Bond Street	79	C4	Ormond Terrace	72	B3	Palmerston Grove	50	B4
Offington Drive	32	B2	Oliver Plunkett Avenue			Ormond View	4	B3	Palmerston Park	50	A4
Offington Lawn	32	B2	(Dún Laoghaire)	60	B4	Ormond Way	4	B3	Palmerston Place	78	D2
Offington Park	32	B2	Oliver Plunkett Avenue			Orpen Close	59	E4	Palmerston Road	50	A3
Olaf Road	78	C2	(Ringsend)	41	F4	Orpen Green	59	E4	Palmerston Villas	49	F4
Olcovar	73	D1	Oliver Plunkett Road	60	C4	Orpen Hill	59	E4	Palmerstown Avenue	37	D2
Old Ballymun Road	18	A3	Oliver Plunkett Square	60	C4	Orpen Rise	59	E4	Palmerstown Close	36	C3
Old Bawn Avenue	64	A2	Olney Crescent	56	B1	Orwell Bank	57	D1	Palmerstown Drive	37	E2
Old Bawn Drive	64	A1	Olney Grove	56	B1	Orwell Gardens	57	D1	Palmerstown Green	37	D3
Old Bawn Park	64	A2	Ongar Avenue	12	B4	Orwell Park (Rathgar)	57	D1	Palmerstown Heights	36	C3
Old Bawn Road	64	A1	Ongar Chase	12	B4	Orwell Park (Templeogue)	55	E3	Palmerstown Lawn	36	C3
Old Bawn Terrace	64	A2	Ongar Green	12	B4	Orwell Park Avenue	55	E2	Palmerstown Woods	45	F1
Old Bawn Way	64	A1	Ongar Lodge (Blanchardstown)	24	A2	Orwell Park Close	55	E2	Paradise Place	80	A2
Old Blessington Road	63	E1	Ongar Lodge (Clonsilla)	22	A1	Orwell Park Crescent	55	E2	Parc na Silla Avenue	75	D3
Old Bray Road (Cabinteely)	70	C4	Ongar Park	22	A1	Orwell Park Dale	55	E3	Parc na Silla Close	75	D3
Old Bray Road (Cornelscourt)	70	A2	Ongar Road	22	B1	Orwell Park Drive	55	E2	Parc na Silla Lane	75	D3
Old Bridge Road	55	F3	Ongar Square	12	B4	Orwell Park Glade	55	E2	Parc na Silla Rise	75	D3
Old Cabra Road	39	E1	Ontario Terrace	49	F2	Orwell Park Glen	55	E2	Park Avenue (Blackrock)	59	F4
Old Carrickbrack Road	33	D4	Onward Close	10	B2	Orwell Park Green	55	E2	Park Avenue (Castleknock)	24	A3
Old Castle Avenue	32	C2	Onward Walk	10	B2	Orwell Park Grove	55	E2	Park Avenue (Malahide)	6	B4
Old Conna Grove	76	B1	Ophaly Court	57	F3	Orwell Park Lawns	55	E2	Park Avenue (Rathfarnham)	56	C4
Old Connaught Avenue	73	D3	Oranmore Road	37	E4	Orwell Park Rise	55	E3	Park Avenue (Sandymount)	51	E2
Old Connaught Grove	76	C1	Orby Avenue	69	D3	Orwell Park Road	55	E2	Park Boulevard	14	A1
Old Connaught View	76	C1	Orby Close	69	D3	Orwell Park View	55	E3	Park Close	71	D2
Old Corduff Road	14	B4	Orby Court	69	D3	Orwell Park Way	55	E2	Park Court (Sallynoggin)	71	D2
Old County Glen	48	C2	Orby Lawn	69	D3	Orwell Road	57	D1	Park Court (Sandymount)	51	E2
Old County Road	48	B2	Orby Park	69	D3	Orwell Woods	57	D1	Park Crescent	48	B4
Old Dunleary Road	60	C3	Orby View	69	D3	Osborne Terrace	50	A2	Park Drive (Cabinteely)	70	B3
Old Finglas Road	26	C3	Orby Way	69	D3	Oscar Square	79	C5	Park Drive (Milltown)	50	B4
Old Grange Road	21	E3	Orchard Avenue	22	C2	Oscar Traynor Road	19	E3	Park Drive Avenue	24	A3
Old Kilmainham	39	E4	Orchard Close	23	E2	Osprey Avenue	55	D2	Park Drive Close	24	A3
Old Lamp Road	38	C1	Orchard Court	23	E2	Osprey Drive	55	D2	Park Drive Crescent	24	A3
Old Lucan Road	37	D2	Orchard Green	23	E2	Osprey Lawn	55	D2	Park Drive Green	24	A3
Old Malahide Road	20	A4	Orchard Grove	23	E2	Osprey Park	55	D2	Park Drive Grove	24	A3
Old Mill Court	79	D5	Orchard Lane (Blackrock)	59	F4	Osprey Road	55	D2	Park Drive Lawn	24	A3
Old Naas Road	47	E2	Orchard Lane (Clondalkin)	45	F3	Ossory Road	41	D2	Park Green Avenue	14	C4
Old Navan Road	24	B2	Orchard Lawns	37	D4	Ostman Place	78	B2	Park Grove	59	F4
Old North Road	16	B2	Orchard Road (Ballybough)	41	D1	Otterbrook	56	B3	Park Heath	23	E3
Old North Road	16	C3	Orchard Road (Raheny)	30	C2	Oulart	4	C4	Park Lane (Dún Laoghaire)	61	E3
Old Orchard	55	F4	Orchard Road South	50	A4	Oulton Road	42	B1	Park Lane (Sandymount)	51	E2
Old Orchard Terrace	56	B3	Orchard Square	58	A1	Our Lady's Road	79	B5	Park Lawn	30	A4
Old Quarry	72	B3	Orchardstown Avenue	56	A3	Ovoca Road	79	D6	Park Lodge	24	A2
Old Rectory Park	57	F3	Orchardstown Drive	55	F3	Owen's Avenue	79	A4	Park Manor	23	F4
Old Street	7	D2	Orchardstown Park	56	A3	Owendoher Haven	66	A1	Park Road (Ashtown)	25	E3
Old Yellow Walls Road	6	B1	Orchardstown Villas	56	A3	Owendoher Lodge	66	A1	Park Road (Dún Laoghaire)	61	E3
Oldbridge Close	44	B1	Orchardton	56	B4	Owendore Avenue	56	B3	Park Road (Sallynoggin)	71	D2
Oldbridge Glen	44	B1	Ordnance Survey Road	38	A1	Owendore Crescent	56	B3	Park Street	38	B4
Oldbridge Green	44	B1	Oriel Street Lower	80	D2	Owenstown Park	58	C2	Park Terrace	79	D5
Oldbridge Grove	44	B1	Oriel Street Upper	80	D2	Oxford Road	50	A2	Park View (Cabra)	78	A1
Oldbridge Park	44	B1	Orlagh Avenue	65	E2	Oxford Terrace	41	E2	Park View (Castleknock)	24	C4
Oldbridge View	44	B1	Orlagh Close	65	E2	Oxmantown Lane	78	C3	Park View (Clonsilla)	23	D2
Oldbridge Walk	44	B1	Orlagh Court	65	E2	Oxmantown Road	78	B2	Park View (Portmarnock)	10	C2
Oldbridge Way	44	B1	Orlagh Crescent	65	E2				Park View (Ranelagh)	50	A2
Oldchurch Avenue	45	D3	Orlagh Dale	65	F2				Park View Avenue	49	E3
Oldchurch Close	45	D3	Orlagh Downs	65	F2				Park Villas	24	B3
Oldchurch Court	45	D3	Orlagh Grange	65	F2	**P**			Park Walk	59	F4
Oldchurch Crescent	45	D3	Orlagh Green	65	F2				Park West Avenue	46	B2
Oldchurch Drive	45	D4	Orlagh Grove	65	E2	Pace Avenue	13	D3	Park West Pointe	46	B2
Oldchurch Grove	45	D3	Orlagh Lawn	65	E2	Pace Crescent	13	D3	Park West Road	46	B2
Oldchurch Lawn	45	D4	Orlagh Lodge	65	E2	Pace Road	12	C3	Parkgate Street	78	A3
Oldchurch Park	45	D3	Orlagh Meadows	65	F2	Pace View	13	D3	Parkhill Avenue	54	A2
Oldchurch Way	45	D3	Orlagh Park	65	E1	Pacelli Avenue	31	D1	Parkhill Close	54	A2
Oldcourt	76	C3	Orlagh Rise	65	E2	Pairc Gleann Trasna	64	A2	Parkhill Court	53	F2
Oldcourt Avenue (Bray)	76	C3	Orlagh View	65	F2	Pakenham	60	C3	Parkhill Drive	53	F2
Oldcourt Avenue (Firhouse)	64	B2	Orlagh Way	65	E2	Pakenham Road	60	C3	Parkhill Green	53	F2
Oldcourt Close	64	B2	Ormond Avenue	4	B2	Palmer Park	66	B1	Parkhill Heights	54	A2
Oldcourt Drive	76	C3	Ormond Close	4	B3	Palmers Avenue	36	C3	Parkhill Lawn	54	A2

Parkhill Rise 54 A2
Parkhill Road 53 F2
Parkhill Way 54 A2
Parkhill West 53 F2
Parklands 24 A2
Parklands Avenue 64 C2
Parklands Court 64 C2
Parklands Drive 64 C2
Parklands Road 64 C2
Parklands View 64 C2
Parkmore Drive 56 A1
Parkvale (Baldoyle) 11 D4
Parkvale (Dundrum) 68 A1
Parkview (Ashtown) 25 E3
Parkview (Dean's Grange) 70 A1
Parkview (Swords) 4 A3
Parkwood Avenue 64 A2
Parkwood Grove 64 A2
Parkwood Lawn 64 A2
Parkwood Road 64 A2
Parliament Street 40 B3
Parnell Avenue 49 E2
Parnell Cottages 7 D3
Parnell Court 49 E2
Parnell Place 80 B2
Parnell Road (Bray) 77 D1
Parnell Road (Harold's Cross) 49 D2
Parnell Square East 80 B2
Parnell Square North 80 B2
Parnell Square West 80 B2
Parnell Street (Central Dublin) 80 B2
Parnell Street (Sallynoggin) 71 D1
Parslickstown Avenue 13 F2
Parslickstown Close 13 F2
Parslickstown Court 13 F2
Parslickstown Drive 14 A2
Parslickstown Gardens 13 F2
Parslickstown Green 13 F2
Partridge Terrace 47 F1
Patrician Villas 59 E3
Patrick Doyle Road 57 E1
Patrick Street (Central Dublin) 79 D5
Patrick Street (Dún Laoghaire) 61 D4
Patrickswell Place 26 A1
Pea Field 59 E2
Pearse Avenue 70 D2
Pearse Brothers Park 66 B1
Pearse Close 71 D1
Pearse Drive 71 D2
Pearse Gardens 70 C2
Pearse Green 71 D2
Pearse Park 71 D2
Pearse Road 70 D2
Pearse Square (Bray) 73 E4
Pearse Square (Central Dublin) 81 D4
Pearse Street (Central Dublin) 81 D4
Pearse Street (Sallynoggin) 71 D2
Pearse Villas 71 D2
Peartree Field 59 E4
Peck's Lane 24 B3
Pelletstown Manor 25 F3
Pemberton 76 B3
Pembroke Cottages
  (Donnybrook) 50 C3
Pembroke Cottages (Ringsend) 41 F3
Pembroke Gardens 50 C1
Pembroke Lane 81 C5
Pembroke Park 50 B2
Pembroke Place 50 C2
Pembroke Road 50 B1
Pembroke Row 81 C6
Pembroke Square 41 E4
Pembroke Street 41 F4
Pembroke Street Lower 81 C5
Pembroke Street Upper 81 C6
Penrose Street 41 E4
Percy French Road 48 A3
Percy Lane 50 B1

Percy Place 81 D5
Peter Row 81 A5
Peter Street 81 A5
Peter's Place 81 B6
Petrie Road 79 C6
Pheasant Run The Drive 13 D3
Pheasant Run The Grove 13 D3
Pheasant Run The Park 13 D3
Phibblestown House 12 B4
Phibsborough Avenue 40 B1
Phibsborough Road 78 D1
Philipsburgh Avenue 28 A4
Philipsburgh Terrace 28 A4
Philomena Terrace 41 F4
Phoenix Avenue 24 B3
Phoenix Court 24 B3
Phoenix Drive 24 B3
Phoenix Gardens 24 C3
Phoenix Place 24 B3
Phoenix Street 38 B4
Phoenix Street North 78 C3
Pickford's Terrace 41 E3
Pig Lane 80 C1
Pigeon House Road 42 A4
Pim Street 79 B5
Pimlico 79 C5
Pine Avenue 69 F2
Pine Copse Road 67 E1
Pine Court (Blackrock) 59 F4
Pine Court (Portmarnock) 10 B2
Pine Grove Park 4 C2
Pine Grove Road 4 C2
Pine Haven 59 D2
Pine Lawn (Dean's Grange) 60 A4
Pine Lawn (Tallaght) 64 A1
Pine Lodge 10 C2
Pine Road 42 A4
Pine Valley Avenue 67 E2
Pine Valley Drive 67 E2
Pine Valley Grove 67 E3
Pine Valley Park 67 D2
Pine Valley Way 67 E3
Pinebrook Avenue 28 C2
Pinebrook Close 13 E4
Pinebrook Crescent 28 C2
Pinebrook Downs 13 E4
Pinebrook Drive 28 D2
Pinebrook Glen 13 E4
Pinebrook Grove 28 D2
Pinebrook Heights 13 E4
Pinebrook Lawn 13 E4
Pinebrook Rise 28 D2
Pinebrook Road 28 D2
Pinebrook Vale 13 E4
Pinebrook View 13 E4
Pinehurst 39 E1
Pinetree Crescent 53 F2
Pinetree Grove 53 F2
Pineview Avenue 64 A2
Pineview Drive 64 A2
Pineview Grove 64 A2
Pineview Lawn 64 A2
Pineview Park 64 A2
Pineview Rise 64 A2
Pineview Road 64 A2
Pinewood 75 D1
Pinewood Avenue 17 E4
Pinewood Close 77 D3
Pinewood Court 13 E3
Pinewood Crescent 17 E4
Pinewood Drive 17 F4
Pinewood Green 17 F4
Pinewood Grove 17 F4
Pinewood Park 56 A4
Pinewood Villas 17 E4
Pinewoods 48 C1
Pleasants Street 81 A6
Plums Road 68 B1

Plunkett Avenue (Finglas West) 16 B4
Plunkett Avenue (Foxrock) 69 F3
Plunkett Court 60 C4
Plunkett Crescent 16 B3
Plunkett Drive 16 B4
Plunkett Green 16 B4
Plunkett Road 16 C4
Poddle Close 48 C3
Poddle Green 48 C4
Poddle Park 48 C4
Poolbeg Street 80 B3
Poole Street 79 C5
Poplar Row 41 D1
Poppintree Park Lane West 17 D3
Portan Road 12 B1
Porter's Avenue 23 D2
Porter's Road 23 D2
Portersfield 23 D2
Portersgate Avenue 22 B2
Portersgate Close 22 B2
Portersgate Court 22 B2
Portersgate Crescent 22 B2
Portersgate Drive 22 B2
Portersgate Grove 22 B2
Portersgate Heights 22 B1
Portersgate Lawn 22 B2
Portersgate View 22 B2
Portersgate Way 22 B2
Porterstown Road 22 C3
Portland Place 40 C1
Portland Row 80 C1
Portland Street North 40 C1
Portmahon Drive 79 A5
Portmarnock Avenue 10 C2
Portmarnock Crescent 10 C2
Portmarnock Drive 10 B2
Portmarnock Grove 10 C2
Portmarnock Park 10 B2
Portmarnock Rise 10 C2
Portmarnock Walk 10 B2
Portobello Harbour 49 E1
Portobello Road 49 F2
Pottery Road 70 B2
Power's Court 81 D5
Premier Square 26 B2
Price's Place 50 A2
Prices Lane 80 B3
Priestfield Cottages 79 B6
Primrose Avenue 78 D1
Primrose Grove 20 B3
Primrose Lane 34 C2
Primrose Road 20 A3
Primrose Street 78 D1
Prince Arthur Terrace 49 F3
Prince's Street North 80 B3
Prince's Street South 80 C3
Princeton 58 B2
Prior Walk Manor Grove 55 F1
Priorswood Road 20 A3
Priory Avenue 59 E3
Priory Drive 59 D3
Priory East 25 F4
Priory Grove 59 D3
Priory Hall (Donaghmede) 21 D3
Priory Hall (Stillorgan) 59 D3
Priory North 25 F3
Priory Road 49 D3
Priory West 25 F4
Proby Garden 59 F3
Proby Square 59 F3
Promenade Road 42 A4
Prospect Avenue 66 A2
Prospect Avenue (Glasnevin) 27 D4
Prospect Court 66 A2
Prospect Downs 66 A2
Prospect Drive 66 A2
Prospect Glen 66 A2
Prospect Grove 66 A2

Prospect Heath 66 A2
Prospect Hills 26 B2
Prospect Lane 50 B4
Prospect Lawn 70 B3
Prospect Manor 66 A2
Prospect Meadow 66 A2
Prospect Square 27 D4
Prospect View 66 A2
Prospect Way 27 D4
Prussia Street 78 B1
Pucks Castle Lane 74 B4
Purley Park 10 B1
Putland Road 77 E2

Q

Quarry Drive 48 A4
Quarry Road 39 F1
Quarryfield Court 46 A4
Queen Street 78 C3
Queen's Park 60 B3
Queen's Road 61 D3
Quinn Avenue 79 A4
Quinn's Road 75 F4
Quinsborough Road 77 D1

R

Radcliff Hall 51 E2
Radlett Grove 10 B2
Rafters Avenue 48 B2
Rafters Lane 48 B2
Rafters Road 48 B2
Raglan Lane 50 C2
Raglan Road 50 C2
Raheen Avenue 63 D1
Raheen Close 63 D1
Raheen Court 63 D1
Raheen Crescent 63 D1
Raheen Drive (Ballyfermot) 46 C1
Raheen Drive (Tallaght) 63 D1
Raheen Green 63 E1
Raheen Lawn 77 F2
Raheen Park (Ballyfermot) 46 C1
Raheen Park (Bray) 77 E2
Raheen Park (Tallaght) 63 D1
Raheen Road 63 D1
Raheny Park 30 B2
Raheny Road 30 A1
Railway Avenue (Baldoyle) 11 E4
Railway Avenue (Inchicore) 47 F1
Railway Avenue (Malahide) 7 D2
Railway Court 7 D2
Railway Street 80 C2
Rainsford Cottages 75 E1
Rainsford Street 79 C4
Ralahine 71 E4
Raleigh Square 48 B2
Ramillies Road 38 A4
Ramleh Close 50 B4
Ramleh Park 50 B4
Ramley View 23 E3
Rampart Lane 50 C3
Ranelagh Avenue 50 A2
Ranelagh Road 50 A3
Range Lodge Avenue 21 E3
Raphoe Road 48 B2
Rath Geal 44 C3
Rathbeale Court 5 D3
Rathbeale Crescent 4 C3
Rathbeale Rise 4 C3
Rathbeale Road 4 C3
Rathborne Avenue 25 E3
Rathborne Close 25 E3

Name	Page	Grid
Rathborne Place	25	E3
Rathborne Way	25	E3
Rathclaren	76	C2
Rathdown Avenue	56	B2
Rathdown Crescent	56	B2
Rathdown Drive	56	B2
Rathdown Park	56	B2
Rathdown Road (Carrickmines)	74	B1
Rathdown Road (Phibsborough)	78	C1
Rathdown Square	78	B1
Rathdown Terrace	68	A2
Rathdown Villas	56	B1
Rathdrum Road	49	D2
Rathfarnham Park	56	B2
Rathfarnham Road	56	B2
Rathfarnham Wood	56	C3
Rathgar Avenue	49	E4
Rathgar Road	49	E4
Rathgar Villas	49	E4
Rathingle Road (Hilltown, north)	4	B4
Rathingle Road (Hilltown, south)	8	B1
Rathlin Road	27	E3
Kathlyon Park	65	D2
Rathmichael Dales	75	D4
Rathmichael Haven	74	C4
Rathmichael Manor	75	D3
Rathmichael Park	75	E3
Rathmichael Road	74	C3
Rathmichael Woods	75	E3
Rathmines Avenue	49	F3
Rathmines Park	49	F3
Rathmines Road Lower	49	F2
Rathmines Road Upper	49	F3
Rathmines Wood	49	F2
Rathmintin Crescent	62	C2
Rathmintin Drive	62	C2
Rathmore	10	A4
Rathmore Avenue (Stillorgan)	58	C4
Rathmore Avenue (Tyrellstown)	14	A1
Rathmore Crescent	14	A1
Rathmore Drive	14	A1
Rathmore Grove	14	A1
Rathmore Park	30	A2
Rathsallagh Avenue	75	E3
Rathsallagh Drive	75	E3
Rathsallagh Grove	75	E3
Rathsallagh Park	75	E3
Rathvale Avenue	20	B4
Rathvale Drive	20	B4
Rathvale Grove	20	B4
Rathvale Park	20	B4
Rathvilly Drive	25	F2
Rathvilly Park	25	F2
Ratoath Avenue	25	F1
Ratoath Drive	25	F1
Ratoath Estate	26	A4
Ratoath Road (Cabra)	39	E1
Ratoath Road (Finglas West)	25	F2
Ratra Park	25	F4
Ratra Road	25	E4
Ravens Court	26	A1
Ravens Rock Road	68	C2
Ravensdale Drive	48	C4
Ravensdale Park	48	C4
Ravensdale Road	41	E2
Ravenswell Road	73	E4
Ravenswood Avenue	12	C4
Ravenswood Crescent	13	D4
Ravenswood Drive	12	C4
Ravenswood Green	12	C4
Ravenswood Lawn	13	D4
Ravenswood Rise	12	C4
Ravenswood Road	12	C4
Ravenswood View	12	C4
Rawson Court	81	D6
Raymond Street	79	D6
Raymor Park	23	F2
Rectory Slopes	76	B2
Red Cow Lane	78	C3
Redberry	34	C4
Redesdale Crescent	58	C3
Redesdale Road	58	C3
Redfern Avenue	10	B2
Redmond's Hill	A5	B5
Redwood Avenue	54	A3
Redwood Close	54	A2
Redwood Court (Churchtown)	57	D2
Redwood Court (Tallaght)	53	F3
Redwood Drive	54	A3
Redwood Grove	59	E2
Redwood Heights	54	A2
Redwood Lawns	54	A2
Redwood Park	54	A2
Redwood Rise	54	A2
Redwood View	54	A2
Redwood Walk	54	A3
Reginald Street	79	C5
Rehoboth Avenue	79	B6
Rehoboth Place	79	B6
Reuben Avenue	79	B5
Reuben Street	79	B5
Reuben Walk	79	B5
Rialto Buildings	79	A5
Rialto Cottages	79	A5
Rialto Drive	79	A6
Rialto Street	79	A5
Ribh Avenue	29	F2
Ribh Road	29	E2
Richelieu Park	51	F3
Richmond	60	A4
Richmond Avenue (Ballybough)	41	D1
Richmond Avenue (Monkstown)	60	C3
Richmond Avenue South	50	A4
Richmond Cottages	80	C1
Richmond Cottages North	80	C1
Richmond Court	57	E1
Richmond Crescent	80	C1
Richmond Green	60	C3
Richmond Grove	60	B3
Richmond Hill (Monkstown)	60	C3
Richmond Hill (Rathmines)	49	F2
Richmond Mews	49	F2
Richmond Park (Bray)	76	B3
Richmond Park (Monkstown)	60	B3
Richmond Road	27	F4
Richmond Street	80	C1
Richmond Street South	49	F2
Richmond Villas	49	F2
Richview Park	50	A4
Riddlesford	77	D3
Ridge Hall	75	E1
Ridge Hill	75	E1
Ridgewood Avenue	8	B1
Ridgewood Cedars	8	B1
Ridgewood Close	8	B1
Ridgewood Court	8	A1
Ridgewood Green	8	B1
Ridgewood Park	8	B1
Ridgewood Square	8	B1
Ring Street	47	F1
Ring Terrace	47	F1
Ringsend Park	42	A4
Ringsend Road	41	E4
Ripley Court	76	C3
Ripley Hills	76	C3
River Close	75	E2
River Gardens	27	D3
River Lane Grove	75	E3
River Road (Ashtown)	25	D3
River Road (Castleknock)	24	A2
River Valley Avenue	4	C4
River Valley Close	4	B3
River Valley Court	4	B3
River Valley Drive	4	C4
River Valley Grove	4	C4
River Valley Heights	4	C4
River Valley Lawn	4	C4
River Valley Park	4	C4
River Valley Rise	4	C4
River Valley Road	4	B4
River Valley View	4	B3
River Valley Way	4	B4
Riverdale Apartments	76	B1
Riverlane	76	C1
Rivermount Cottages	26	C3
Riverpark View	13	F3
Riversdale	58	A4
Riversdale Avenue	56	C1
Riversdale Avenue (Clondalkin)	46	A4
Riversdale Avenue (Palmerstown)	37	D2
Riversdale Crescent	45	F3
Riversdale Drive	45	F3
Riversdale Green	45	F2
Riversdale Grove	37	D2
Riversdale Park (Clondalkin)	45	F2
Riversdale Park (Palmerstown)	37	D2
Riversdale Road	45	F3
Riverside	45	F3
Riverside Avenue	19	E3
Riverside Cottages	56	A3
Riverside Crescent	19	E3
Riverside Drive (Coolock)	19	E3
Riverside Drive (Palmerstown)	37	D2
Riverside Drive (Rathfarnham)	57	D2
Riverside Grove	19	E3
Riverside Park	19	E3
Riverside Road	19	E3
Rivervale	25	E3
Riverview	37	D2
Riverview Court	38	A3
Riverwood Avenue	23	E4
Riverwood Chase	23	D3
Riverwood Close	23	D3
Riverwood Court	23	D3
Riverwood Crescent	23	D3
Riverwood Dale	23	D3
Riverwood Dene	23	D3
Riverwood Drive	23	D3
Riverwood Gardens	23	D3
Riverwood Glebe	23	D3
Riverwood Glen	23	D3
Riverwood Green	23	E3
Riverwood Grove	23	D3
Riverwood Hall	23	E3
Riverwood Heath	23	D3
Riverwood Lawn	23	D3
Riverwood Park	23	E3
Riverwood Place	23	D3
Riverwood Road	23	D3
Riverwood Terrace	23	D3
Riverwood Vale	23	D3
Riverwood View	23	D3
Riverwood Way	23	E3
Robert Emmett Close	79	C4
Robert Street	40	C1
Robert Street South	79	B5
Robin Villas	37	D2
Robinhood Road	47	D3
Robinsons Court	79	C5
Robswall	7	F3
Rochestown Avenue	70	B1
Rochestown Park	71	D2
Rochfort Avenue	35	F4
Rochfort Close	35	F3
Rochfort Crescent	35	F4
Rochfort Park	35	F3
Rochfort Way	35	F4
Rock Hill	59	F2
Rock Lodge	72	A4
Rock Road	59	E1
Rockfield	34	C4
Rockfield Apartments	58	A4
Rockfield Avenue	55	E1
Rockfield Close	23	E2
Rockfield Drive (Clondalkin)	53	D1
Rockfield Drive (Clonsilla)	23	E3
Rockfield Drive (Kimmage)	55	F1
Rockfield Park	23	E2
Rockford Manor	60	B4
Rockford Park	60	B4
Rockford Terrace	60	A4
Rockfort Avenue	72	B2
Rocks Yard Lane	61	F4
Rockview	67	F3
Rockville Crescent	60	A3
Rockville Drive	60	A3
Rockville Road	60	A3
Rockwood	34	C4
Rocwood	69	E1
Roebuck Avenue	58	B2
Roebuck Castle	58	A2
Roebuck Downs	58	A2
Roebuck Drive	48	A4
Roebuck Road	58	B2
Rollins Court	71	D1
Rollins Villas	71	D1
Roncalli Road	31	D1
Rope Walk Place	41	F4
Rory O'Connor Park	60	B4
Ros Mor View Apartments	65	E1
Rosary Gardens East	61	D3
Rosary Gardens West	61	D3
Rosary Road	79	B5
Rosbeg Court	31	D1
Rosberry	44	B1
Rose Park	70	B1
Rosebank (Clondalkin)	45	F2
Rosebank (Tallaght)	64	A1
Rosedale	12	C4
Roseglen Avenue	30	C1
Roseglen Road	30	B1
Rosehaven	23	E3
Roselawn	35	E2
Roselawn Avenue	23	F2
Roselawn Close	23	F2
Roselawn Court	24	A2
Roselawn Crescent	23	E2
Roselawn Drive	23	F2
Roselawn Glade	23	E2
Roselawn Grove	23	F2
Roselawn Park	77	E3
Roselawn Road	23	E2
Roselawn View	23	F2
Roselawn Walk	23	F2
Roselawn Way	24	A2
Rosemount Avenue	29	E2
Rosemount Court (Booterstown)	59	D1
Rosemount Court (Goatstown)	58	A3
Rosemount Crescent	58	A1
Rosemount Estate	57	F3
Rosemount Glade	58	A1
Rosemount Park	57	F3
Rosemount Park Drive	15	E3
Rosemount Park Road	15	D3
Rosemount Road	40	A1
Rosemount Terrace (Booterstown)	59	D1
Rosemount Terrace (Central Dublin)	78	C3
Rosery Terrace	41	F4
Roseville Court	73	E4
Rosewood Grove	35	F4
Rosmeen Gardens	61	E4
Rosmeen Park	61	E4
Ross Road	81	A4
Ross Street	78	B2
Rosse Court	35	F4
Rossfield Avenue	52	C4
Rossfield Close	52	C4
Rossfield Drive	52	C4
Rossfield Gardens	52	C4
Rossfield Park	53	D4

Name	Page	Ref
Rossfield Way	52	C4
Rosslyn Court	77	D2
Rossmore Avenue (Ballyfermot)	37	F4
Rossmore Avenue (Templeogue)	55	E3
Rossmore Close	55	E3
Rossmore Crescent	55	E3
Rossmore Drive (Ballyfermot)	37	F4
Rossmore Drive (Templeogue)	55	E3
Rossmore Grove	55	E3
Rossmore Lawns	55	E3
Rossmore Park	55	E3
Rossmore Road (Ballyfermot)	37	F3
Rossmore Road (Templeogue)	55	E3
Rossmore Terrace	37	F3
Rostrevor Road	57	D1
Rostrevor Terrace	57	D1
Rothe Abbey	48	B1
Rowan Park	60	A3
Rowan Park Avenue	60	A4
Rowanbyrn	60	A4
Rowans Road	68	B2
Rowlagh Avenue	36	B4
Rowlagh Crescent	36	A4
Rowlagh Gardens	36	B4
Rowlagh Green	36	B4
Rowlagh Park	36	B4
Royal Canal Bank	78	D1
Royal Canal Park	25	F3
Royal Marine Park	73	F4
Royal Oak	18	C3
Royal Terrace East	61	D4
Royal Terrace West	61	D4
Royse Road	40	B1
Royston	48	B4
Royston Village	48	B4
Ruby Hall	70	B1
Rugby Road	50	A2
Rugged Lane	22	C4
Rushbrook	23	F2
Rushbrook Avenue	55	D2
Rushbrook Crescent	55	D2
Rushbrook Grove	55	D2
Rushbrook Park	55	D2
Rushbrook Road	55	D2
Rushbrook View	55	D2
Rushbrook Way	55	D2
Rusheeney Avenue	13	D4
Rusheeney Close	13	D4
Rusheeney Court	13	D4
Rusheeney Crescent	13	D3
Rusheeney Green	13	D3
Rusheeney Grove	13	D4
Rusheeney Manor	13	D3
Rusheeney Park	13	D4
Rusheeney View	13	D4
Rusheeney Way	13	D4
Russell Avenue (Ballybough)	40	C1
Russell Avenue (Jobstown)	62	C1
Russell Avenue East	41	E2
Russell Court	62	C1
Russell Crescent	62	C1
Russell Downs	62	C1
Russell Drive	62	C1
Russell Lane	62	C1
Russell Lawns	62	C1
Russell Meadows	62	C1
Russell Place	62	C1
Russell Rise	62	C1
Russell Street	40	C1
Rutland Avenue	49	D2
Rutland Grove	49	D2
Rutland Place	80	B2
Rutland Place North	80	C1
Rutland Street	80	C1
Rutledge Terrace	79	C6
Ryder's Row	80	A3
Ryecroft	77	D2

S

Name	Page	Ref
Sackville Avenue	41	D1
Sackville Place	80	B3
Saddlers Avenue	13	F3
Saddlers Close	14	A3
Saddlers Court	49	F2
Saddlers Crescent	13	F3
Saddlers Drive	13	F3
Saddlers Glade	13	F3
Saddlers Grove	13	F3
Saddlers Lawn	13	F3
Saddlers Place	49	F2
Saint Agnes Park	48	B3
Saint Agnes Road	48	B3
Saint Agnes Terrace	48	A3
Saint Aidan's Drive	58	A2
Saint Aidan's Park Avenue	28	B4
Saint Aidan's Park Road	28	B4
Saint Alban's Park	51	E3
Saint Alban's Road	79	C6
Saint Alphonsus Road	27	E4
Saint Andrew Street	81	B4
Saint Andrews Drive	35	E2
Saint Andrews Fairway	35	E3
Saint Andrews Green	35	F2
Saint Andrews Grove	7	D2
Saint Andrews Park	4	C2
Saint Andrews Wood	35	F2
Saint Anne's	55	F1
Saint Anne's Avenue	30	A3
Saint Anne's Drive	30	A3
Saint Anne's Park (Killester)	29	F4
Saint Anne's Park (Shankill)	73	E1
Saint Anne's Road	40	C1
Saint Anne's Road South	49	D2
Saint Anne's Square	59	F2
Saint Anne's Square Lower	10	B4
Saint Anne's Terrace (Raheny)	30	A2
Saint Anne's Terrace (Ranelagh)	50	A2
Saint Anthony's Avenue	45	F4
Saint Anthony's Crescent (Dolphin's Barn)	79	A5
Saint Anthony's Crescent (Greenhills)	55	D1
Saint Anthony's Road	79	A5
Saint Aongus Court	54	C3
Saint Aongus Crescent	54	C3
Saint Aongus Green	54	C3
Saint Aongus Grove	54	C3
Saint Aongus Lawn	54	C3
Saint Aongus Park	54	C3
Saint Aongus Road	54	C3
Saint Assam's Avenue	30	B2
Saint Assam's Drive	30	B2
Saint Assam's Park	30	B2
Saint Assam's Road East	30	B2
Saint Assam's Road West	30	B2
Saint Attracta Road	26	C4
Saint Aubyn's Court	75	E2
Saint Augustine Street	79	C4
Saint Augustine's Park	59	F4
Saint Begnet's Villas	72	A2
Saint Berach's Place	30	B1
Saint Brendan's Avenue	29	E1
Saint Brendan's Cottages	41	F4
Saint Brendan's Crescent	54	C1
Saint Brendan's Drive	29	E1
Saint Brendan's Park	29	E1
Saint Brendan's Road	40	B1
Saint Brendan's Terrace	29	D1
Saint Bricin's Park	78	B3
Saint Bridget's Avenue	41	E1
Saint Bridget's Drive	54	C1
Saint Brigid's Church Road	59	E4
Saint Brigid's Close	29	D2
Saint Brigid's Cottages	46	B4
Saint Brigid's Crescent	29	D2
Saint Brigid's Drive (Clondalkin)	45	F4
Saint Brigid's Drive (Killester)	29	D2
Saint Brigid's Green	29	D2
Saint Brigid's Grove	29	D2
Saint Brigid's Lawn	29	D2
Saint Brigid's Park (Blanchardstown)	23	F2
Saint Brigid's Park (Clondalkin)	45	F4
Saint Brigid's Park (Cornelscourt)	70	A3
Saint Brigid's Road (Clondalkin)	45	F4
Saint Brigid's Road (Killester)	29	D2
Saint Brigid's Road Lower	40	C1
Saint Brigid's Road Upper	40	C1
Saint Broc's Cottages	50	C3
Saint Canice's Park	27	D2
Saint Canice's Road	27	D2
Saint Catherine's Avenue	79	C6
Saint Catherine's Park	71	F1
Saint Catherine's Road	71	F1
Saint Claire's Terrace	76	C3
Saint Clare's Avenue	49	E2
Saint Clare's Terrace	49	E2
Saint Clement's Road	40	C1
Saint Colomba's Road Lower	40	C1
Saint Columba's Road	54	C1
Saint Columba's Road Upper	40	C1
Saint Columbanus Avenue	57	E1
Saint Columbanus Road	57	E1
Saint Columbas Heights	4	C3
Saint Columbas Rise	4	C3
Saint Columcills Drive	5	D3
Saint Columcills Park	5	D3
Saint Conleth's Road	55	D1
Saint Cronan's Avenue	4	B3
Saint Cronan's Close	4	B3
Saint Cronan's Court	4	B3
Saint Cronan's Grove	4	B3
Saint Cronan's Lawn	4	B3
Saint Cronan's View	4	B3
Saint Cronan's Way	4	B3
Saint David's	28	C2
Saint David's Wood	28	C2
Saint Declan's Road	28	B4
Saint Dominic's Avenue	64	B1
Saint Dominic's Road	64	B1
Saint Dominic's Terrace	64	B1
Saint Donagh's Crescent	21	D4
Saint Donagh's Park	21	D4
Saint Donagh's Road	21	D4
Saint Eithne Road	26	C4
Saint Enda's Drive	56	B4
Saint Enda's Park	56	B4
Saint Enda's Road	49	E4
Saint Finbar's Road	26	B4
Saint Finbar's Close	54	C1
Saint Finian's Avenue	35	D3
Saint Finian's Close	35	D3
Saint Finian's Crescent	35	D3
Saint Fintan Road	26	C4
Saint Fintan's Crescent	32	C3
Saint Fintan's Park (Dean's Grange)	70	B1
Saint Fintan's Park (Howth)	32	B3
Saint Fintan's Road	32	B3
Saint Fintan's Terrace	37	E2
Saint Fintan's Villas	60	B4
Saint Gabriel's	70	C3
Saint Gabriel's Road	29	F4
Saint Gall Gardens North	57	E1
Saint Gall Gardens South	57	E2
Saint Gatien Court	56	B4
Saint George's Avenue (Ballybough)	40	C1
Saint George's Avenue (Killiney)	71	F4
Saint Gerard's Road	55	D1
Saint Helen's Road	59	D1
Saint Helena's Drive	26	B2
Saint Helena's Road	26	A2
Saint Helier's Copse	59	E3
Saint Ignatius Road	40	C1
Saint Ita's Road	27	E3
Saint James Court	51	D2
Saint James's Avenue	41	D1
Saint James's Road	47	F4
Saint James's Terrace (Dolphin's Barn)	79	B6
Saint James's Terrace (Sandymount)	51	D1
Saint James's Wood	39	E4
Saint Jarlath Road	26	C4
Saint John's	51	E3
Saint John's Avenue	45	E4
Saint John's Close	45	E4
Saint John's Court (Clondalkin)	45	E4
Saint John's Court (Coolock)	28	C1
Saint John's Court (Santry)	18	B4
Saint John's Crescent	45	E4
Saint John's Drive	45	E4
Saint John's Gate	45	E4
Saint John's Lawn	45	E4
Saint John's Park	60	C4
Saint John's Park East	45	E4
Saint John's Road (Clondalkin)	45	E4
Saint John's Road (Sandymount)	51	E2
Saint John's Road West	39	E3
Saint John's Way	45	E4
Saint John's Wood (Clondalkin)	45	E4
Saint John's Wood (Clontarf)	29	D4
Saint John's Wood (Terenure)	56	C1
Saint Joseph's Avenue (Ballybough)	41	D1
Saint Joseph's Avenue (Drumcondra)	40	C1
Saint Joseph's Parade	80	A1
Saint Joseph's Place	78	B2
Saint Joseph's Road	78	B2
Saint Joseph's Square	42	C1
Saint Kevin's Avenue	79	D5
Saint Kevin's Cottages	81	A6
Saint Kevin's Court	57	D1
Saint Kevin's Gardens	57	D1
Saint Kevin's Parade	79	D6
Saint Kevin's Park (Dartry)	57	D1
Saint Kevin's Park (Stillorgan)	58	C4
Saint Kevin's Road	49	E2
Saint Kevin's Square	77	D1
Saint Kevin's Terrace	77	D1
Saint Kevin's Villas	71	D1
Saint Killian's Avenue	54	C1
Saint Killian's Park	45	F3
Saint Laurence Road	38	A3
Saint Lawrence Road (Clontarf)	28	C4
Saint Lawrence Road (Howth)	33	D1
Saint Luke's Crescent	57	F1
Saint Maelruans Park	64	A1
Saint Magdalen Terrace	41	F4
Saint Malachy's Drive	55	D1
Saint Malachy's Road	27	E3
Saint Margaret's	59	E2
Saint Margaret's Avenue	30	D1
Saint Margaret's Close	72	A2
Saint Margaret's Park	7	D3
Saint Margaret's Road (Finglas)	16	C3
Saint Margaret's Road (Malahide)	7	D2
Saint Margaret's Terrace	7	D2
Saint Mark's Avenue	36	B4
Saint Mark's Crescent	36	B4
Saint Mark's Drive	36	B4
Saint Mark's Green	36	B4
Saint Mark's Grove	36	A4
Saint Marnocks Avenue	10	B4
Saint Martin's Drive	48	C4
Saint Martin's Park	48	C4
Saint Mary's Avenue	56	B3
Saint Mary's Avenue West	38	C4

Saint Mary's Crescent	48	A3
Saint Mary's Drive	48	A3
Saint Mary's Park (Crumlin)	48	A3
Saint Mary's Park (Finglas)	25	E1
Saint Mary's Place	33	E2
Saint Mary's Road (Ballsbridge)	50	B1
Saint Mary's Road (Crumlin)	48	A3
Saint Mary's Road (North Wall)	41	E2
Saint Mary's Road North	41	E2
Saint Mary's Street	61	D3
Saint Mary's Terrace	80	A2
Saint Mel's Avenue	54	C1
Saint Michael's Close	79	D4
Saint Michael's Cottages	21	D2
Saint Michael's Estate	39	D4
Saint Michael's Hill	79	D4
Saint Michael's Road	27	E3
Saint Michael's Terrace	79	D6
Saint Mochan's Street	78	D3
Saint Mobhi Boithirin	27	D3
Saint Mochtas Avenue	23	D2
Saint Mochtas Chase	23	D2
Saint Mochtas Close	23	D2
Saint Mochtas Drive	23	D2
Saint Mochtas Glen	23	D2
Saint Mochtas Green	23	D2
Saint Mochtas Grove	23	D2
Saint Mochtas Lawns	23	D2
Saint Mochtas Road	23	D2
Saint Mochtas Vale	23	D2
Saint Mura's Terrace	41	E2
Saint Nathy's Villas	57	E3
Saint Nessan's Close	33	D2
Saint Nicholas Place	81	B4
Saint Oliver's Park	46	A1
Saint Pappin's Green	27	D1
Saint Pappin's Road	27	D1
Saint Patrick's Close	81	A5
Saint Patrick's Cottages	56	B4
Saint Patrick's Crescent	60	C4
Saint Patrick's Park (Clondalkin)	45	E2
Saint Patrick's Park (Clonsilla)	23	F2
Saint Patrick's Road (Ballybough)	40	C1
Saint Patrick's Road (Clondalkin)	45	E2
Saint Patrick's Road (Dalkey)	72	B2
Saint Patrick's Road (Walkinstown)	55	D1
Saint Patrick's Terrace	38	C4
Saint Paul's Drive	55	D1
Saint Peter's Crescent	47	F4
Saint Peter's Drive	47	F4
Saint Peter's Road (Bray)	73	E4
Saint Peter's Road (Phibsborough)	40	A1
Saint Peter's Road (Walkinstown)	47	F4
Saint Peter's Terrace	33	D2
Saint Raphaels	68	C1
Saint Ronan's Avenue	45	E1
Saint Ronan's Close	45	E1
Saint Ronan's Crescent	45	E1
Saint Ronan's Drive	36	A4
Saint Ronan's Gardens	45	E1
Saint Ronan's Green	45	E1
Saint Ronan's Park	36	A4
Saint Ronan's Way	45	E1
Saint Samson	20	C2
Saint Stephen's Green East	50	A1
Saint Stephen's Green North	81	B5
Saint Stephen's Green South	81	B5
Saint Stephen's Green West	81	B5
Saint Sylvester Villas	7	D3
Saint Teresa Place	27	D4
Saint Teresa Road	27	D4
Saint Teresa's Road	48	B4
Saint Theresa's Gardens	79	C6
Saint Thomas Mead	58	C2
Saint Thomas Road (Dolphin's Barn)	79	C5
Saint Thomas Road (Mount Merrion)	58	C2
Saint Vincent Street South	79	D6
Saint Vincent Street West	48	A1
Saint Vincent's Park	60	A3
Saint Werburgh's	5	E4
Saintbury Avenue	71	F4
Salamanca	58	B3
Sallowood View	18	B3
Sally Park	65	D1
Sallymount Avenue	50	B2
Sallymount Gardens	50	B2
Sallymount Terrace	50	A3
Sallynoggin Park	70	C2
Sallynoggin Road	70	C2
Sallypark Close	55	D2
Salthill	60	C3
Salzburg	58	B3
Sampsons Lane	80	B3
Sandford Avenue (Dolphin's Barn)	79	C6
Sandford Avenue (Ranelagh)	50	B3
Sandford Close	50	B3
Sandford Gardens	79	C6
Sandford Road	50	B3
Sandford Wood	4	C2
Sandwith Street Lower	81	D4
Sandwith Street Upper	81	D4
Sandycove Avenue East	72	A1
Sandycove Avenue North	72	A1
Sandycove Avenue West	72	A1
Sandycove Point	72	A1
Sandycove Road	72	A1
Sandyford Downs	68	B3
Sandyford Hall Avenue	68	C4
Sandyford Hall Court	68	C4
Sandyford Hall Crescent	68	C4
Sandyford Hall Drive	68	C4
Sandyford Hall Green	68	C4
Sandyford Hall Grove	68	C4
Sandyford Hall Lawn	68	C4
Sandyford Hall Park	68	C3
Sandyford Hall Rise	68	C4
Sandyford Hall Walk	68	C4
Sandyford Road (Dundrum)	58	A4
Sandyford Road (Sandyford)	68	A1
Sandyford Village	68	B3
Sandyhill Avenue	17	F4
Sandyhill Close	17	F3
Sandyhill Court	17	F3
Sandyhill Gardens	17	F4
Sandymount Avenue	51	D2
Sandymount Castle Drive	51	E2
Sandymount Castle Park	51	E2
Sandymount Castle Road	51	E2
Sandymount Court	51	E1
Sandymount Green	51	E2
Sandymount Road	51	D1
Sans Souci Park	59	D2
Santry Avenue	18	A3
Santry Close	18	C3
Santry Court	18	C3
Santry Villas	18	C3
Santry Way	18	B3
Santry Woods	18	A3
Sarah Curran Avenue	56	B4
Saran Wood	76	B4
Sarsfield Park	34	C2
Sarsfield Road	38	C4
Sarsfield Street (Phibsborough)	80	A1
Sarsfield Street (Sallynoggin)	71	D1
Sarto Lawn (Baldoyle)	21	F4
Sarto Lawn (Sutton)	31	D1
Sarto Park	31	D1
Sarto Road	31	D1
Saul Road	48	D2
Saval Park Gardens	72	A3
Saval Park Road	72	A3
Scholarstown Interchange	64	C2
Scholarstown Park	65	F1
Scholarstown Road	65	F1
School Street	79	C4
School's Road	76	C3
Schoolhouse Lane	18	C4
Scott Park	77	E3
Scribblestown Avenue	25	E2
Scribblestown Close	25	F2
Scribblestown Grove	25	F2
Scribblestown Park	25	F2
Scribblestown Place (Finglas)	25	E2
Scribblestown Road (Ashtown)	25	D2
Scribblestown Road	25	F2
Sea Road	6	C2
Sea View Terrace	33	D2
Seabury	51	E2
Seabury Avenue	6	B1
Seabury Close	6	B2
Seabury Court	6	B2
Seabury Crescent	6	B2
Seabury Dale	6	B2
Seabury Downs	6	B2
Seabury Drive	6	B2
Seabury Gardens	6	A1
Seabury Glen	6	B1
Seabury Green	6	B2
Seabury Grove	6	B2
Seabury Heights	6	A2
Seabury Lane	6	B2
Seabury Lawns	6	A2
Seabury Meadows	6	A1
Seabury Orchard	6	B1
Seabury Park	6	A2
Seabury Place	6	B2
Seabury Road	6	A2
Seabury View	6	A2
Seabury Walk	6	B2
Seabury Wood	6	A1
Seacliff Avenue	21	F4
Seacliff Drive	21	F4
Seacliff Road	21	F4
Seacourt	29	F4
Seacrest	77	D2
Seafield	75	F3
Seafield Avenue (Clontarf)	29	F4
Seafield Avenue (Monkstown)	60	B3
Seafield Close	58	C1
Seafield Court (Killiney)	75	F2
Seafield Court (Malahide)	7	D2
Seafield Crescent	58	C1
Seafield Downs	43	D1
Seafield Drive	58	C1
Seafield Grove	29	F4
Seafield Park	58	C1
Seafield Road (Ballybrack)	75	E2
Seafield Road (Booterstown)	58	C1
Seafield Road East	29	E4
Seafield Road West	29	E4
Seafort Avenue	51	E1
Seafort Gardens	51	D1
Seafort Parade	59	E1
Seafort Villas	51	E1
Seagrange Avenue	21	F3
Seagrange Drive	21	F4
Seagrange Road	21	F3
Seagrave	10	A4
Seamount	59	D1
Seamount Drive	7	E3
Seamount Grove	7	E3
Seamount Heights	7	E3
Seamount Park	7	E3
Seamount Road	7	E3
Seamount View	5	E4
Seamus Ennis Road	26	B1
Sean MacDermott Street Lower	80	C2
Sean MacDermott Street Upper	80	B2
Sean Moore Road	42	A4
Sean O'Casey Avenue	80	C1
Seapark (Clontarf)	29	F4
Seapark (Malahide)	7	E3
Seapark Drive	43	D1
Seapark Hill	7	E3
Seapark Road	29	F4
Seapoint Avenue	60	B2
Seapoint Court	73	F4
Seapoint Road	73	F4
Seatown Road	5	E2
Seatown Villas	5	D2
Seatown Walk	5	E3
Seaview Avenue	41	E2
Seaview Avenue North	42	A1
Seaview Lawn	75	E3
Seaview Park	75	E3
Seaview Terrace	51	D3
Seaview Wood	75	E3
Second Avenue	80	D2
Sefton	70	C1
Selskar Terrace	50	A2
Serpentine Avenue	51	D2
Serpentine Park	51	D1
Serpentine Road	51	D1
Serpentine Terrace	51	D2
Seskin View Avenue	64	A1
Seskin View Drive	64	B1
Seskin View Park	64	B2
Seskin View Road	64	B1
Setanta Place	81	C4
Seven Oaks (Drumcondra)	27	F3
Seven Oaks (Inchicore)	38	C4
Seville Place	80	D2
Seville Terrace	80	D1
Seymour Road	73	F4
Shackleton	13	E3
Shamrock Place	80	D1
Shamrock Street	78	D1
Shamrock Terrace	80	D1
Shamrock Villas	49	E3
Shanagarry	57	E1
Shanard Avenue	27	E1
Shanard Road	27	E1
Shanboley Road	28	A1
Shancastle Avenue	36	B3
Shancastle Close	36	B3
Shancastle Crescent	36	B3
Shancastle Drive	36	B3
Shancastle Lawns	36	B3
Shancastle Park	36	B3
Shandon Crescent	26	C4
Shandon Drive	40	A1
Shandon Gardens	26	C4
Shandon Mill	27	D4
Shandon Park (Monkstown)	60	A3
Shandon Park (Phibsborough)	26	C4
Shandon Road	40	A1
Shangan Avenue	18	A4
Shangan Crescent	18	A4
Shangan Gardens	18	B4
Shangan Green	18	B4
Shangan Road	18	A4
Shanganagh Cliffs	75	F3
Shanganagh Grove	75	F4
Shanganagh Road	27	E4
Shanganagh Road (Ballybrack)	75	E2
Shanganagh Terrace	75	E1
Shanganagh Vale	74	C1
Shanganagh Wood	75	E3
Shanglas Road	28	A1
Shanid Road	49	D4
Shanliss Avenue	18	B4
Shanliss Drive	18	B4
Shanliss Gardens	18	A4
Shanliss Grove	18	B4
Shanliss Park	27	F1
Shanliss Road	18	A4
Shanliss Walk	18	B4

Name	Page	Grid
Shanliss Way	18	B4
Shanowen Avenue	27	E1
Shanowen Crescent	27	F1
Shanowen Drive	27	E1
Shanowen Grove	27	E1
Shanowen Hall	27	E1
Shanowen Park	27	E1
Shanowen Road	27	F1
Shanowen Square	27	E1
Shanrath Road	28	A1
Shantalla Avenue	28	A1
Shantalla Drive	28	A1
Shantalla Park	28	A1
Shantalla Road	28	A1
Shanvarna Road	28	A1
Sharavogue	71	E1
Shaw Street	81	C4
Shaw's Lane	50	C1
Sheelin Avenue	75	E2
Sheelin Drive	75	E2
Sheelin Hill	75	E1
Sheephill Avenue	14	C3
Sheephill Park	14	B3
Sheepmoor Avenue	13	F4
Sheepmoor Close	23	D1
Sheepmoor Crescent	13	F4
Sheepmoor Gardens	13	F4
Sheepmoor Green	13	F4
Sheepmoor Grove	13	F4
Sheepmoor Lawn	13	F4
Sheepmoor Way	13	F4
Shelbourne Lane	50	C2
Shelbourne Road	50	C1
Shelerin Road	22	C2
Shellysbanks Road	42	B4
Shelmalier Road	41	E2
Shelmartin Avenue	28	A4
Shelmartin Terrace	28	A4
Shelton Drive	48	B4
Shelton Gardens	48	B4
Shelton Grove	48	B4
Shelton Park	48	B4
Sheriff Street Lower	80	D2
Sheriff Street Upper	41	E3
Sherkin Gardens	27	F3
Sherrard Avenue	40	C1
Sherrard Street Lower	40	C1
Sherrard Street Upper	80	B1
Shielmartin Drive	32	B3
Shielmartin Road	32	B3
Ship Street Great	81	A4
Ship Street Little	81	A4
Shrewsbury	51	D2
Shrewsbury Hall	73	D1
Shrewsbury Lawn	70	C4
Shrewsbury Lodge	70	C3
Shrewsbury Park	51	D2
Shrewsbury Road (Ballsbridge)	51	D3
Shrewsbury Road (Shankill)	73	D1
Shrewsbury Woods	70	C4
Sidmonton Avenue	77	E1
Sidmonton Court	77	E2
Sidmonton Gardens	77	E2
Sidmonton Road	77	E2
Sidmonton Square	77	E1
Sigurd Road	78	B2
Silchester Court	61	E4
Silchester Crescent	71	D1
Silchester Park	71	D1
Silchester Road	61	E4
Silloge Avenue	17	F4
Silloge Gardens	17	F4
Silloge Road	17	F4
Silver Birches	58	A4
Silverberry	34	C4
Silverdale	34	C4
Silverpines (Bray)	76	C2
Silverpines (Leopardstown)	69	D2
Silverwood	34	C4
Silverwood Road	56	A3
Simmonscourt Road	51	D2
Simmonscourt Square	51	D2
Simmonscourt Terrace	50	C3
Simon's Ridge	68	A3
Sion Hill	59	E2
Sion Hill Avenue	49	E3
Sion Hill Road	28	A3
Sion Road	71	E2
Sir John Rogerson's Quay	41	E3
Sirthorpe Lane	50	B2
Sitric Place	78	C2
Sitric Road	78	C2
Skelligs Court	14	C4
Skelly's Lane	28	C1
Skreen Road	39	D1
Skyview House	72	C3
Slademore Avenue	20	B4
Slademore Close	20	B4
Slademore Court	20	B3
Slademore Drive	20	B3
Slane Road	48	C2
Slaney Close	26	C3
Slaney Court	26	C3
Slaney Road	26	C3
Slate Cabin Lane	68	A4
Slemish Road	39	D1
Slieve Rua Drive	58	C4
Slievebloom Park	47	F2
Slievebloom Road	47	F3
Slievemore Road	48	A2
Slievenamon Road	48	B1
Sloperton	60	C3
Smithfield	78	C3
Smyth's Villas	61	D3
Snowdrop Road	20	B3
Snowdrop Walk	20	B3
Snugborough Road	14	C4
Snugborough Road Extension	23	D2
Somerton	70	C2
Somerville Avenue	48	A3
Somerville Drive	48	A3
Somerville Park	48	A3
Sommerville	57	F3
Sonesta	6	C2
Sorrel Avenue	22	C2
Sorrel Dale	22	C2
Sorrel Drive	22	C2
Sorrel Heath	22	C2
Sorrento Drive	72	B3
Sorrento Lawn	72	C3
Sorrento Road	72	C3
South Avenue	58	C3
South Bank	5	D2
South Bank Road	42	B4
South Brown Street	79	C5
South Circular Road (Dolphin's Barn)	48	C1
South Circular Road (Islandbridge)	39	D3
South Dock Road	41	E4
South Dock Street	41	E4
South Great George's Street	81	B4
South Hill (Dartry)	57	E1
South Hill (Howth)	32	C3
South Hill Avenue	59	D2
South Hill Park	59	D2
South Lotts Road	41	E4
South Park	70	B2
South Park Drive	70	B2
Southern Cross	76	B4
Southern Cross Avenue	39	D4
Southwood Park	59	E2
Spa Road (Inchicore)	38	C4
Spa Road (Phoenix Park)	39	D2
Spawell Link	55	E3
Spencer Dock	D2	D2
Spencer Row	80	C2
Spencer Street	41	E1
Spencer Villas	61	E4
Spences Terrace	79	C5
Sperrin Road	48	A1
Spiddal Road	37	E4
Spire View	25	F4
Spire View Lane	49	E3
Spittal Hill	5	E2
Spring Garden Lane	80	C3
Spring Garden Street	41	D1
Springdale Road	29	F2
Springfield	39	D1
Springfield Avenue	56	B2
Springfield Crescent	56	A3
Springfield Drive	56	A3
Springfield Park (Dean's Grange)	69	F2
Springfield Park (Templeogue)	56	A3
Springfield Road	56	A2
Springhill Avenue	60	A4
Springhill Park (Dalkey)	71	F2
Springhill Park (Dean's Grange)	60	A4
Springlawn Close	23	E1
Springlawn Court	23	E1
Springlawn Drive	23	E1
Springlawn Road	23	E1
Springvale	66	A2
Stable Lane	78	C3
Stamer Street	81	A6
Stanford Green	47	F3
Stanhope Street	78	C2
Stannaway Avenue	48	B4
Stannaway Drive	48	C3
Stannaway Road	48	C3
Stapolin Lawns	21	F3
Station Court	75	E4
Station Court Hall	23	D3
Station Court Park	23	D3
Station Court View	23	D3
Station Court Way	23	E3
Station Road (Clondalkin)	45	F2
Station Road (Killiney)	71	F4
Station Road (Portmarnock)	10	A4
Station Road (Raheny)	30	A2
Station Road (Sallynoggin)	71	E1
Station Road (Shankill)	75	E4
Station Road (Sutton)	11	E4
Station Road (Sutton)	32	A1
Station View	23	E3
Steamville Road	20	C4
Steeven's Lane	39	F3
Stella Avenue	27	E3
Stephen Street Lower	81	B4
Stephen Street Upper	81	A4
Stephen's Lane	81	D5
Stephen's Place	81	D5
Stephen's Road	48	B1
Sterling Square	12	B2
Stiles Court	29	D4
Stillorgan Grove	59	E4
Stillorgan Heath	68	C1
Stillorgan Park	59	E4
Stillorgan Park Avenue	59	E4
Stillorgan Road (Donnybrook)	51	D4
Stillorgan Road (Foxrock)	69	F2
Stillorgan Road (Mount Merrion)	59	D3
Stillorgan Wood	68	C1
Stirling Park	57	D2
Stirrup Lane	78	D3
Stocking Avenue	65	D3
Stocking Lane	65	E3
Stocklidle Lane	9	D3
Stockton Court	24	B3
Stockton Drive	24	B3
Stockton Green	24	B3
Stockton Lawn	24	B3
Stockton Park	24	B3
Stokes Place	81	B5
Stonebridge Avenue	22	B1
Stonebridge Close	75	E4
Stonebridge Drive	22	B1
Stonebridge Road (Clonsilla)	22	B1
Stonebridge Road (Shankill)	75	D3
Stonecroft	75	E2
Stonemasons Way	67	D2
Stonepark Abbey	56	C4
Stonepark Orchard	56	C3
Stoneview Place	61	E3
Stoney Road (Dundrum)	58	A4
Stoney Road (East Wall)	41	E2
Stoneybatter	40	A3
Stonylea Terrace	77	D3
Store Street	80	C3
Stormanstown Road	27	D1
Stradbrook Gardens	60	B3
Stradbrook Hall	60	B3
Stradbrook Lawn	60	A3
Stradbrook Park	60	B3
Stradbrook Road	60	A3
Stralem Court	22	A1
Stralem Grove	22	A1
Stralem Mews	22	A1
Stralem Terrace	22	A1
Strand Mews	51	E2
Strand Road (Baldoyle)	11	E3
Strand Road (Bray)	77	E1
Strand Road (Killiney)	75	F1
Strand Road (Portmarnock)	10	B3
Strand Road (Sandymount)	51	E1
Strand Road (Sutton)	32	B2
Strand Street (Malahide)	7	D2
Strand Street (Ringsend)	41	F4
Strand Street Great	80	A3
Strand Street Little	80	A3
Strandmill Avenue	10	B4
Strandmill Park	10	B4
Strandmill Road	10	B4
Strandville Avenue North	41	D2
Strangford Gardens	41	E2
Strangford Road East	41	E2
Strathmore Road	71	F4
Streamville Court	75	E2
Suffolk Street	81	B4
Sugarloaf Crescent	77	D3
Suir Road	48	B1
Summer Arch	80	C1
Summer Street North	80	C1
Summer Street South	79	C5
Summerfield Avenue	23	E1
Summerfield Close	23	E1
Summerfield Green	23	E1
Summerfield Lawns	23	E1
Summerfield Meadows	23	E1
Summerfield Rise	23	E1
Summerhill	80	C1
Summerhill Parade (Ballybough)	80	C1
Summerhill Parade (Dún Laoghaire)	61	E3
Summerhill Place	80	C1
Summerhill Road	61	E3
Summerseat Court	12	B2
Summerset Avenue	12	B2
Summerset Crescent	12	B2
Summerset Drive	12	B3
Summerset Green	12	B2
Summerset Walk	12	B3
Summerset Way	12	B2
Summerville	42	C1
Sunbury Gardens	49	F4
Suncroft Drive	62	C1
Suncroft Park	62	C1
Sundale Close	62	C2
Sundale Crescent	62	C1
Sundale Grove	62	C1
Sundale Heights	62	C1

Sundale Lawn	62	B1
Sundale Meadow	62	B1
Sundale Parade	62	B1
Sundale Park	62	C1
Sundale Road	62	C2
Sundale Villas	62	C1
Sundale Walk	62	B1
Sundrive Park	49	D3
Sundrive Road	48	C3
Sunnybank Court	57	F3
Susan Terrace	79	C6
Susanville Road	41	D1
Sussex Road	50	B2
Sussex Street	61	D3
Sutton Downs	31	E1
Sutton Grove	31	E1
Sutton Lawns	11	D4
Sutton Park	11	D4
Swallowbrook Crescent	13	D3
Swallowbrook View	13	E3
Swallowwood View	18	B3
Swan Alley (Christchurch)	79	C4
Swan Alley (Phibsborough)	80	A1
Swan Grove	50	A2
Swan's Nest Avenue	30	B1
Swan's Nest Road	30	B1
Swanbrook	77	D4
Swanville Place	49	F3
Sweetbriar Lane	58	B4
Sweetman's Avenue	59	F2
Sweetmount Avenue	57	E4
Sweetmount Drive	57	E4
Sweetmount Park	57	F4
Swift's Alley	79	C4
Swift's Grove	19	E2
Swiftbrook Avenue	62	C1
Swiftbrook Close	62	C1
Swiftbrook Drive	62	C1
Swiftbrook Park	62	C1
Swilly Road	39	E1
Swords Manor Avenue	4	B3
Swords Manor Court	4	B3
Swords Manor Crescent	4	B2
Swords Manor Drive	4	B3
Swords Manor Grove	4	B3
Swords Manor View	4	B3
Swords Manor Way	4	B3
Swords Plaza	5	D3
Swords Road (Malahide)	6	B2
Swords Road (Santry)	18	C3
Swords Road (Whitehall)	27	F3
Swords Road (Whitehall)	28	A2
Swords Street	78	B2
Sybil Hill Avenue	29	F3
Sybil Hill Road	29	E3
Sycamore Avenue (Cabinteely)	70	A4
Sycamore Avenue (Castleknock)	23	E3
Sycamore Avenue (Tallaght)	54	A2
Sycamore Close (Cabinteely)	70	A4
Sycamore Close (Tallaght)	54	A2
Sycamore Crescent	58	D3
Sycamore Drive (Castleknock)	23	E3
Sycamore Drive (Tallaght)	54	A2
Sycamore Grove	70	A4
Sycamore Lawn	23	E3
Sycamore Park (Castleknock)	23	F3
Sycamore Park (Finglas East)	17	D4
Sycamore Park (Tallaght)	54	A2
Sycamore Road (Dundrum)	57	E4
Sycamore Road (Finglas East)	17	D4
Sycamore Road (Fox & Geese)	46	C3
Sycamore Road (Mount Merrion)	59	D3
Sycamore Street	81	A4
Sycamore View	23	E3
Sycamore Walk	70	A4
Sydenham Mews	61	D4
Sydenham Road (Ballsbridge)	51	D2
Sydenham Road (Dundrum)	58	A3
Sydenham Villas	58	A4
Sydney Avenue	59	F2
Sydney Gate	51	E3
Sydney Parade Avenue	51	E3
Sydney Terrace	59	F2
Sylvan Avenue	54	A1
Sylvan Close	54	A2
Sylvan Drive	54	A1
Synge Lane	81	A6
Synge Place	81	A6
Synge Street	81	A6
Synnott Place	40	C1
Synnott Row	40	C1

T

Taaffe's Place	41	D1
Talbot Avenue	6	B2
Talbot Court (Castleknock)	24	A2
Talbot Court (Malahide)	6	B2
Talbot Downs	24	A2
Talbot Lodge	59	E3
Talbot Park	6	B2
Talbot Place	80	C2
Talbot Road (Killiney)	72	A4
Talbot Road (Malahide)	6	B2
Talbot Street	80	C2
Tallaght Bypass	54	B4
Tallaght Road	54	E3
Tamarisk Avenue	54	A2
Tamarisk Close	54	A2
Tamarisk Court	54	A2
Tamarisk Dale	54	A2
Tamarisk Drive	54	B2
Tamarisk Grove	54	A2
Tamarisk Heights	54	A2
Tamarisk Lawns	54	A2
Tamarisk Park	54	A2
Tamarisk View	54	A2
Tamarisk Walk	54	A2
Tamarisk Way	54	A2
Tandy's Lane	34	B4
Taney Avenue	58	A3
Taney Court	58	A3
Taney Crescent	58	A3
Taney Drive	57	F3
Taney Grove	58	A3
Taney Lawn	57	F3
Taney Park	57	F3
Taney Rise	58	A3
Taney Road	58	A3
Tara Crescent	64	C2
Tara Hill Crescent	56	B3
Tara Hill Grove	56	B4
Tara Hill Road	56	B3
Tara Lawn	21	D4
Tara Street	80	C3
Taylor Lane	79	c4
Taylor's Court	66	A1
Taylor's Lane	66	B1
Teeling Way	41	F2
Temple Bar	80	B3
Temple Cottages	78	D2
Temple Court	18	B2
Temple Crescent	60	A2
Temple Gardens (Milltown)	50	A4
Temple Gardens (Santry)	18	B2
Temple Hill	60	A2
Temple Lane	80	B2
Temple Lane South	81	B4
Temple Lawns	18	B2
Temple Manor Avenue	55	D2
Temple Manor Close	55	D2
Temple Manor Court	55	D1
Temple Manor Drive	55	D1
Temple Manor Grove	55	D1
Temple Manor Way	55	D1
Temple Park	57	E1
Temple Park Avenue	60	A2
Temple Place	50	A2
Temple Road (Blackrock)	60	A2
Temple Road (Milltown)	57	E1
Temple Square	50	A4
Temple Street	80	B1
Temple Street West	78	B3
Temple View Avenue	20	C3
Temple View Close	20	C3
Temple View Copse	20	C3
Temple View Crescent	20	C3
Temple View Downs	20	C3
Temple View Drive	20	C3
Temple View Green	20	C3
Temple View Grove	20	C3
Temple View Lawn	20	C3
Temple View Park	20	C3
Temple View Place	20	C3
Temple View Rise	20	C3
Temple View Row	20	C3
Temple View Square	20	C3
Temple View Walk	20	C3
Temple Villas	78	B3
Templemore Avenue	49	F4
Templeogue Lodge	55	E3
Templeogue Road	56	A2
Templeogue Wood	55	E3
Templeroan Avenue	65	F1
Templeroan Close	65	F1
Templeroan Court	65	F1
Templeroan Crescent	65	F1
Templeroan Downs	56	A4
Templeroan Drive	65	F1
Templeroan Green	65	F1
Templeroan Grove	65	F1
Templeroan Meadows	56	A4
Templeroan Mews	65	F1
Templeroan Park	55	F4
Templeroan View	65	F1
Templeroan Way	65	F1
Templeville Avenue	55	F2
Templeville Drive	55	F2
Templeville Park	56	A2
Templeville Road	55	F2
Terenure Court	56	B1
Terenure Park	56	B1
Terenure Road East	56	C1
Terenure Road North	56	B1
Terenure Road West	56	A1
Terminal Road North	42	C2
Terminal Road South	42	C3
Termon Court	17	F3
Texas Lane	6	C2
The Alders	60	B3
The Avenue (Ballyboden)	65	F1
The Avenue (Hartstown)	12	B4
The Avenue (Mulhuddart)	13	F3
The Avenue (Swords)	5	E2
The Avenue (Swords, Melrose Park)	9	E1
The Avenue (Templeogue)	55	E2
The Bawn	7	D3
The Bawn Grove	7	D3
The Beeches	21	D4
The Belfry	30	C1
The Birches	69	F3
The Boulevard	14	A1
The Bramblings	29	D3
The Burgage	72	B3
The By	69	F3
The Castlelands	56	C3
The Cedars (Loughlinstown)	75	E2
The Cedars (Monkstown)	60	B3
The Chase	69	D2
The Cloisters (Drumcondra)	28	A3
The Cloisters (Terenure)	49	D4
The Close (Ballyboden)	65	F1
The Close (Kilmore)	19	D4
The Close (Lucan)	35	D4
The Close (Mount Merrion)	58	C2
The Close (Swords)	9	F1
The Close (Tallaght)	53	F2
The Close (Templeogue)	55	E2
The Coombe	79	C5
The Coppice	37	D2
The Coppins	69	F3
The Cottages	62	A1
The Cottages (Firhouse)	64	B3
The Court (Clontarf)	42	A1
The Court (Mulhuddart)	13	F3
The Court (Raheny)	30	B3
The Court (Santry)	19	D3
The Court (Shankill)	75	F4
The Court (Swords)	5	E2
The Court (Tallaght, Belgard Hts)	53	E3
The Court (Tallaght, Kingswood Hts)	53	F2
The Court (Templeogue)	55	E2
The Courtyard (Clonsilla)	23	D2
The Courtyard (Foxrock)	69	F2
The Cove	6	C2
The Crescent (Ballyboden)	65	F1
The Crescent (Castleknock)	24	B4
The Crescent (Donnybrook)	50	C3
The Crescent (Hartstown)	12	B4
The Crescent (Lucan)	44	A1
The Crescent (Malahide)	7	F3
The Crescent (Marino)	28	B4
The Crescent (Mulhuddart)	14	A2
The Crescent (Santry)	19	D3
The Crescent (Sutton)	11	E4
The Crescent (Swords)	5	E2
The Crescent (Swords, Melrose Park)	9	F1
The Crescent (Tallaght, Belgard Hts)	53	E3
The Crescent (Tallaght, Kingswood Hts)	53	F2
The Crescent (Tallaght)	64	A1
The Dale (Tallaght)	53	F3
The Dell	67	F2
The Dingle	37	D2
The Drive (Ballyboden)	66	A1
The Drive (Bray)	73	E3
The Drive (Lucan)	44	A1
The Drive (Mulhuddart)	13	F3
The Drive (Swords)	9	E1
The Drive (Tallaght)	64	B1
The Drive (Templeogue)	55	E2
The Dunes	10	B3
The Elms	51	E4
The Fairways	73	E3
The Fosters	58	C2
The Gables	44	C3
The Gallops (Leopardstown)	68	C3
The Gallops (Swords)	4	B2
The Garth	53	F2
The Georgian Village	24	B4
The Glade (Palmerstown)	37	D2
The Glade (Tallaght)	53	E2
The Glebe	35	D3
The Glen (Ballyboden)	66	A1
The Glen (Raheny)	30	B3
The Grange (Galloping Green)	69	E1
The Grange (Kill O' The Grange)	70	B1
The Green (Ballyboden)	65	F1
The Green (Beaumont)	28	B4
The Green (Bray)	73	E3
The Green (Malahide)	7	D2
The Green (Mulhuddart)	13	F3
The Green (Santry)	19	D3
The Green (Swords)	5	E2

The Green
  (Swords, Melrose Park) 9 F1
The Green (Tallaght) 54 A2
The Green (Templeogue) 55 F2
The Green Road 72 C3
The Grove (Ballyfermot) 38 A3
The Grove (Bray) 73 E3
The Grove (Lucan) 34 C4
The Grove (Sandymount) 51 D1
The Grove (Swords) 9 F1
The Grove
  (Tallaght, Belgard Hts) 64 B1
The Grove
  (Tallaght, Kingswood Hts) 53 F2
The Haggard 33 E2
The Hall 67 E3
The Haven 56 C1
The Heath (Tallaght) 53 F3
The Heath (Templeogue) 55 E2
The Hedgerows 69 E3
The Heights 9 F1
The Hill (Malahide) 7 D4
The Hill (Monkstown) 60 C3
The Hill (Stillorgan) 59 D4
The Hole In The Wall Road 21 D2
The Island 38 A3
The Larches 75 E2
The Laurels (Clontarf) 29 F4
The Laurels (Dundrum) 57 F3
The Laurels (Terenure) 56 B1
The Lawn (Ballyboden) 65 F1
The Lawn (Bray) 73 E3
The Lawn (Finglas) 26 A1
The Lawn (Swords) 9 F1
The Lawn (Tallaght) 53 E3
The Lighthouse 7 F3
The Links 10 A4
The Lodge 71 D1
The Mall (Clonsilla) 23 D2
The Mall (Hartstown) 12 B4
The Mall (Lucan) 34 C2
The Mall (Malahide) 7 D2
The Malthouse 39 F4
The Maltings 73 E4
The Manor 55 F2
The Maples 57 F1
The Meadows 29 E3
The Meadows East 53 E3
The Meadows West 53 E3
The Mews (Ballsbridge) 50 C1
The Mews (Clontarf) 42 B1
The Mews (Hartstown) 12 B4
The Mews (Malahide) 7 F3
The Mews (Sandymount) 51 D3
The Moorings 7 E2
The New Park 64 B1
The New Road (North) 15 E4
The New Road (South) 24 C1
The Nurseries (Ballybrack) 75 E1
The Nurseries (Bray) 76 C2
The Nurseries (Sallynoggin) 71 E2
The Nurseries (Stillorgan) 69 D1
The Nurseries (Swords) 8 C1
The Oaks (Clontarf) 30 A4
The Oaks (Dundrum) 57 F3
The Oaks (Loughlinstown) 75 D2
The Oaks (Swords) 8 B1
The Oaks (Tallaght) 53 E2
The Old Forge 44 A1
The Old Hill 35 D2
The Orchard (Ard na Greine) 20 C3
The Orchard (Killester) 29 D3
The Orchard (Lucan) 34 C2
The Orchard (Monkstown) 60 B3
The Orchard (Palmerstown) 37 D2
The Orchard (Terenure) 55 F1
The Oval 37 E2
The Paddock 25 E4

The Paddocks 12 B4
The Palms 58 B2
The Park (Beaumont) 28 B1
The Park (Lucan) 44 A1
The Park (Santry) 19 D3
The Park (Swords) 9 E1
The Park (Tallaght) 53 F2
The Park (Templeogue) 55 F2
The Pines (Castleknock) 24 B3
The Pines (Killester) 29 E2
The Poplars 60 B3
The Priory 56 C4
The Rise (Ballyboden) 66 A1
The Rise (Ballymount) 53 F2
The Rise (Dalkey) 72 A2
The Rise (Glasnevin) 27 E2
The Rise (Malahide) 7 E2
The Rise (Mount Merrion) 58 C2
The Rise (Swords) 9 F1
The Rise (Tallaght) 53 E3
The Rookery 65 E1
The Slopes 60 C3
The Square (Ringsend) 41 F4
The Square (Santry) 19 D3
The Stables 12 B4
The Steeples 38 A4
The Stiles Road 29 D4
The Thatch Road 28 A2
The Thicket 69 F4
The Tramyard 48 A1
The Turrets 51 D1
The Vale 37 D2
The View (Santry) 19 D3
The View
  (Tallaght, Kingswood Hts) 53 F2
The View (Tallaght) 64 B1
The Villa 9 E1
The Village (Ashtown) 25 D3
The Village (Clonsilla) 22 C2
The Village (Drumcondra) 27 F3
The Village (Raheny) 30 B3
The Village Gate 72 B3
The Walk (Tallaght) 64 B1
The Walk (Templeogue) 55 E2
The Warren 6 B2
The Waterside 45 F2
The Weir 38 A3
The Willows 26 C3
The Wood 64 B1
The Woods 73 E3
Third Avenue 80 D2
Thomas Court 40 A4
Thomas Davis Street 79 D4
Thomas Davis Street West 48 A1
Thomas Lane 80 B2
Thomas Moore Road 47 F3
Thomas Street 79 C4
Thomastown Road 71 D3
Thomond 75 E4
Thomond Road 38 A4
Thor Place 78 B2
Thormanby Lawns 33 E2
Thormanby Lodge 33 E2
Thormanby Road 33 E2
Thormanby Woods 33 E3
Thorncastle Street 41 F3
Thorncliffe Park 57 E1
Thorndale Avenue 28 C2
Thorndale Crescent 28 C2
Thorndale Drive 28 C2
Thorndale Grove 28 C2
Thornfield Square 45 F3
Thornhill Road (Bray) 76 B1
Thornhill Road (Mount Merrion) 58 C4
Thornleigh Avenue 4 C1
Thornleigh Court 4 C1
Thornleigh Green 4 C1
Thornleigh Row 4 C1

Thornville Avenue 30 C1
Thornville Drive 30 C1
Thornville Park 30 C1
Thornville Road 30 C1
Three Rock Close 54 C1
Three Rock Road 68 C2
Tibradden Close 54 C1
Tibradden Drive 54 C1
Tibradden Grove 54 C1
Tibradden Road 66 B4
Ticknock Dale 67 F3
Ticknock Grove 67 F3
Ticknock Hill 67 F3
Ticknock Road 67 F3
Ticknock Way 67 F3
Timber Mills Apartments 29 D2
Tinker's Hill 22 A4
Tivoli Avenue 49 E3
Tivoli Close 61 D4
Tivoli Road 61 D4
Tivoli Terrace East 61 D3
Tivoli Terrace North 61 D3
Tivoli Terrace South 61 D3
Tolka Cottages 26 C2
Tolka Estate 26 C2
Tolka Estate Road 26 C2
Tolka Quay Road 42 A4
Tolka Road 41 D1
Tolka Valley Road 25 F2
Tolka Valley Road 26 A3
Tolka Valley View 25 F2
Tonduff Close 54 C1
Tonlegee Avenue 29 F1
Tonlegee Drive 29 F1
Tonlegee Road 20 B4
Tonlegee Road 29 E1
Torca Road 72 B3
Torcaill 10 B2
Torquay Road 69 E2
Torquay Wood 69 E2
Tory Square 14 B4
Tournville Lodge 56 B2
Tower Avenue 49 E4
Tower Road (Castleknock) 37 E1
Tower Road (Clondalkin) 45 F3
Townsend Street 80 C3
Townyard Lane 7 D2
Trafalgar Terrace 60 B2
Tramway Court 32 A1
Tranquility Grove 19 E4
Treepark Avenue 54 A2
Treepark Close 54 A2
Treepark Drive 54 A2
Treepark Road 54 A2
Trees Avenue 58 C3
Trees Road Lower 58 C3
Trees Road Upper 58 C3
Treesdale 59 D3
Tresilian 69 F4
Trim Road 19 E4
Trimblestown 58 A2
Trimleston Avenue 51 F4
Trimleston Drive 59 D1
Trimleston Gardens 59 D1
Trimleston Park 59 D1
Trimleston Road 59 D1
Trinity Street 81 B4
Tritonville Avenue 51 D1
Tritonville Court 51 D1
Tritonville Road 51 D1
Tubber Lane Road 34 A3
Tubbermore Road 72 B2
Tuckett's Lane 33 D2
Tudor Lawns 69 E2
Tudor Road 50 A4
Tulip Court 20 A3
Tully Hall Avenue 44 B1
Tully Hall Close 44 B1

Tully Hall Court 44 B1
Tully Hall Crescent 44 B1
Tully Hall Drive 44 B1
Tully Hall Green 44 A1
Tully Hall Park 44 B1
Tully Hall Rise 44 B1
Tully Hall Way 44 B1
Tullyvale 74 C2
Turlough Gardens 41 E1
Turlough Parade 28 B3
Turnapin Cottages 19 D2
Turnapin Green 18 C2
Turnapin Grove 19 D2
Turnapin Lane 18 C2
Turnberry 11 D4
Turnpike Road 46 C4
Turret Road 37 D3
Turvey Avenue 39 D4
Tuscany Downs 30 A1
Tuscany Park 11 D4
Tymon Close 64 A2
Tymon Crescent 63 F2
Tymon Grove 64 A1
Tymon Lane 55 D3
Tymon Lawn 64 A2
Tymon North Apartments 55 D4
Tymon North Avenue 54 B3
Tymon North Gardens 54 C3
Tymon North Grove 54 C3
Tymon North Lawn 54 C3
Tymon North Park 54 C3
Tymon North Road 54 C3
Tymonville Avenue 54 B2
Tymonville Court 54 B3
Tymonville Crescent 54 B2
Tymonville Drive 54 B2
Tymonville Grove 54 B2
Tymonville Lawn 54 B3
Tymonville Park 54 B2
Tymonville Road 54 B3
Tynan Hall Avenue 53 F1
Tynan Hall Grove 53 F1
Tynan Hall Park 53 F2
Tyrconnell Park 47 F1
Tyrconnell Road 47 F1
Tyreconwell Street 48 A1
Tyrellstown Road 13 F1
Tyrellstown The Boulevard 14 A1
Tyrellstown Way 14 A1
Tyrone Place 48 A1

U

Ulster Street 40 A1
Ulster Terrace 80 D1
Ulverton Close 72 B2
Ulverton Court 72 B2
Ulverton Road 72 B2
Upper Cliff Road 33 E2
Upper Dargle Road 76 B1
Upper Glen Road 38 A2
Uppercross Road 79 A5
Usher Street 79 C4
Usher's Island 78 C3
Usher's Quay 78 C3

V

Vale View Avenue 70 B3
Vale View Close 70 B3
Vale View Grove 70 B3
Vale View Lawn 70 B3
Valentia Parade 40 C1
Valentia Road 27 E3

Name	Page	Grid
Valeview Crescent	26	A2
Valeview Drive	26	A2
Valley Avenue	74	C2
Valley Close	74	C2
Valley Drive	74	C2
Valley Park Drive	25	F2
Valley Park Road	25	E2
Valley View (Loughlinstown)	74	C2
Valley View (Swords)	4	B3
Valley Walk	74	C2
Vauxhall Avenue	79	B5
Vavasour Square	50	C1
Venetian Hall	29	E3
Ventry Drive	26	A4
Ventry Park	26	A4
Ventry Road	26	A4
Verbena Avenue (Foxrock)	69	F3
Verbena Avenue (Kilbarrack)	31	D1
Verbena Grove	21	F4
Verbena Lawns	21	E4
Verbena Park	21	E4
Verdemont Apartments	23	F1
Vergemount Hall	50	B4
Vergemount Park	50	C4
Vernon Avenue (Clontarf)	42	C1
Vernon Avenue (Killester)	29	E3
Vernon Drive	29	E3
Vernon Gardens	42	C1
Vernon Grove (Clontarf)	42	C1
Vernon Grove (Rathgar)	49	F4
Vernon Heath	29	E4
Vernon Park	29	E4
Vernon Rise	29	E3
Vernon Street	81	A6
Verona Apartments	68	B3
Veronica Terrace	41	F4
Verschoyle Avenue	62	A2
Verschoyle Drive	62	A1
Verschoyle Glen	62	A2
Verschoyle Green	62	A2
Verschoyle Heights	62	A2
Verschoyle Park	62	A2
Verschoyle Place	81	D5
Verschoyle Vale	62	A2
Vesey Mews	60	C3
Vesey Place	60	C3
Vesey Terrace	34	C2
Vevay Crescent	77	D2
Vevay Road	77	D2
Vico Road	72	B4
Victoria Avenue (Bray)	77	E1
Victoria Avenue (Donnybrook)	50	C3
Victoria Lane	56	C1
Victoria Quay	78	B3
Victoria Road (Clontarf)	42	A1
Victoria Road (Dalkey)	72	C3
Victoria Road (Killiney)	71	F3
Victoria Road (Terenure)	56	C1
Victoria Street	49	F2
Victoria Terrace	57	F3
Victoria Village	49	F2
Victoria Villas	28	B4
Viking Place	78	C3
Viking Road	78	B2
Villa Bank	40	B1
Villa Blanchard	23	F2
Villa Park Avenue	39	D1
Villa Park Gardens	25	F4
Villa Park Road	39	D1
Village Court	56	B3
Villarea Park	61	E4
Villiers Road	49	F4
Violet Hill Drive	26	C3
Violet Hill Park	26	C3
Violet Hill Road	26	C3
Virginia Drive	25	F2
Virginia Heights	53	E4
Virginia Park	25	F2
Viscount Avenue	18	C2

W

Wade's Avenue	30	A2
Wadelai Green	27	D1
Wadelai Road	27	D1
Wainsfort Avenue	55	F2
Wainsfort Crescent	55	F2
Wainsfort Drive	55	F1
Wainsfort Gardens	55	F2
Wainsfort Grove	56	A1
Wainsfort Manor Crescent	55	E1
Wainsfort Manor Drive	55	F1
Wainsfort Manor Green	55	E1
Wainsfort Manor Grove	55	F2
Wainsfort Park	55	F1
Wainsfort Road	55	F2
Waldemar Terrace	57	F3
Walker's Cottages	50	A2
Walker's Court	50	A2
Walkinstown Avenue	47	E2
Walkinstown Crescent	47	E3
Walkinstown Drive	47	E3
Walkinstown Green	47	E3
Walkinstown Parade	47	E3
Walkinstown Park	47	E3
Walkinstown Road	47	F4
Walnut Avenue (Tallaght)	54	A1
Walnut Avenue (Whitehall)	27	F2
Walnut Close	54	A1
Walnut Court	27	F2
Walnut Drive	54	A1
Walnut Lawn	27	E3
Walnut Park	27	F2
Walnut Rise	27	F2
Walsh Road	27	E3
Walsh's Cottages	60	C4
Waltersland Road	69	D1
Waltham Terrace	59	E2
Wanford Close	71	E2
Warburton Terrace	77	E1
Ward's Hill	79	D5
Warner's Lane	50	A2
Warren Avenue	23	E3
Warren Close	23	E3
Warren Crescent	23	E3
Warren Green (Carpenterstown)	23	E3
Warren Green (Sutton)	11	E4
Warren Street	49	F2
Warrenhouse Road	11	D3
Warrenmount Place	79	D5
Warrenstown Close	14	B3
Warrenstown Court	14	A3
Warrenstown Downs	14	A3
Warrenstown Drive	14	A3
Warrenstown Garth	14	A3
Warrenstown Green	14	B3
Warrenstown Grove	14	B3
Warrenstown Lawn	14	A3
Warrenstown Park	14	A3
Warrenstown Place	14	A3
Warrenstown Rise	14	B3
Warrenstown Row	14	B3
Warrenstown Walk	14	B3
Warrenstown Way	14	A3
Warrington Place	81	D5
Wasdale Grove	56	C1
Wasdale Park	56	C1
Washington Lane	56	A3
Washington Park	56	A3
Washington Street	49	E2
Waterfall Road	29	F2
Watergate	64	A1
Waterloo Avenue	80	D1
Waterloo Lane	50	B2
Waterloo Road	50	B2
Watermeadow Drive	63	F1
Watermeadow Park	64	A1
Watermill Avenue	30	A2
Watermill Close	64	A2
Watermill Drive	30	A2
Watermill Grove	64	A2
Watermill Lane	30	B2
Watermill Lawn	64	A2
Watermill Park	30	A2
Watermill Road	30	A2
Waterside Avenue	5	F4
Waterside Close	5	F4
Waterside Court	5	F4
Waterside Crescent (Portmarnock)	10	B1
Waterside Crescent (Swords)	5	F4
Waterside Drive	5	F4
Waterside Green	5	F4
Waterside Grove	5	F4
Waterside Lawn	5	F4
Waterside Park	5	F4
Waterside Place	5	F4
Waterside Rise	5	F4
Waterside Road	5	F4
Waterside Walk	5	F4
Waterside Way	5	F4
Waterstown Avenue	37	D2
Waterville	14	C4
Waterville Row	23	F1
Waterville Terrace	24	A1
Watery Lane (Clondalkin)	46	A3
Watery Lane (Swords)	5	D2
Watling Street	79	C4
Watson Avenue	71	D4
Watson Drive	71	D4
Watson Park	71	D4
Watson Road	71	D3
Waverley Avenue	28	A4
Weaver Square	79	C5
Weaver's Street	79	C5
Weirview Drive	69	D1
Weldon's Lane	11	D3
Wellington Court	77	D1
Wellington Gardens	50	A3
Wellington Lane (Ranelagh)	50	B2
Wellington Lane (Templeogue)	55	E2
Wellington Park	55	E2
Wellington Place	50	B2
Wellington Place North	80	A1
Wellington Quay	80	A1
Wellington Road (Phoenix Park)	39	E3
Wellington Road (Ranelagh)	50	B2
Wellington Street	61	D3
Wellington Street Lower	80	A1
Wellington Street Upper	80	A1
Wellmount Avenue	25	F2
Wellmount Court	26	A1
Wellmount Crescent	25	F2
Wellmount Drive	25	F2
Wellmount Green	25	F2
Wellmount Parade	26	A1
Wellmount Park	25	F2
Wellmount Road	26	A2
Wellpark Avenue	27	F3
Wellview Crescent	13	F2
Wellview Green	13	F2
Wellview Grove	13	F2
Wellview Park	13	F2
Wendell Avenue	10	C2
Werburgh Street	81	A4
Wesley Heights	68	A1
Wesley Lawns	67	F1
Wesley Place	49	E2
Wesley Road	49	E4
West End Village	23	E1
West Haven	13	D3
West Park Drive	27	D2
West Pier Howth Harbour	33	D1
West Road	41	E2
West Terrace	38	C4
Westbourne Avenue	45	D3
Westbourne Close	45	D3
Westbourne Court	45	D3
Westbourne Drive	44	C3
Westbourne Green	45	D3
Westbourne Grove	45	D3
Westbourne Lodge	55	E4
Westbourne Park	45	D3
Westbourne Road	56	C1
Westbourne View	45	D3
Westbrook	48	B4
Westbrook Lawns	62	B2
Westbrook Park	34	B3
Westbrook Road	57	F2
Westbury	59	D4
Westbury Avenue	34	C4
Westbury Close	34	C4
Westbury Court	34	C3
Westbury Park	34	C4
Western Road	79	C6
Western Way	78	D2
Westerton Rise	57	F4
Westfield Park	77	E2
Westfield Road	49	D3
Westland Row	81	C4
Westminster Lawns	69	E1
Westminster Road	69	F3
Westmoreland Street	80	B3
Weston Avenue	34	A2
Weston Close	34	A2
Weston Court	34	A2
Weston Crescent	34	A2
Weston Drive	34	A2
Weston Green	34	A2
Weston Heights	34	A3
Weston Lawn	34	A2
Weston Meadow	34	A2
Weston Park	57	E3
Weston Road	57	E3
Weston Way	34	A2
Westpark	54	A4
Westpark Estate	29	E1
Westway	14	C3
Westway Close	14	C3
Westway Grove	14	C3
Westway Lawns	14	C4
Westway Park	14	C3
Westway View	14	C3
Westwood Avenue	25	E2
Westwood Road	25	E2
Wexford Street	81	A5
Wheatfield	76	C3
Wheatfield Grove	10	B2
Wheatfield Road (Palmerstown)	37	D3
Wheatfield Road (Portmarnock)	10	B2
Wheatfields Avenue	36	C4
Wheatfields Close	36	B4
Wheatfields Court	36	C4
Wheatfields Crescent	36	B4
Wheatfields Drive	36	C4
Wheatfields Grove	36	C4
Wheatfields Park	36	C4
Whelan House Flats	41	F4
White Oak	58	A2
White's Road	24	B4
White's Villas	72	B2
Whiteacre Close	18	B4
Whiteacre Court	18	B4
Whiteacre Crescent	18	B4
Whitebank Road	42	B4
Whitebarn Road	57	D3
Whitebeam Avenue	50	B4
Whitebeam Road	50	B4
Whitebeams Road	68	B1
Whitebrook Park	63	D1

Whitechapel Avenue	23	D1
Whitechapel Green	23	D1
Whitechapel Grove	23	D1
Whitechapel Lawn	23	D1
Whitechapel Park	23	D1
Whitechapel Road	23	D1
Whitechurch Avenue	66	B2
Whitechurch Close	66	B2
Whitechurch Court	66	B2
Whitechurch Crescent	66	B2
Whitechurch Drive	66	B2
Whitechurch Green	66	B2
Whitechurch Grove	66	B2
Whitechurch Hill	66	B2
Whitechurch Lawn	66	B2
Whitechurch Park	66	B2
Whitechurch Place	66	B2
Whitechurch Road	66	B1
Whitechurch View	66	B2
Whitechurch Way	66	B2
Whitecliff	66	B1
Whitefriar Place	81	A5
Whitehall Close	55	E1
Whitehall Gardens	55	F1
Whitehall Park	55	E1
Whitehall Road (Churchtown)	57	D3
Whitehall Road (Kimmage)	55	E1
Whitehall Road West	55	E1
Whitehall Square	48	A4
Whitehorn Crescent	36	C4
Whitehorn Drive	37	D4
Whitehorn Gardens	36	C4
Whitehorn Park	36	C4
Whitehorn Way	36	C4
Whitestown Avenue	13	F4
Whitestown Crescent	13	F4
Whitestown Drive (Killinarden)	63	E1
Whitestown Drive (Mulhuddart)	13	F3
Whitestown Gardens	13	F4
Whitestown Green	13	F4
Whitestown Grove	13	F4
Whitestown Park	13	F4
Whitestown Road	63	E1
Whitestown Walk	13	F4
Whitethorn Avenue	28	C2
Whitethorn Crescent	28	C2
Whitethorn Grove	28	C2
Whitethorn Park	28	C2
Whitethorn Rise	28	C2
Whitethorn Road (Beaumont)	28	C2
Whitethorn Road (Milltown)	57	F1
Whitton Road	49	E4
Whitworth Place	40	C1
Whitworth Road	40	B1
Wicklow Street	81	B4
Wigan Road	40	B1
Wilderwood Grove	55	D3
Wilfield	51	D2
Wilfield Park	51	D2
Wilfield Road	51	D2
Wilfrid Road	49	E3
Willans Avenue	12	B4
Willans Drive	12	B4
Willans Green	12	B4
Willans Grove	12	B4
Willans Park	12	B4
Willans Rise	12	B4
Willans Row	12	B4
Willans Way	12	B4
Willbrook Lawn	56	B4
Willbrook Park	56	B4
Willbrook Road	56	B3
Willbrook Street	56	B3
William Place South	79	D6
William Street North	80	C1
William Street South	81	B4
William's Park	49	F2
Willie Nolan Road	11	D3
Willington Avenue	55	D2
Willington Court	55	D2
Willington Crescent	55	D2
Willington Drive	55	D2
Willington Green	55	D2
Willington Grove	55	D2
Willington Park	55	D2
Willow Avenue (Clondalkin)	45	E4
Willow Avenue (Loughlinstown)	74	C1
Willow Bank	60	C3
Willow Court (Clondalkin)	52	D1
Willow Court (Clonsilla)	22	C1
Willow Court (Loughlinstown)	74	C2
Willow Crescent	74	C2
Willow Drive (Clondalkin)	45	E4
Willow Drive (Clonsilla)	22	C1
Willow Field	51	E2
Willow Gate	57	E4
Willow Green	22	C1
Willow Grove (Clondalkin)	52	C1
Willow Grove (Cornelscourt)	70	B3
Willow Mews	51	E3
Willow Park	74	C1
Willow Park Avenue	27	D1
Willow Park Close	17	E4
Willow Park Crescent	17	E4
Willow Park Drive	26	C1
Willow Park Grove	17	E4
Willow Park Lawn	17	E4
Willow Park Road	17	E4
Willow Place (Booterstown)	59	D1
Willow Place (Loughlinstown)	74	C2
Willow Road (Dundrum)	57	E4
Willow Road (Fox & Geese)	46	C2
Willow Terrace	59	E1
Willow Vale	75	D1
Willow Wood Close	22	B1
Willow Wood Downs	22	C1
Willow Wood Green	22	B1
Willow Wood Grove	22	B1
Willow Wood Lawn	22	B1
Willow Wood Park	22	B1
Willow Wood Rise	22	B1
Willow Wood View	22	B1
Willow Wood Walk	22	B1
Willowbank Drive	56	B4
Willowbank Park	56	B4
Willowfield Avenue	58	A3
Willowfield Park	58	A3
Willsbrook Avenue	35	E2
Willsbrook Crescent	35	E2
Willsbrook Drive	35	E2
Willsbrook Gardens	35	E2
Willsbrook Green	35	E2
Willsbrook Grove	35	E2
Willsbrook Place	35	E2
Willsbrook Road	35	E2
Willsbrook View	35	E2
Willsbrook Way	35	E2
Wilmont Avenue	61	F4
Wilson Crescent	58	C2
Wilson Road	58	C2
Wilton Place	81	C6
Wilton Terrace	81	C6
Windele Road	27	E3
Windermere	22	A1
Windgate Rise	33	E3
Windgate Road	33	E3
Windmill	23	D2
Windmill Avenue (Crumlin)	48	B3
Windmill Avenue (Swords)	4	C3
Windmill Crescent	48	B3
Windmill Lane	80	D3
Windmill Lawns	4	C3
Windmill Park	48	B3
Windmill Rise	4	C3
Windmill Road	48	B2
Windrush	75	E4
Windsor Avenue	28	A4
Windsor Drive	60	B4
Windsor Park	60	B4
Windsor Road	50	A3
Windsor Terrace (Dún Laoghaire)	61	E3
Windsor Terrace (Harold's Cross)	49	E2
Windsor Villas	28	A4
Winetavern Street	79	D4
Winton Avenue	49	E4
Winton Grove	49	D4
Winton Mews	49	E4
Winton Road	50	B2
Wolfe Tone Avenue	61	D3
Wolfe Tone Quay	78	B3
Wolfe Tone Square East	77	D3
Wolfe Tone Square Middle	77	D3
Wolfe Tone Square North	77	D3
Wolfe Tone Square South	77	D3
Wolfe Tone Square West	77	D3
Wolfe Tone Street	80	A3
Wolseley Street	79	C6
Wolverton Glen	72	A2
Wood Lane	78	C3
Wood Quay	79	D4
Wood Street	81	A5
Wood Way	44	C2
Woodbank Avenue	25	E2
Woodbank Drive	25	E2
Woodberry (Carpenterstown)	23	F3
Woodberry (Lucan)	34	C4
Woodbine Avenue	58	C1
Woodbine Close	30	A1
Woodbine Drive	30	A1
Woodbine House Apartments	58	C1
Woodbine Park (Booterstown)	59	C1
Woodbine Park (Raheny)	30	A1
Woodbine Road (Booterstown)	58	C1
Woodbine Road (Raheny)	20	C4
Woodbrook Court	23	D3
Woodbrook Crescent	23	D3
Woodbrook Downs	73	D2
Woodbrook Hall	23	D3
Woodbrook Lawn	77	D3
Woodbrook Park (Carpenterstown)	23	D3
Woodbrook Park (Templeogue)	55	F3
Woodbrook Square	23	D3
Woodcliff Heights	33	E2
Wooddale Close	64	C2
Wooddale Crescent	64	C2
Wooddale Drive	64	C2
Wooddale Green	64	C2
Wooddale Grove	65	D2
Wooddale View	64	C2
Woodfarm Acres	37	D2
Woodfarm Avenue	37	E3
Woodfarm Drive	37	D3
Woodfield	65	F2
Woodford	69	D2
Woodford Avenue	46	B3
Woodford Close	46	B3
Woodford Court	46	B3
Woodford Crescent	46	A3
Woodford Downs	46	B3
Woodford Drive	46	A3
Woodford Garth	46	A3
Woodford Green	46	B3
Woodford Grove	46	B3
Woodford Heights	46	B3
Woodford Hill	46	B3
Woodford Lawn	46	B3
Woodford Meadows	46	A3
Woodford Parade	46	A3
Woodford Park	46	B3
Woodford Park Road	46	A3
Woodford Rise	46	B3
Woodford Road	46	A3
Woodford View	46	B3
Woodford Villas	46	A3
Woodford Walk	46	A3
Woodford Way	46	B3
Woodhaven	57	F1
Woodhazel Close	18	A4
Woodhazel Terrace	18	A4
Woodhazel Way	18	A4
Woodlands (Blanchardstown)	13	E4
Woodlands (Portmarnock)	10	B2
Woodlands Avenue (Cabinteely)	70	C3
Woodlands Avenue (Stillorgan)	59	D3
Woodlands Drive (Stillorgan)	59	D3
Woodlands Park (Cabinteely)	70	D3
Woodlands Park (Stillorgan)	59	D3
Woodlands Road	70	C3
Woodlawn Avenue	19	D3
Woodlawn Close	19	D3
Woodlawn Court	19	D3
Woodlawn Crescent	57	E2
Woodlawn Drive	19	D3
Woodlawn Green	19	D3
Woodlawn Park (Churchtown)	57	E3
Woodlawn Park (Kilmore)	19	D3
Woodlawn Park Avenue	64	C1
Woodlawn Park Drive	64	C1
Woodlawn Park Grove	64	C1
Woodlawn Rise	19	D3
Woodlawn View	19	D3
Woodlawn Walk	19	D3
Woodlawn Way	19	D3
Woodley Park	58	B4
Woodley Road	71	D3
Woodpark	24	A2
Woodpark The Avenue	67	F2
Woodpark The Close	67	F2
Woodpark The Court	67	F2
Woodpark The Crescent	67	E2
Woodpark The Drive	67	F2
Woodpark The Glade	67	E2
Woodpark The Glen	67	F2
Woodpark The Green	67	F2
Woodpark The Grove	67	E2
Woodpark The Heath	67	E2
Woodpark The Heights	67	F2
Woodpark The Hill	67	F2
Woodpark The Lawn	67	F2
Woodpark The Meadow	67	F2
Woodpark The Rise	67	E2
Woodpark The View	67	F2
Woodpark The Walk	67	F2
Woodscape	34	C4
Woodside	29	F4
Woodside Drive	56	C2
Woodside Grove	57	D2
Woodstock Gardens	50	B3
Woodstown Abbey	65	E2
Woodstown Avenue	65	D2
Woodstown Close	65	D2
Woodstown Court	65	D2
Woodstown Crescent	65	D2
Woodstown Dale	65	D2
Woodstown Drive	65	D2
Woodstown Gardens	65	D2
Woodstown Green	65	D2
Woodstown Heath	65	D2
Woodstown Heights	65	D2
Woodstown Hill	65	D2
Woodstown Lane	65	E2
Woodstown Lawn	65	D2
Woodstown Meadows	65	D2
Woodstown Parade	65	D2
Woodstown Park	65	D2
Woodstown Place	65	E2
Woodstown Rise	65	E2
Woodstown Road	65	D2
Woodstown Vale	65	D2

Woodstown Walk 65 D2
Woodstown Way 65 F3
Woodstown Way (Firhouse) 65 D2
Woodthorpe 59 D4
Woodvale Avenue 13 E4
Woodvale Crescent 13 E4
Woodvale Drive 13 E4
Woodvale Garth 22 C1
Woodvale Green 13 E4
Woodvale Grove 13 E4
Woodvale Park 13 E4
Woodview (Blackrock) 59 E2
Woodview (Lucan) 34 B3
Woodview Close 21 D4
Woodview Cottages 56 B2
Woodview Drive 77 D3
Woodview Grove 23 E2
Woodview Heights 34 B3
Woodview Park (Castleknock) 24 B3
Woodview Park (Donaghmede) 21 D4
Woodville Avenue 35 E2
Woodville Close 35 F2
Woodville Court 19 E4
Woodville Green 35 E2
Woodville Grove 35 E2
Woodville Lawn 35 E2
Woodville Walk 35 E2
Wyattville Close 75 D1
Wyattville Hill 75 D1
Wyattville Park 75 D1
Wyattville Road 75 D1
Wyckham Bypass 67 F1
Wyckham Grove 67 F1
Wyckham Park Road 67 F1
Wyckham Place 67 F1
Wynberg Park 60 B3
Wyndham Park 77 D1
Wynnefield Road 49 F3
Wynnsward Drive 58 A1
Wynnsward Park 58 A1
Wyteleaf Grove 20 C3
Wyvern 72 A4

X

Xavier Avenue 80 D1

Y

Yale 58 B2
Yeates Way 46 B2
Yellow Meadows Avenue 46 A3
Yellow Meadows Drive 46 A3
Yellow Meadows Grove 46 A3
Yellow Meadows Lawn 46 A3
Yellow Meadows Park 46 A3
Yellow Meadows Vale 46 A3
Yellow Nook Avenue 70 C3
Yellow Road 28 A2
Yellow Walls Road 6 C2
Yewlands Terrace 56 B1
York Avenue 49 F3
York Road (Dún Laoghaire) 61 D3
York Road (Rathmines) 49 F4
York Road (Ringsend) 41 F3
York Street 81 B5
York Terrace 61 D3

Z

Zion Road 56 C1
Zoo Road 39 E2

Suburbs & Districts

Ard na Greine 20 B3
Artane 29 D2
Ashtown 25 D3
Baldoyle 21 F3
Balgriffin 20 C1
Ballinteer 67 E2
Ballsbridge 50 C1
Ballyboden 65 F1
Ballybough 41 D1
Ballybrack 75 E1
Ballycorus 74 A4
Ballyfermot 37 E4
Ballymorris 76 C3
Ballymount 46 C4
Ballymun 18 A4
Beaumont 28 B2
Blackrock 59 E1
Blanchardstown 23 F1
Bluebell 47 E2
Booterstown 59 D1
Bray 77 D2
Bray Commons 76 B2
Cabinteely 70 B4
Cabra 39 E1
Cabra West 26 B4
Carpenterstown 23 D3
Carrickmines 74 A1
Castleknock 24 A3
Chapelizod 38 A3
Christchurch 40 A3
Churchtown 57 D3
City Quay 40 C3
Cloghran 8 C2
Clondalkin 44 C3
Clonee 12 B2
Clonsilla 22 C1
Clonskeagh 58 A1
Clontarf 42 C1
Coolock 29 E1
Cornelscourt 70 A3
Crumlin 48 B3
Dalkey 72 B2
Darndale 20 B3
Dartry 57 E1
Dean's Grange 70 A1
Dolphin's Barn 48 C1
Donaghmede 21 D3
Donnybrook 50 C3
Donnycarney 28 C3
Drimnagh 48 A2
Drumcondra 27 F3
Dún Laoghaire 61 D3
Dundrum 57 F3
East Wall 41 E2
Edenmore 30 A1
Edmondstown 66 A3
Finglas 26 A1
Finglas East 26 B1
Finglas South 26 A2
Finglas West 16 B4
Firhouse 64 C1
Fox & Geese 46 C3
Foxrock 69 F3
Galloping Green 69 D1
Glasnevin 27 D2
Goatstown 58 B3
Greenhills 54 C2
Harold's Cross 49 D2
Hartstown 12 C4
Hilltown 4 B4
Howth 33 E2
Huntstown 12 C3
Inchicore 38 C4
Irishtown 42 A4
Irishtown (Bray) 77 D4
Islandbridge 39 D3

Jobstown 62 C2
Kilbarrack 30 C1
Kill O' The Grange 70 C1
Killester 29 D3
Killinarden 63 E3
Killiney 71 E3
Kilmainham 39 E4
Kilmore 19 D4
Kilnamanagh 54 A2
Kimmage 48 C4
Knocklyon 65 E2
Leopardstown 69 D3
Loughlinstown 75 D2
Lucan 34 C3
Malahide 6 C2
Marino 28 B4
Milltown 50 B4
Monkstown 60 B3
Mooretown 4 B2
Mount Merrion 58 C3
Mulhuddart 13 F3
Newcourt 77 E3
North Wall 41 E3
Old Connaught 73 D4
Oldcourt 76 C3
Outlands 4 B1
Palmerstown 37 D2
Park West 46 B1
Phibsborough 40 B1
Poppintree 17 E2
Portmarnock 10 A1
Raheny 30 B2
Ranelagh 50 A2
Rathfarnham 56 C2
Rathgar 49 E4
Rathmichael 74 C4
Rathmines 49 F3
Ridgewood 8 B1
Ringsend 41 F4
Ronanstown 45 E1
Sallynoggin 71 D1
Sandyford 68 B3
Sandymount 51 D2
Santry 18 B4
Shankill 75 E4
Stillorgan 59 D4
Sutton 11 E4
Swords 4 C3
Tallaght 53 F4
Templeogue 55 E3
Terenure 56 B1
Tyrellstown 14 A1
Walkinstown 47 E3
Whitehall 27 F2
Windmill Lands 4 B3

Landmarks - Buildings

Abberley Court Hotel 54 A4
Abbey & Peacock Theatre 80 B3
Abbey Presbyterian Church 80 A2
Abbey Street Station (LUAS) 80 B3
Adult & Community
  Education Office (Cabinteely) 70 C3
Alexandra College 57 E1
Alexandra Quay 42 A3
All Hallows Missionary College 27 F3
All Saints Church of Ireland 59 F3
All Saints Church Raheny –
  Church of Ireland 30 A2
All Saints Parish Church 78 D1
Allied Irish Bank 51 D2
Ambassador Theatre 80 B2
American College Dublin 81 D5
An Post (Swords) 5 D3

An Post Dublin 2 Delivery
  Office 80 D3
An Post Glenageary
  Sorting Office 71 D1
An Post Tallaght Delivery Centre 54 A3
Andrews Lane Theatre 80 B4
Annabeg House Nursing Home 75 D1
Annamoe Nursing Home 77 E2
Apple of my Eye Creche 17 D3
Arbour Hill Prison 78 B3
Archbishop McQuaid Senior
  National School 75 D2
Archbishop Ryan National
  School 35 F4
Archbishop's House 27 F4
Ardeeshal Lodge Nursing Home 61 D4
Ardscoil Eanna 48 B2
Ardscoil Ris 28 B4
Arena (Malahide) 7 E2
Arlington Hotel 80 B3
Artane Castle Shopping Centre 28 C2
Artane Library 29 D2
Artane Oratory of the
  Resurrection 29 D2
Ashfield College 55 F3
Ashfield House Nursing Home 61 D3
Ashling Hotel 78 B3
Ashtown Station 25 D3
Aston Hotel 80 B3
B & Q, Lucan 36 C3
Bahai National Centre 50 B2
Balally Station (LUAS) 58 A4
Baldoyle Delivery Office 11 D3
Baldoyle Library 11 E3
Ballinteer Centre (Superquinn) 67 E2
Ballinteer Community School 67 E1
Ballyboden Public Library 56 A4
Ballydowd Prison 36 A2
Ballyfermot Boys & Girls
  National School 38 A4
Ballyfermot Mental Health
  Centre 37 D4
Ballyfermot Music Centre 37 F4
Ballyfermot Senior College 37 F4
Ballymount Fire Station 53 E1
Ballymount Industrial Estate 47 D4
Ballymun Junior
  Comprehensive School 18 A4
Ballymun Senior
  Comprehensive School 18 A4
Ballymun Shopping Centre 18 A4
Ballyroan Boys School 56 B4
Ballywaltrim Business Centre 76 C4
Balymun Public Library 27 E1
Bank of Ireland (Central Dublin) 81 B4
Bawnogue Shopping Centre 45 D3
Bayside Station 11 D4
Beaumont Hospital 28 C1
Beechwood Church 50 A3
Beechwood Station (LUAS) 50 A3
Belgard Station (LUAS) 53 F3
Belgrove School 42 C1
Beneavin College 26 C1
Bethany Church 55 E1
Bewleys Hotel (Ballsbridge) 51 D2
Bewleys Hotel (Newlands Cross) 45 F4
BIM Fish Plant 33 D1
Bishop Galvin Primary School 55 E3
Blackhorse Station (LUAS) 47 F1
Blackrock Clinic 59 E2
Blackrock College Venture
  Group 59 E1
Blackrock Delivery Office 59 F2
Blackrock Hospice 59 F2
Blackrock Post Office 59 F2
Blackrock Station 59 F2
Blanchardstown Village
  Shopping Centre 23 F2

Blanchardstown Community School	13	F4
Blanchardstown Garda Station	23	F1
Blanchardstown Institute of Technology	14	B3
Blanchardstown Public Library	23	F2
Blanchardstown Shopping Centre	23	E1
Bloomfield Shopping Centre	61	D3
Blue Feather School of Languages	60	B3
Bluebell Industrial Estate	47	D2
Bluebell Station (LUAS)	47	F2
Bon Secours Hospital	27	D3
Booterstown Station	59	E1
Bord Failte	81	A4
Bord na Mona	76	C3
Boulevard Shopping Centre	73	F4
Boulevard Shopping Precinct	77	D1
Bray Bus Station	77	E1
Bray Business Park	76	C4
Bray Cineplex	73	E4
Bray District Court House	77	D3
Bray Head Inn	77	E2
Bray Methodist Church	77	D1
Bray Public Library	77	D1
Bray Retail Park	76	B4
Bray Shopping Centre	73	E4
Bray Social Welfare	77	D1
Bray Station	77	E1
Bray Town Council	77	D1
Bray Urban District Council	76	C3
Bray VEC / Bray Senior College	77	D1
Brook House School	75	C2
Broombridge Station	26	B3
Brothers & Sisters in Christ Saint Francois	59	E3
Bru Chaoimhin Nursing Home	79	C5
Brymore Nursing Home	33	E2
Buckley Galleries	61	F4
Burlington Hotel	50	B2
Bus Eireann	78	D1
Busarus Station (LUAS)	80	C2
Butt Bridge	80	C3
Calvary Bible Baptist Church	77	D1
Calvary South Church	75	E1
Camden De-luxe Hotel	81	A5
Camp Ireland	60	A3
Canadian Embassy Residence	71	F4
Cappagh Hospital	16	A4
Cappagh Schopping Centre	25	F2
Capuchin Friary	30	A1
Car Ferry Terminal	42	C3
Caritas College	37	E3
Carmelite Church	81	A5
Carmelite Monastery	59	D4
Carnegie Library (Cabinteely)	70	C4
Carnegie Library (Sandyford)	68	B3
Carrickhill Nursery Montessori School	10	C2
Carysfort National School	59	F3
Casino (National Monument)	28	B3
Castle Hotel	72	A3
Castle Park School	72	B2
Castlefarm Water & Drainage Depot	5	D2
Castleknock College	24	A4
Castleknock Community College	23	E4
Castleknock National School	24	B3
Castleknock Station	24	A2
Castleknock Travelodge	24	B2
Castletymon Shopping Centre	54	C3
CBS St Declan's	26	B4
CBS St Joseph's School	39	E1
CDVEC - College of Technology	78	D2
CDVEC – St Kevin's College	48	C2
CDVEC Dublin Institute of Technology	49	F3
CDVEC Rathmines Senior College	49	F3
Central Bus Station	80	C3
Central Hotel	81	B4
Central Mental Hospital	57	E2
Central Remedial Clinic	29	E4
Central Statistics Office	49	F2
Chamber of Commerce	77	E1
Chanel College Secondary School for Boys	29	D1
Chapelizod Boys & Girls National School	38	A3
Chapelizod National School	38	A3
Charlemont Clinic	49	F2
Charlemont Station (LUAS)	50	A2
Charleyville Primary School	55	E4
Charlotte Quay Dock	41	E4
Cherry Orchard Church of the Most Holy Sacrament	46	B1
Cherry Orchard Hospital	37	D4
Cherry Orchard Station	46	C1
Child's World Creche	45	F4
Children's Sunshine Home	69	E2
Christ Church - Church of Ireland (Ranelagh)	50	A2
Christ Church (Bray)	77	D2
Christ Church (Sandymount)	51	E1
Christ Church Cathedral	79	D4
Christ Church Rathgar	49	E4
Christ Church Taney	58	A3
Christian Brothers	80	C4
Church of Ireland College of Education	49	F3
Church of Ireland House	50	A3
Church of Ireland Theological College	57	D2
Church of Jesus Christ of Latter Day Saints	77	D1
Church of Our Lady Help of Christians	25	F4
Church of Our Lady Mother of Divine Grace Raheny	30	A2
Church of Our Lady of Dolours	79	B6
Church of Our Lady of Good Counsel (Ballyboden)	66	B2
Church of Our Lady of Good Counsel (Drimnagh)	48	A2
Church of Our Lady of Perpetual Succour	70	A2
Church of Our Lady of Refuge	49	F2
Church of Our Lady of the Miraculous Medal	57	F1
Church of Our Lady of the Rosary	49	E3
Church of Our Lady of the Wayside	47	E2
Church of Our Lady of Victories	27	E1
Church of Our Lady Queen of Peace	51	E3
Church of Our Mother of Divine Grace	27	D2
Church of St Aengus	54	C3
Church of St Agnes Crumlin	48	B3
Church of St Bernadette	48	C2
Church of St Canice	26	B1
Church of St Catherine & St James	79	C6
Church of St Ciaran	22	B1
Church of St Colmcille	65	E1
Church of St John the Baptist	42	C1
Church of St John Vianney	29	D1
Church of St Luke the Evangelist	19	E4
Church of St Nicholas of Myra	79	D4
Church of St Peter the Apostle	44	E1
Church of St Stephen	72	A4
Church of St Thomas the Apostle	23	F3
Church of St Vincent de Paul	28	B3
Church of the Annunciation	25	F1
Church of the Apostles	75	D1
Church of the Ascension Batally Parish	68	B2
Church of the Assumption (Booterstown)	59	D1
Church of the Assumption (Milltown)	50	B4
Church of the Assumption (Walkinstown)	47	F3
Church of the Divine Mercy	36	A4
Church of the Good Shepherd Churchtown	57	D3
Church of the Holy Child	28	A2
Church of the Holy Family (Central Dublin)	78	B2
Church of the Holy Family (Kill O' The Grange)	70	B1
Church of the Holy Spirit (Ballyboden)	56	A4
Church of the Holy Spirit (Greenhills)	55	D1
Church of the Immaculate Conception (Clondalkin)	45	F4
Church of the Immaculate Conception (Sallynoggin)	71	D2
Church of the Most Holy Redeemer	77	D1
Church of The Most Precious Blood	26	B4
Church of the Nativity of Our Lord	28	B1
Church of the Sacred Heart	50	C3
Church of the Three Patrons	49	E4
Church of the Transfiguration (Bawnogue)	45	D3
Churchtown Business Park	57	E3
City Hall	80	A4
Citylink Business Park	47	D2
Citywest Business Park	52	A3
Clancy Barracks	39	D3
Clarence Hotel	81	A4
Classic Cinema	49	E3
Cleraun Study Centre	58	C2
Clondalkin Delivery Office	45	F2
Clondalkin Industrial Estate	44	B3
Clondalkin Library	46	A3
Clondalkin Park	45	E3
Clondalkin Station	45	F2
Clonkeen College	70	B3
Clonkeen Montessori School	70	B2
Clonsilla Station	22	B2
Clonskeagh Hospital	50	C4
Clonskeagh Mosque	58	A2
Clontarf & Howth Road National School	28	B4
Clontarf Castle	29	D4
Clontarf Court Hotel	42	C1
Clontarf Presbyterian Church	28	B4
Clontarf Road Station	41	F1
Cloverhill Courthouse	36	C4
Cloverhill Industrial Estate	45	F1
Cloverhill Remand Centre	36	C4
Cloverhill Visitors Centre	36	C4
Cobalt Gallery	80	B2
Coiaiste Choilm	5	D4
Colaiste Cois Life School	35	D3
Colaiste Eanna Cabra	26	B4
Colesberg Nursing Home	73	E4
College of Commerce	57	F3
Collinstown Park Community College	36	B4
Cornelscourt Shopping Centre	70	B3
Computer Services Board	78	A3
Connolly Station	80	D2
Connolly Station (LUAS)	80	C1
Convent of Mercy	29	E1
Convent of Sisters of Mercy	48	A2
Convent of St Louis	49	F3
Convent of the Holy Faith (Central Dublin)	79	D5
Convent of the Holy Faith (Finglas)	26	A1
Convent of The Holy Faith (Glasnevin)	27	D3
Cookstown Industrial Estate	53	F4
Cookstown Station (LUAS)	53	E3
Coolmine Station	23	E3
Coombe Womens Hospital	79	B6
Corduff Shopping Centre	14	B3
Corpus Christi Church	27	E3
Corpus Christi National School	27	E3
Council Offices (Dún Laoghaire)	61	E4
Cowper Station (LUAS)	50	A4
Crannton School	57	E1
Cross & Passion College for Girls	28	B3
Crowne Plaza Hotel	18	C2
Crumlin Delivery Office	48	B3
Crumlin Public Library	48	A3
Crumlin Shopping Centre	48	C2
Custom House	80	C3
Custom House Harbour	80	C1
Dalkey Station	72	B3
Dalkey Island Hotel	72	C3
Dalkey Lodge Nursing Home	72	B3
Dalkey Public Library	72	B2
Dalkey Town Hall	72	B2
Daughters of Charity	60	A3
Daughters of Charity Convent	19	E4
Daughters of Charity Social Development Centre	60	A2
Davenport Hotel	80	C4
Davis Gallery	80	A3
De La Salle Brothers School	26	B1
De La Salle College	37	F4
De La Salle Provincialate	29	D4
De la Salle School	57	D3
Dean's Grange Branch Library	70	B1
Deansgrange Cemetery	70	A1
Deansgrange Business Park	70	B1
Deansrath Community College	45	D3
Deer Park Hotel	33	D2
Defence Forces Headquarters	78	A3
Dental Hospital	80	C4
Department of Defence	27	E3
Department of Education	80	B2
Department of Marine Harbour Masters Office	33	D1
Department of Social Welfare	34	C2
Diabetic Day Centre	80	A1
DIT (Pembroke St Upper)	81	C5
DIT (Peter Row)	81	A5
DIT Research & Development	80	B2
DIT Mountjoy Square	80	C1
Dodsboro Shopping Centre	34	B3
Dolphin's Barn Post Office	79	B6
Dominican College	27	F3
Donaghmede Shopping Centre	21	D4
Donore Presbyterian	81	B6
Dorset College	40	C1
Doyle Montrose	58	C1
Doyles Hotel	51	E4
Drimnagh Station (LUAS)	48	A1
Drumcondra National School	27	F4
Drumcondra Station	40	C1
Dublin Airport	8	
Dublin Bus	78	A3
Dublin Bus Garage	50	C3
Dublin Bus Phibsborough Garage	78	D2
Dublin Castle	81	A4
Dublin City Council	22	C1
Dublin City University (DCU)	27	E2
Dublin College of Catering	80	B2

Name	Page	Grid
Dublin Corporation (Allingham St)	79	C5
Dublin Corporation (Grangegorman Lower)	78	C2
Dublin Corporation Water Division	42	A4
Dublin County Council	68	A3
Dublin Fire Brigade Training Centre	28	B3
Dublin Institute for Advanced Studies	50	B2
Dublin Institute of Technology	80	A2
Dublin Zoo	39	E2
Dublinia	79	D4
Duke Gallery	81	B4
Dún Laoghaire & Rathdown Church	61	D3
Dún Laoghaire & Rathdown County Council	61	D3
Dún Laoghaire Christian Institute	61	D3
Dún Laoghaire College of Art & Design	70	C1
Dún Laoghaire Community College	61	D3
Dún Laoghaire District Court	61	D3
Dún Laoghaire Evangelical Church	61	D4
Dún Laoghaire Garda Station	61	D3
Dún Laoghaire Harbour Carlisle Terminal	61	E3
Dún Laoghaire Methodist Church	61	D3
Dún Laoghaire Public Library	61	D3
Dún Laoghaire Shopping Centre	61	D3
Dún Laoghaire Station	61	D3
Dún Laoghaire VEC Senior College Blackrock	60	A2
Dundrum College	57	F4
Dundrum Library	57	F3
Dundrum Methodist Church	67	F2
Dundrum Station (LUAS)	57	F3
Dunnes Stores	4	C2
Earls Court Industrial Estate	57	E3
East Coast Area Health Board	33	E2
East Coast Area Health Board Central Purchasing Section	37	D4
East Point Business Park	41	F2
Eastlink Bridge	41	F3
Eastlink Toll	41	F3
Edenmore An Post	29	F1
Edenmore Special Needs School	30	A1
Edmondstown National School	66	A3
Elmhurst Private Convalescent Home	27	C2
Employment Exchange (Cabra)	39	E1
Employment Exchange (Clondalkin)	45	F3
Employment Exchange (Tallaght)	54	A4
Esker Church	34	C3
Esker School	34	C3
Esplanade Hotel	77	E2
Fairfield College	49	F4
Fairways / Rathfarnham Shopping Centre	56	A3
FÁS (Cabra West)	26	B3
FÁS (Clonsilla)	23	D2
FÁS (Loughlinstown)	75	D2
FÁS (Mulhuddart)	13	F2
FÁS Community Centre	44	E1
FÁS Training Centre	26	B4
FÁS Workshop	19	F2
Fatima Station (LUAS)	79	B5
Fettercairn Church	53	D4
Fingal Adult Education Centre	5	D3
Fingal Cemetery	20	C2
Fingal Community College	5	D3
Fingal County Council	23	D2
Fingal County Council Offices	23	E1
Fingal House	5	D2
Finglas Library	26	B1
Finglas Main Centre	26	B1
Finglas Parochial School	26	A1
Finglas Social Welfare Office	26	A1
Fios Feasa Scoil Chronain Naofa	77	D2
Firhouse Community College	64	B2
Firhouse National School	64	C1
Firhouse Shopping Centre	64	C1
First Church of Christ Scientist	50	C2
Fitzwilliam Hotel	81	B5
Focus Theatre	80	C6
Fonthill Abbey	56	B4
Forte Travel Lodge	5	D4
Fortfield Delivery Office	56	A1
Four Courts	78	D3
Four Courts Station (LUAS)	78	D3
Four Seasons Hotel	51	D2
Franciscan Church of Adam & Eve	79	D4
Franciscan Missionary Sisters for Africa	51	E2
Frank Sherwin Bridge	78	B3
Friar Mathew Bridge	78	D3
Gael Scoil Mide	30	C1
Gaelscoil Inchicore	39	D4
Gaiety Theatre	81	B4
Garda Headquarters	39	E2
Garda Siochana HQ	81	B6
Garda Station (Bray)	77	D2
Garda Station (Kilmainham)	39	E4
Garda Station (Rathfarnham)	56	B3
Garda Traffic Department	81	A4
Gate Theatre	80	B2
General Post Office	80	B3
Glasnevin (Prospect) Cemetery	26	C3
Glasnevin National School	27	D3
Glasthule Post Office	61	E4
Glen College	37	F2
Glen Hilton Nursing Home	73	E4
Glenageary & Killiney National School	72	A3
Glenageary Station	71	E1
Goldenbridge Convent	48	A1
Goldenbridge Station (LUAS)	48	B1
Gonzaga College	50	B3
Good Shepherd National School	57	D3
Gort Muire	67	F1
Gort na Mona	71	D1
Government Buildings	81	C5
Grand Canal Dock Station	41	E4
Grand Canal Wharf	41	E4
Grand Hotel	7	E2
Grattan Bridge	80	A3
Green Acres Creche	37	D2
Green Isle Hotel	52	C1
Greendale Community School	30	C1
Greendale Shopping Centre	30	C1
Greenhills Community College	55	D1
Gresham Hotel	80	B2
Griffeen Valley National School	35	E4
Griffith College Dublin	49	E2
Grosvenor Creche	49	E3
Grosvenor Road Baptist Church	49	E3
Grove Nursing Home	71	F4
Guardian Angels Church	60	A3
Guardian Angels National School	60	A3
Guinness Brewery	78	B3
Guinness Storehouse	79	B4
Ha'penny Bridge	80	B3
Hampstead Private Hospital	27	D3
Harcourt Nursing Home	80	B6
Harcourt Station (LUAS)	81	B6
Harmonstown Delivery Office	29	E2
Harmonstown Station	29	E2
Harold National School	61	E4
Harold's Cross Primary School	49	D4
Hartstown Shopping Centre	22	B1
Hawthorn Hotel	5	D3
Herbert Park Hotel	50	C2
Heritage Centre & Tourist Office	73	E4
Heuston Station	78	A3
Heuston Station (LUAS)	78	B3
Highfield Private Hospital & Alzheimer Care Centre	28	A2
Hillcrest Shopping Centre	34	B3
Hilton Hotel	20	C2
Hollybrook Hotel	28	C4
Holy Child Community School	71	D2
Holy Cross Primary School	57	F4
Holy Family Junior School	4	B4
Holy Family School	60	C4
Holy Family Senior School	4	B4
Holy Rosary Convent	29	E1
Holy Rosary Primary School	64	B2
Holy Spirit School	17	F4
Holy Trinity Church (Donaghmede)	21	D4
Holy Trinity Church (Killiney)	71	F3
Holy Trinity Church (Rathmines)	49	F3
Holycross College	27	F4
Horizon Montessori School	55	F2
Horticultural Training Unit	59	E4
Hospital Station (LUAS)	53	E4
Hotel Abbey	80	B3
Hotel Capri	80	B3
Hotel Conrad	81	B6
Hotel Ibis	46	B4
House of St Mary of the Servants	13	F4
Howth Castle Museum of Transport	33	D2
Howth Hill Lodge Nursing Home	33	E3
Howth Junction Station	21	E4
Howth Presbyterian Church	32	C1
Howth Public Library	33	E2
Howth Station	33	D1
Huge Lane Municipal Art Gallery	80	A2
Hunt's Post Office	51	F4
IDA Enterprise Centre	54	B4
IFSC	80	D3
Ilac Centre	80	A3
Immaculate Conception House	29	F4
Inchicore Vocational School	39	D4
Incorporated Law Society	78	C3
Institute for Public Administration	50	C1
Iona Centre	65	E1
Irish Film Centre	81	A4
Irish Missionary Union	57	D1
Irish Sisters of Charity Chapel	51	E3
Irish Tourist Board	81	D6
Irish Wheelchair Association	29	E4
Iscamil School	81	B5
Island View Hotel	7	E2
Italian Embassy	34	C2
Iveagh Hostel	79	D4
James Connolly Memorial Hospital	24	A1
James Joyce Bridge	78	C3
James Joyce Centre	80	B2
James Joyce Tower	61	F3
James's Station (LUAS)	79	B4
Jamestown Road Baptist Church	26	B1
Janelle Shopping & Leisure Centre	26	B2
Jensen Hotel	45	F3
Jervis Centre Station (LUAS)	80	B3
Jervis Shopping Centre	80	A3
John F Kennedy Estate	47	D2
John McCormick Bridge	41	E2
John Paul II School	6	C2
Jury's Hotel	79	D4
Jury's Inn Custom House	80	D3
Kevin Street College (DIT)	81	A5
Kevin Street Garda Station	81	A5
Kilakee House	53	F4
Kilbarrack Secondary School	30	B1
Kilbarrack Shopping Centre	30	B1
Kilbarrack Station	30	B1
Kilbride Church	76	B3
Kildare Place School	49	F3
Kill O' The Grange Parish Office	70	B1
Killester Station	29	D3
Killinarden Community School	63	E2
Killiney Shopping Centre	71	D3
Killiney Station	75	F1
Kilmacud Station (LUAS)	68	B1
Kilmainham Congregational Church	39	D4
Kilmainham Gaol (Museum)	39	D4
Kilmainham Post Office	39	D4
Kilnamanagh Shopping Centre	54	A3
King's Inns	78	D2
Kingdom Hall of Jehovah's Witnesses (Bray)	77	D3
Kingdom Hall of Jehovah's Witnesses (Cloghran)	9	D2
Kingdom Hall of Jehovah's Witnesses (Clondalkin)	45	F3
Kingdom Hall of Jehovah's Witnesses (Monkstown)	60	C4
Kingfisher Guesthouse	80	B2
Kingswood Art Gallery	52	B3
Kingswood Station (LUAS)	54	A2
Kinvara House	77	E1
Kylemore Station (LUAS)	47	E2
Ladyswell National School	14	A3
Lambert Puppet Theatre & Museum	60	B3
Lambkins Montessori	33	E3
Language & Commercial Centre	27	F3
Larkhill School	27	F1
Leeson Court Hotel	81	C6
Leeson Park School of Music	50	B2
Legionaires of Christ	68	C3
Leinster House	80	C4
Leopardstown Park Hospital	69	D3
LIDL	16	C3
Lifegate Bible Baptist Church	54	A3
Liffey Valley Shopping Centre	36	C3
Lindsay Road Infants School	27	E4
Little Rascal's Nursery	28	B2
Little Sisters of the Poor Convent	58	B2
Littlepace Shopping Centre	13	D3
Loreto Abbey	56	C3
Loreto College	4	B4
Loreto Convent (Bray)	77	D2
Loreto Convent (Foxrock)	69	F2
Loreto High School	56	B3
Loreto National School	56	C3
Loreto Primary School	72	B2
Loughlinstown Health Centre	75	D2
Lucan Community College	34	C3
Lucan Methodist Church	34	C3
Lucan Presbyterian Church	34	C2
Lucan Studio	34	C2
Lucan Veterinary Hospital	35	D2
Lucena Clinic	77	D2
Luke Kelly Bridge	41	D1
Lycee Francais d'Irlande	69	F1
M S The National Care Centre	56	C1
Madonna House School	59	E3
Magic Years Montessori	23	F1
Malahide Castle	6	C3
Malahide Community School	7	D4
Malahide Library	7	D2
Malahide Presbyterian Church	7	D2
Malahide Schools	7	D2
Malahide Station	7	D2
Manresa House	30	A4
Mansion House	80	B5

Maple House Hotel 27 E4
Margaret Aylward Community
College 28 A2
Marianist Community 75 E1
Marine Hotel 32 A1
Marino College 28 B4
Marino Institute of Education 28 B3
Marino School 77 D2
Marist Convent 48 C3
Marist National School 49 D2
Marley Montessori School 56 B2
Martello Tower (Monkstown) 60 B2
Martello Tower (Sandymount) 51 E2
Mary Help of Christians 25 F4
Mary Immaculate School 69 E1
Mary Queen of Angels 37 E3
Maryfield Nursing Home 37 F3
Mater Dei Institute 40 C1
Mater Misericordiae Hospital 40 B1
Mater Private Hospital 80 A1
Mayberry Industrial Estate 53 F3
Mayfair Hotel 73 F4
McKee Barracks 78 A1
Meanscoil Naomh Scoil 48 B3
Mellowes Bridge 78 C3
Melody School of Music 55 E1
Mercy College 29 E1
Merrion Shopping Centre 51 E3
Mespil Hotel 81 D6
Met Office 27 D3
Methodist Church Blackrock 60 A2
Methodist Church Drimnagh 48 A3
Millennium Bridge 80 A3
Milltown Station (LUAS) 57 E1
Missionaries of Africa 55 F3
Monastery of Our Lady of
Charity of Refuge 80 C2
Monastery Shopping Centre 45 F3
Monkstown & Richmond
Cheshire Home 60 B3
Monkstown Community
Centre 60 C4
Monkstown Park Christian
Brothers School 60 C3
Monkstown Primary School 60 C3
Montessori & After School Care 27 E2
Montessori & Day Care 23 F1
Moran Hotel 46 C4
Morgan Hotel 80 B3
Morrison Hotel 80 A3
Mother of Divine Grace School
& College 26 C1
Mount Anville School 58 B3
Mount Carmel Hospital 57 D2
Mount Jerome Cemetery 49 D2
Mount Sackville Convent 37 E2
Mount Temple Comprehensive
School 28 C4
Mountjoy Prison 40 B1
Mountjoy Square 80 B1
Mountview Church St Philip
the Apostle 22 C1
Moymel Shopping Centre 23 F1
Mulhuddart National School 13 F3
Museum Station (LUAS) 78 B3
Naiscoil Ide Raheny 30 A2
Nangor Medical Centre 45 D3
National Archives 81 A5
National College of Art &
Design 79 C4
National Gallery 80 C4
National Library 80 C4
National Maternity Hospital 81 D5
National Monument Round
Tower 45 F3
National Museum 81 C5
National Museum
(Collins Barracks) 78 B3

National Rehabilitation Hospital
St Joseph's College 70 C2
National Training College
Rehabilitation Institute 51 E1
National University of Ireland 81 D5
Natural History Museum 81 C5
NDNSP School 27 D3
Neilstown Shopping Centre 44 E1
New Boys National School 11 D3
New International Hotel 77 E1
Newgrove School 21 E3
Newman College Belmont
Campus 69 E1
Newpark School 60 A4
Northside Shopping Centre 19 E4
Novena of Grace Saint Francis
Xavier 18 A4
Nutgrove Office Park 57 E3
Nutgrove Shopping Centre 57 E4
O'Brien's Ferryman 80 D3
O'Connell Bridge 80 B3
O'Donovan Rossa Bridge 79 D4
Oblate Church of Mary
Immaculate 47 F1
Oisin Art Gallery 41 E1
Olivia Theatre 80 B1
OLV Primary School 27 D1
Olympia Theatre 81 A4
Omni Park Shopping Centre 18 B4
OmniPlex Cinema 18 B4
Open University 80 D4
OPW 81 C5
Order of St Camillus 59 D2
Ordnance Survey Ireland 38 A1
Orthopaedic Hospital 29 E4
O'Scanall Vet Hospital 5 D4
Our Lady of Consolation Church 28 B3
Our Lady of Dolours Church 27 D3
Our Lady of Good Counsel
Church 71 D3
Our Lady of Good Counsel
Schools 71 D3
Our Lady of Lourdes Church 80 C2
Our Lady of Mercy Church 29 E2
Our Lady of Mount Carmel
Church 64 C1
Our Lady of the Wayside
National School 47 E2
Our Lady Queen of Peace
Church 77 D3
Our Lady Star of the Sea 51 E1
Our Lady's Convent 56 A2
Our Lady's Hospice 49 E2
Our Lady's Manor Nursing
Home 72 B1
Our Lady's School 56 A2
Palmerstown Catholic Church 37 D2
Parish Church of Saint Stephen 81 D5
Parish of Our Lady Mother
of The Church 24 B3
Park Hotel 20 B3
Parliament Hotel 81 A4
Parnell Centre 80 A2
Parnell Road Fire Station 49 D2
Parnell West Hotel 80 A2
Patrician College 25 F2
Pavillion Theatre 61 D3
Pearse Museum 66 C1
Pearse Station 80 D4
People's College 80 A2
Phatos House Kitchen City 46 C4
Phoenix Park Special School 25 E4
Plunkett College 27 F2
Pobalscoil Rosmini Post
Primary School 28 A3
Portmarnock Community School 10 B2
Portmarnock Golf Links Hotel 10 C3
Portmarnock National School 10 B4

Portmarnock Post Office 10 B3
Portmarnock Station 10 A4
Portuguese Embassy 69 F2
Post Primary School Colaiste
Ebin 25 F1
Presentation School 77 E3
Presentation Secondary School
(Monkstown) 60 B4
Presentation Secondary School
(Terenure) 56 B1
Priorswood Post Office 19 F3
Priory Studios 59 D3
Provincialate Our Lady's Grove 58 A2
Quakers 50 B2
Queen of Angels National
School 68 B2
Radisson Hotel 59 D2
Raglan Lodge 50 C2
Raheny Public Library 30 A2
Raheny Shopping Centre 30 A2
Raheny Station 30 A2
Ranelagh Station (LUAS) 50 A2
Rathdown Senior School 71 E1
Rathfarnham National School 56 A3
Rathfarnham Parish Church 56 B2
Rathgar Methodist Church 49 E4
Rathgar School 49 E4
Rathmichael Primary School
& Parochial Hall 75 E3
Rathmines Post Office 49 F3
Red Cow Station (LUAS) 46 C4
Redemptorists Marianella
Pastoral Centre 57 D1
Regency Airport Hotel 27 F3
Registry of Births Deaths &
Marriages (Bray) 77 D1
Rehabilitation Centre 51 F4
Religious Society of Friends 57 E2
Rialto Parish Centre 79 A6
Rialto Station (LUAS) 79 A5
Richview Architecture 50 C4
Rickard House 60 A3
Riverbank Theatre 79 D4
Riversdale Community Centre 14 B3
Riverside Clinic 57 D2
Riverview Business Park 46 B2
Rochestown Lodge Hotel 71 D3
Rosary College 25 F4
Rosary College (Crumlin) 48 B3
Roselawn Shopping Centre 23 F2
Rosemount Shopping Centre 56 A4
Roseville Nursing Home 77 E2
Rotunda Hospital 80 B2
Round Tower School 44 C4
Roy O'More Bridge 78 C3
Royal Dublin Society (RDS) 51 D3
Royal Dublin Society's
Showground 51 D2
Royal Hibernian Exhibition
Centre 81 C5
Royal Hospital Kilmainham 79 A4
Royal Hotel 77 D1
Royal Marine Hotel 61 D3
Royal Victoria Eye & Ear Hospital 81 C6
Russell Court Hotel 81 B5
Sachs Hotel 50 B2
Sacred Heart Church
(Huntstown) 13 E3
Sacred Heart Church
(Killinarden) 63 E2
Sacred Heart Church Sruleen 45 E4
Sacred Heart Community 50 A2
Sacred Heart Foundation
Little Sisters of the Poor 29 E3
Sacred Heart House 40 C1
Sacred Heart Missionaries 59 E2
Sacrament of the Lord's Supper 60 C3
Saint Agnes National School 48 B3

Saint Aidan's Community
School 62 B1
Saint Aidan's Primary School 62 C1
Saint Aidan's Secondary School 27 F2
Saint Alphonsus & Saint
Columbus Church 75 E1
Saint Andrew's 59 F2
Saint Andrew's Church 7 D2
Saint Andrew's Church 80 C4
Saint Andrew's Church of
Ireland 34 C2
Saint Andrew's National School 7 D2
Saint Andrew's Newcourt
School 77 E3
Saint Andrew's Presbyterian
Church 77 D1
Saint Andrew's School 59 D1
Saint Anne's Church
(Portmarnock) 10 B4
Saint Anne's Church (Shankill) 75 E4
Saint Anne's National School 53 D4
Saint Anthony's Church 42 A1
Saint Anthony's House 42 A1
Saint Attracta's Junior National
School Meadowbrook 67 E1
Saint Audoen's Church 79 D4
Saint Basil's Training Centre 54 B4
Saint Benedict's Church 30 B1
Saint Brendan's 70 C2
Saint Brendan's Church 29 E1
Saint Brendan's Hospital 78 C1
Saint Bricin's Military Hospital 78 B2
Saint Brigid's Church
(Blanchardstown) 23 F2
Saint Brigid's Church
(Cabinteely) 70 C4
Saint Brigid's Church
(Castleknock) 24 B3
Saint Brigid's Church (Killester) 29 E3
Saint Brigid's Church (Stillorgan) 59 E4
Saint Brigid's Girls School
(Cabinteely) 70 B4
Saint Brigid's Girls School
(Killester) 29 D2
Saint Brigid's National School
(Castleknock) 24 B3
Saint Brigid's National School
(Stillorgan) 59 E4
Saint Brigid's Primary School 52 C4
Saint Brigid's School 29 E3
Saint Canice's Church 26 A1
Saint Canice's National School 26 B1
Saint Catherine's Church 79 C4
Saint Clare's Convent
San Damiano 49 E2
Saint Clare's Home 27 D2
Saint Clare's Primary School 49 E2
Saint Columba's 48 B3
Saint Columba's Church 27 E4
Saint Columba's College 67 D3
Saint Columba's School 27 E4
Saint Columbanus Church 75 D2
Saint Columcille Senior School 65 E1
Saint Columcille's Boys
National School 5 E3
Saint Columcille's Church 5 D3
Saint Columcille's Girls 5 E3
Saint Columcille's Hospital
& Convent 75 D2
Saint Cronan's 77 D2
Saint Cronan's Primary School 4 C3
Saint Damian's Religious
Institution 51 D2
Saint David's Christian
Community 28 C2
Saint Dominic's Church 64 B1
Saint Dominic's College 26 A4
Saint Dominic's Senior School 64 A1

Saint Fergal's Boys National
School 26 A1
Saint Fergal's Church 76 C3
Saint Fergal's Junior School 76 C3
Saint Finbar's National School 26 B4
Saint Finian's Pastorate 81 C6
Saint Finian's River Valley 4 B4
Saint Finian's School 25 F2
Saint Fintan's Church 32 B1
Saint Fintan's High School 32 A1
Saint Francis Church 19 F3
Saint Francis School 19 F2
Saint Francis Xavier's School 23 F2
Saint Francis Xavier's Church 80 B1
Saint Gabriel's Church 29 F4
Saint Helen's Christian
Brothers Provincialate 60 C3
Saint Helen's School 7 F4
Saint James Church Crinken 73 D2
Saint James's Hospital 79 A5
Saint John Bosco's 25 F4
Saint John of God Hospital 59 E4
Saint John of God School 71 D1
Saint John the Evangelist
Church (Coolock) 20 B4
Saint John the Evangelist
Church (Dún Laoghaire) 60 C4
Saint John the Evangelist
Church (Kilbarrack) 30 C1
Saint John the Evangelist
Church (Sandymount) 51 E2
Saint John's Church 45 F3
Saint Joseph's Boys School 28 B4
Saint Joseph's Centre 73 D1
Saint Joseph's Church
(Phibsborough) 80 A1
Saint Joseph's Church (Terenure) 56 C1
Saint Joseph's Church Glasthule 61 E4
Saint Joseph's College
Presbyterian Convent 35 D2
Saint Joseph's Hospital
(Clonsilla) 22 A2
Saint Joseph's Hospital
(Edenmore) 29 F2
Saint Joseph's Presentation
Convent 56 B1
Saint Joseph's Primary School 61 D4
Saint Joseph's School for Boys 56 C1
Saint Joseph's School for the
Visually Handicapped 28 A4
Saint Joseph's Church
(Ballymun) 17 F3
Saint Joseph's Church
(Darndale) 19 F3
Saint Joseph's Girl's School 16 B4
Saint Joseph's School (Ballymun) 17 F3
Saint Joseph's School (Darndale) 19 F3
Saint Jude the Apostle 55 E3
Saint Kevin's Parish Church 54 B2
Saint Kevin's Primary School 71 D1
Saint Kevin's National School 16 B4
Saint Kilian's Church 54 A1
Saint Kilian's School 58 B2
Saint Laurence College 75 D1
Saint Laurence's Church
of Ireland 38 A3
Saint Laurence's School 16 B4
Saint Loman's Hospital 36 A2
Saint Lorcan's Boys National
School 37 E2
Saint Louise's Junior & Senior
Schools 37 E3
Saint Luke's Hospital 57 D1
Saint Luke's Oaklands Hospital 57 D1
Saint Luke's Church 14 A3
Saint Mac Dara's College 55 D3
Saint Maelruain's Church
of Ireland 54 A4

Saint Maelruain's School 63 D1
Saint Maelruan's Senior
National School 64 A2
Saint Malachy's Boys
National School 30 A1
Saint Malachy's School 26 B2
Saint Maria Secondary School 65 F1
Saint Martin Apostolate
& Chapel 80 A2
Saint Martin de Porres Church 64 A2
Saint Martin de Porres
National School 63 F2
Saint Mary of the Angels 78 D3
Saint Mary's 56 B3
Saint Mary's & Saint Demyanas
Church 76 C2
Saint Mary's Boys National
School 35 D2
Saint Mary's Church
(Ballsbridge) 81 D6
Saint Mary's Church
(Donnybrook) 50 C2
Saint Mary's Church (Howth) 33 E2
Saint Mary's Church (Lucan) 35 D2
Saint Mary's Church of Ireland 48 A3
Saint Mary's College CSSP 49 F2
Saint Mary's Community School 54 A4
Saint Mary's Convent 54 A4
Saint Mary's Dominican College
/ Muckross Park College 50 B3
Saint Mary's Friary 54 A4
Saint Mary's Holy Faith School 29 D2
Saint Mary's Hospital 38 B3
Saint Mary's Primary School 35 D2
Saint Mary's School & Clinic
for the Deaf 26 A3
Saint Mary's School
(Ballyboden) 66 B1
Saint Mary's School
(Donnybrook) 50 C3
Saint Mary's School (Marino) 41 E1
Saint Mary's School (Tallaght) 53 E4
Saint Mary's Hospital 11 D3
Saint Mary's Secondary School 11 D3
Saint Mathias Church 71 E4
Saint Michael's Church
(Dún Laoghaire) 61 D3
Saint Michael's Church
(Inchicore) 39 D4
Saint Michael's College 51 E3
Saint Michael's Hospital 61 D3
Saint Michael's House 25 F3
Saint Michael's House
Short-Term Training Centre 27 D2
Saint Michael's School 37 F2
Saint Michan's Catholic Church 78 D3
Saint Michan's Church of Ireland 78 D3
Saint Mobhi's Church 27 D3
Saint Mochta's School 23 D2
Saint Monica's Church 30 A1
Saint Monica's Convent 80 B1
Saint Nessan's School 11 D4
Saint Oliver Plunkett Junior
School 26 B2
Saint Oliver Plunkett National
School (Malahide) 7 D3
Saint Oliver Plunkett National
School (Monkstown) 60 C3
Saint Oliver Plunkett's Church 26 B2
Saint Oliver's Park Community
Hall & Pre School 46 A1
Saint Pappan's Church 18 C4
Saint Patrick's Cathedral 79 D5
Saint Patrick's Church (Dalkey) 72 B2
Saint Patrick's Church
(Monkstown) 60 C3
Saint Patrick's Hospital 79 A4

Saint Patrick's National School
(Dalkey) 72 B2
Saint Patrick's National School
(Drumcondra) 27 E4
Saint Patrick's Teacher's Centre 27 E3
Saint Patrick's Church 14 B3
Saint Patrick's Junior School 14 B4
Saint Paul of the Cross
Mount Argus 49 D3
Saint Paul's CBS 78 C3
Saint Paul's Church (Bray) 73 E4
Saint Paul's Church
(Christchurch) 78 C3
Saint Paul's Church
(Sallynoggin) 71 E1
Saint Paul's Church Ayrefield 20 B4
Saint Paul's College 29 E3
Saint Peter the Apostle School 45 E1
Saint Peter's Church 73 E3
Saint Peter's College 29 D3
Saint Peter's National School 73 E4
Saint Philomena's School
Ravenswell 73 E4
Saint Philip's Church 57 E1
Saint Philip's School 22 C1
Saint Phillip & Saint James 59 E2
Saint Pius Cross Church 56 A2
Saint Ronan's Church 44 C3
Saint Rosalie's Convent 10 C1
Saint Saviour's Priory 80 A2
Saint Stephen's Green
Shopping Centre 81 B5
Saint Sylvester's Church 7 D2
Saint Thomas Aquinas School 60 C4
Saint Thomas's Church 62 C2
Saint Vincent de Paul Church 36 B4
Saint Vincent's Centre Chapel 25 E4
Saint Vincent's Centre Day
Centre 25 E4
Saint Vincent's Centre VTC 25 E4
Saint Vincent's Hospital 28 A4
Saint Vincent's National School 25 E4
Saint Vincent's School 27 D4
Saint Vincent's University
Hospital 51 E4
Saints Peter & Paul Church 11 E3
Sally Park Nursing Home 55 D4
Sallynoggin Public Library 71 D2
Salthill & Monkstown Station 60 C3
San Remo Nursing Home 77 E2
Sandford National School 50 B3
Sandford Parish Church 50 B3
Sandford Park School 50 B3
Sands Hotel 10 C2
Sandycove & Glasthule Station 61 E4
Sandyford Church 68 B3
Sandyford Station (LUAS) 69 D2
Sandymount Station 51 D2
Santa Sabina Dominican
Convent 32 B1
Santry Garda Station 27 F1
Sarsfield House 38 B4
Savoy Theatre 80 B2
School of Irish Studies 51 D2
Scoil Aine 45 F4
Scoil an tSeachtar Laoch 18 A4
Scoil Chaitlin Maude 63 D2
Scoil Chaitriona 27 E3
Scoil Chiarain 13 D4
Scoil Chiarain 13 E4
Scoil Cholmcille 75 D1
Scoil Chualann 77 E3
Scoil Daibheid Naola / Scoil
Naisiunta 28 C1
Scoil Eanna na Magoine Muire 57 E2
Scoil Eanna Naisiunta Aengusa
Naofa 54 C3
Scoil Eithne 30 A1

Scoil Eoin 30 C1
Scoil Fhorsa 19 E4
Scoil Lorcain 60 B2
Scoil Maighdine Muire 67 E2
Scoil Mhuire (Ballyfermot) 38 A4
Scoil Mhuire (Clonsilla) 13 F4
Scoil Mhuire Bearn Eadair 33 D2
Scoil Mobhi 27 E3
Scoil Muire Gan Smal 47 F1
Scoil Naisciunta Muire na
Deagh Comhairle 48 A2
Scoil Naisiunta Caitriona 29 E1
Scoil Naisiunta Iosa 54 C3
Scoil Naisiunta Naomh Iosef 54 C3
Scoil Naisunta Bhride 37 E3
Scoil Naisiunta Muire agus Josef 25 F2
Scoil Naisunta na Monatan 28 C3
Scoil Naomh Padraig 56 A4
Scoil Neasain 29 E2
Scoil Oilibhir 23 D1
Scoil Phobail Chuil Mhin 23 D1
Scoil Santain 64 B1
Scoil Thomais Primary School 23 F3
Scoil Treasa 64 C1
Scoll UI Chonalll 42 A1
Sean Heuston Bridge 78 B3
Sean O'Casey Bridge 80 C3
Seapoint Station 60 B2
Senior College Colaiste Ebin 25 F1
Senior College Sallynoggin 71 D2
Shanganagh Castle 73 D1
Shankill Library 75 E4
Shankill Station 75 F3
Shannagh Bay Nursing Home 77 E1
Sharavogue 71 E1
Sheridan Imax 80 A3
Shieling Hotel 30 B2
Sisters of Charity (Howth) 33 E3
Sisters of Charity (Sandymount) 51 E2
Sisters of Mercy 48 A1
Sisters of Our Lady of Apostles 50 C1
Sisters of St Peter Claver 56 C1
Skylon Hotel 27 F3
Smithfield Station (LUAS) 78 D3
Smurfit School of Business 59 E3
Social Welfare Office
(Dún Laoghaire) 60 C3
Social Welfare Services Office
(Ballyfermot) 37 F4
South City Business Park 63 E2
South Hill Evangelist Church 59 D2
Southern Cross Business Park 76 C3
Spa Hotel 34 B2
Spencer Dock 41 E3
Stephens Green Station (LUAS) 81 B5
Stewart's Hospital 37 E2
Stewart's School 37 E2
Stillorgan Church Library 59 E4
Stillorgan Park Hotel 59 D3
Stillorgan Plaza Ormonde
Cinema 59 D4
Stillorgan Reservoir 69 D2
Stillorgan Senior College 59 D3
Stillorgan Shopping Centre 59 D4
Stillorgan Station (LUAS) 68 C1
Strand Lounge Hotel 77 E2
Stratford College 56 C1
Suir Road Station (LUAS) 48 B1
Sundrive Nursery 49 D3
Sundrive Shopping Centre 49 D3
Sunny Bank Hotel 27 D4
Superquinn Shopping Centre 34 C3
Supervalu Shopping Centre 29 D3
Sutton Castle 32 C3
Sutton Close Shopping Centre 32 A1
Sutton Methodist Church 32 B1
Sutton Nursing Home 32 A1
Sutton Park School 32 C3

Entry	Page	Grid
Sutton Station	32	A1
Swan Shopping Centre	49	F3
Swords Boys School	5	D3
Swords Fire Station	5	D2
Swords Health Centre	5	D3
Swords Leisure Centre	5	D3
Swords Old Boro National School	5	D3
Sydney Parade Station	51	E3
Synagogue	56	B1
T.J. Mitchell Ltd Gallery	81	C5
Talbot Memorial Bridge	80	C3
Tallaght Garda Station	54	A4
Tallaght Hospital	53	E4
Tallaght Institute of Technology	54	A4
Tallaght Library	53	F4
Tallaght Station (LUAS)	53	F4
Tallaght Theatre	54	B2
Tara Nursing Home	77	E2
Tara Street Station	80	C3
Taylor Galleries	80	B5
Team Theatre Company	80	C3
Temple Street Children's Hospital	80	B1
Temple Theatre	80	B1
Templeogue College	55	F2
Terenure College	56	A2
Terenure Library	56	B1
The Abbey	47	F3
The Anne Sullivan Centre	69	D2
The Baily Court Hotel	33	E2
The Bizzie Kids Bungalow	21	D4
The Children's House	59	D4
The Church of Jesus Christ of Latter Day Saints (Glasnevin)	26	C3
The Church of Jesus Christ of Latter Day Saints (Terenure)	56	C1
The Church of St Laurence O'Toole	59	D4
The Clarion Hotel	80	D3
The Cottage	32	C1
The Court Hotel	71	F4
The Divine Word Museum	66	C1
The Donaghies School	20	C4
The Gasworks	41	E4
The Guinness Gallery	69	F3
The Kings Hospital School	36	C2
The Lott Art & Picture Gallery	5	D3
The Malthouse	79	B5
The Maple Centre	39	E1
The Merrion Hotel	81	C5
The Mill Shopping Centre	45	F3
The Mont Clare Hotel	80	C4
The National Concert Hall	81	B6
The Old Court House	33	D1
The Park Shopping Centre	70	B4
The Pavillions Shopping Centre	5	D4
The Plaza Clinic	5	D3
The Point Depot	41	F3
The Rathfarnham Convalescent Nursing House	65	F2
The Royal Hospital	50	B2
The Screen Cinema	80	C3
The Shelbourne Hotel	81	C5
The Spire	80	B3
The Square Shopping Centre	53	F4
Thorn Castle	59	E1
Tivoli Theatre	79	D4
Traverslea Consulate of Malta	61	E4
Trinity College	80	C4
Trinity College Enterprise Centre	41	E4
Tudor Galleries	61	F4
Tullow Church	70	A4
UCD Horticulture Unit	51	D4
UCD School of Diagnostic Imaging	51	E4
University College Dublin (UCD)	58	B1
University of Dublin Trinity College School of Pharmacy	51	D3
Verbum Dei Missionaries	75	E4
Verville Retreat	29	E4
Vincentian Community Residence	29	E3
Virgin Mary's School	18	A4
Walkinstown Park	47	E3
Waterways Visitor's Centre	41	E4
Waverley Ambulance Station	79	A1
Weatherwell Business Centre	45	F2
Weatherwell Industrial Estate	45	F2
Wee Care Montessori School	60	B4
Wellington Monument	39	E3
Wesley College	67	F2
West Country Hotel	37	F3
West Finglas Shopping Centre	16	B4
Westbourne Hotel	77	D1
Westbury Hotel	81	B4
Western Industrial Park	46	C2
Westgate Business Park	54	B1
Whitechurch Branch Library	66	A1
Whitechurch Church of Ireland	66	C3
Whitechurch National School	66	B2
Windmill Lane Studios	80	B1
Windy Arbour Station (LUAS)	57	E2
Woodland Court Hotel	77	E3
Woodlands Creche	71	D3
Zion Church	56	C1
Zion Court School	56	C1
Irishtown Stadium	42	A4
Iveagh Grounds	48	B2
Johnstown Park	26	C2
Kilbogget Park	71	D4
Kildonan Park	16	B4
Killiney Golf Course	71	E3
Killiney Park	72	B4
Lansdowne Rugby Ground	51	D1
Le Fanu Park	37	F4
Leopardstown Race Course	69	E3
Liffey Gaels GAA Club	38	C4
Longmeadows Park	38	B4
Lorcan O'Toole Park	48	B4
Luttrellstown Golf Course	22	C4
Malahide Golf Course	10	A3
Markievicz Park	38	A4
Marley Park	67	D2
McAuley Park	29	E2
Mellowes Park	16	C4
Merrion Square	81	C5
Milltown Golf Course	57	E2
Milltown Park	50	B4
National Aquatic Centre	14	C4
National Baseball Facility	52	B1
National Basketball Arena	55	D3
Newlands Golf Course	53	D2
Open Golf Centre	16	B1
Parnell Park	28	C3
Pearse Memorial Park	48	B3
People's Garden	78	A3
Phoenix Park	38	B2
Pope John Paul II Park	26	A4
Poppintree Park	17	E3
Portmarnock Golf Club	11	E2
Portmarnock Golf Links	10	C3
Ringsend Park	41	F4
Rockfield Park	28	C2
Royal Dublin Golf Course	43	E1
Royal Dublin Golf Links	30	C4
Saint Anne's Golf Links	31	D2
Saint Anne's Park	30	A3
Saint Enda's Park	66	C1
Saint Stephen's Green	81	B5
Saint Vincent's GAA	28	B3
Santry Stadium	18	B3
Santry Woods	18	B3
Seagrange Park	11	D4
Sean Moore Park	51	E1
Shanganagh Park	73	E1
Sillogue Golf Course	17	F1
Sillogue Park	17	F2
Stannaway Park	48	B4
Stardust Memorial Park	19	F3
Sutton Golf Links	32	A1
Three Rock Rovers Hockey Club	66	C1
Tolka Park	27	F4
Tolka Valley Park	25	F3
Tolka Valley Park	26	A3
Tymon Park	54	B2
Woodbrook Golf Course	73	E2

Parks - Golf courses - Sports stadia

Entry	Page	Grid
Albert College Park	27	E2
Blackrock College Sports Ground	59	E1
Blackrock Park	59	F2
Botanic Gardens	27	D3
Bray Golf Course	77	F4
Bray Golf Links	73	F3
Brickfields Park	48	B2
Busby Park	56	B2
Cabinteely Park	70	B4
Californian Hills Park	37	F3
Carrickmines Golf Course	74	A2
Castle Golf Course	56	C3
Ceannt Stadium	49	D3
Cherry Orchard Park	46	B1
Clontarf Golf Course	28	C3
Collinstown Park	36	C4
Corduff Park	14	B4
Croke Park	41	D1
Dalymount Park	40	B1
Deer Park	58	C3
Deer Park Golf Course	32	C2
Donaghmede Park	21	E3
Donnybrook	50	C3
Dún Laoghaire Golf Course	61	D4
Eamon Ceannt Park	49	D3
Ellenfield Park	28	A1
Elm Park Golf Course	51	E4
Elmgreen Golf Course	24	C2
Fairview Park	41	E1
Fitzwilliam Square	81	C5
Forest Little Golf Course	8	C2
Garden of Remembrance	80	B2
Greyhound Race Track	41	F4
Harold's Cross Greyhound Stadium	49	E3
Hartstown Park	13	E4
Herbert Park	50	C2
Howth Golf Course	33	D3
Irish National War Memorial Park	38	C4
Irishtown Park	51	F1